PENGUIN BOOKS

Wisdom Man

'Occasionally you read a book that is bigger than itself. A book that strikes chords that are bigger than the individual, bigger than the society. A book that moves to the heart of human existence. *Wisdom Man* is such a book.'

SPENCER LEIGHTON, *Geelong Advertiser*

'One of the most compelling stories you will ever read . . . This is a wonderful book about the life of a wonderful human being. Banjo Clarke was, quite simply, an extraordinary man.'

STEVE STEVENS, *Swan Hill Guardian*

'Banjo Clarke may not yet be as famous as some of the people who befriended him, but his remarkable life story deserves to be known.'

JULIAN BURGESS, *Launceston Examiner*

'an extraordinary man . . . His story is one of racism, cruelty and hardship, yet still filled with forgiveness and love.'

MX Melbourne

'[Banjo] was a spiritual rock, who, despite his own difficulties, could be relied upon to deliver a message of love and forgiveness . . . [This is] a compelling account of one man's life'
JEREMY FENTON, *Northern Rivers Echo*

'[*Wisdom Man*] goes beyond documenting history to explore Mr Clarke's simple morality of forgiveness and compassion . . . People who knew Mr Clarke will find the book a valuable reminder of what the esteemed man stood for, while those who never met him will wish they had.'
JASON WALLACE, *Portland Observer*

'In *Wisdom Man*, Clarke is revealed as a man who believed goodness could change the world . . . The voice that comes through . . . is the voice of reconciliation and it is strong and true.'
Weekend Gold Coast Bulletin

The publisher wishes to advise that this book contains references to and photographs of people who have passed on which may be distressing to some Aboriginal people.

Wisdom Man

BANJO CLARKE

as told to **Camilla Chance**

PENGUIN BOOKS

PENGUIN BOOKS

Published by the Penguin Group
Penguin Group (Australia)
250 Camberwell Road, Camberwell, Victoria 3124, Australia
(a division of Pearson Australia Group Pty Ltd)
Penguin Group (USA) Inc.
375 Hudson Street, New York, New York 10014, USA
Penguin Group (Canada)
10 Alcorn Avenue, Toronto, Ontario, Canada M4V 3B2
(a division of Pearson Penguin Canada Inc.)
Penguin Books Ltd
80 Strand, London WC2R 0RL, England
Penguin Ireland
25 St Stephen's Green, Dublin 2, Ireland
(a division of Penguin Books Ltd)
Penguin Books India Pvt Ltd
11 Community Centre, Panchsheel Park, New Delhi – 110 017, India
Penguin Group (NZ)
Cnr Airborne and Rosedale Roads, Albany, Auckland, New Zealand
(a division of Pearson New Zealand Ltd)
Penguin Books (South Africa) (Pty) Ltd
24 Sturdee Avenue, Rosebank, Johannesburg 2196, South Africa

Penguin Books Ltd, Registered Offices: 80 Strand, London, WC2R 0RL, England

First published by Penguin Books Australia Ltd, 2003
This edition published by Penguin Group (Australia), a division of Pearson Australia Group Pty Ltd, 2005

1 3 5 7 9 10 8 6 4 2

Design by David Altheim © Penguin Group (Australia)
Cover photograph by Simon O'Dwyer/the Age
Typeset in Fairfield Light by Post Pre-press Group, Brisbane Queensland
Printed and bound in Australia by McPherson's Printing Group, Maryborough, Victoria

National Library of Australia
Cataloguing-in-Publication data:

Clarke, Banjo.
Wisdom man.
New ed.
ISBN 0 14 300345 3.
1. Clarke, Banjo. 2. Aboriginal Australians – Biography. 3. Gunditjmara (Australian people).
4. Aboriginal Australians – Social life and customs. I. Chance, Camilla. II. Title.
305.89915

This project has been assisted by the Commonwealth Government through the Australia Council,
its arts funding and advisory body.

www.penguin.com.au

To the future of my people

The River Knows
(Kuuyang – Eel Song)

Shane Howard, Neil Murray and Banjo Clarke

Who's going to save this country now?
Who'll protect its sacred power?
Listen to the south-west wind
Listen can you hear the spirits sing?

See the wild birds fill the sky
Hear the plover's warning cry
Feel the wind and feel the rain
Falling on the river once again

The river knows
The river flows
That old river knows
Watch us come and go

The south-west wind brings Autumn rain
To fill the rivers once again
The eels will make their journey now
Longing for that salty water

Down the Tuuram stones they slither
In their thousands down the river
Headed for the river mouth
Fat and sleek and slowly moving south

All the tribes will gather here
Travel in from everywhere
Food to share and things to trade
Song and dance until it fades

Hear the stories being told
Handed down to young from old
See the fires burning there
Hear the voices echo through the air

Listen can you hear their song?
Singin' as they move along?
Movin' through that country there
All the stories gathered here

The kuuyang* move into the ocean
Restless motion
Even though they go away
The spirits all return to here again

_____

*Eels

ACKNOWLEDGEMENTS

Camilla Chance and Banjo Clarke's family would like to thank the following people for their help and support in making this book possible: above all, Elizabeth (Libby) Clarke, the historian among Banjo's children and a greatly honoured keeper of traditional ways; Camilla is much indebted to her for her input into her father's book. Also our freelance editor Saskia Adams, Andy Alberts, Sonia Borg, Geraldine Briggs, Laura Clare, Yvonne Clarke, Judith Durham, Martin Flanagan (who helped us find a publisher), David Fligelman, Ruth Fligelman, the Right Honourable Malcolm Fraser, AC, CH; Tim Goodall, Belinda Guest (for her help in the search for Louisa Briggs's letters), Reverend Colin Holden, Doctor David Horton, Shane Howard, Helene Jedwab, Paul Kelly, Betty Kenna, Father Michael of the Benedictine Monastery in Camperdown, Neil Murray, David Owen, Susan Pickles, Betty Reynolds, Archie Roach, Reverend David Robarts, Tricia Smith, Marjorie Tipping, Tom Wicking and Rodney Wicks. Lastly, we would like to thank our friends at Penguin Australia: publisher Clare Forster for recognising the value of Banjo's life story; Meredith Rose for her enthusiasm, patience and sensitive editing; and David Altheim for his most powerful cover design.

FOREWORD

Wisdom Man describes the life and times of Banjo Clarke. In reading, it is impossible not to understand Aboriginal people's love and respect for their own place, of their own land. The land's importance to Banjo Clarke and his family can not be over-emphasised. This book is also the story of an Aboriginal person watching and being affected by changes that were dramatically altering the land and the world as he knew it.

If readers can understand this book and its motivation, they will understand the need for reconciliation and, above all, for an understanding of the principles of Aboriginal life and culture and the standards by which Aboriginal people sought to live.

Banjo Clarke was extraordinary. In many ways his life was one of forgiving; a life of kindness and a life of love. He knew what had happened to his ancestors in western Victoria and in other parts of Australia, yet he carried no residual anger.

There is a touching story about a little girl who observed Banjo walking along one of the main streets of Warrnambool, greeting young and old. She turned to her mother and asked, 'Mummy, who is that man who loves everyone?' In many ways, that child's words describe Banjo Clarke most accurately.

I first came to know Banjo and other members of his family during the 1970s when there were problems involving their relationship with the state and the control and ownership of the Framlingham Forest. It took some time for these issues to be resolved, but in the end they were, in ways that respected Aboriginal life and enhanced Aboriginal dignity.

Non-Indigenous Australians who read this book will come away with a better understanding of how many Aboriginal people lived on the edge of what had become mainstream society, but at the same time being touched by it and participating in it. When the world went to war, in 1914 and again in 1939, Banjo Clarke's people were as much involved as other Australians.

The recollections at the conclusion of *Wisdom Man* are examples of the many ways in which Banjo Clarke's life affected everyone who came in contact with him. He was loved and respected by all those who knew him.

The Right Honourable Malcolm Fraser, AC, CH

PREFACE

Our father Banjo Clarke met Camilla Chance in July 1975. It was a meeting that would forever change both their lives. Convinced that knowing about traditional Aboriginal values would help the world counter hatred, greed and lack of caring, Dad asked Camilla to record his life story. He insisted no one be told about the project, fearing that if people knew they might start influencing what he wanted to say. He wanted to speak from an uncluttered spirit. The manuscript's existence was only made public by Camilla at his funeral in March 2000. As his children, we then resolved to ensure that their many years of work together was seen through to publication.

Dad's home on the Framlingham Aboriginal Settlement was always open to those in need – black or white, able or disabled, young or old. Everyone was welcome. For decades he provided an informal, unfunded social-welfare net for the Warrnambool region. People drifted in homeless, broke, wounded, messed up and down and out. They stayed as long as they needed to, and moved on when they were ready. No one could keep count of the number who found shelter and support with him. You could roll up to Dad's to find that a minibus of Aboriginal youth had arrived at the same time that another full of Dutch/English/German backpackers was departing. All would mill around amid the resident army of kids, dogs and recuperating young people. A Japanese film crew might be hovering overhead in a helicopter. 'Where's the old man?' someone would ask.

'He's answering a call from his old mate Malcolm Fraser,' someone else would reply. It was divine bedlam.

Dad was born into the Kirrae Whurrong tribe of the Gunditjmara nation on the Framlingham Mission in the early 1920s. He saw a great many changes in his lifetime, both cultural and technological. One of these was an increasing number of Aboriginal people, including his own children, being educated and employed in positions of responsibility, in both Aboriginal and mainstream organisations. Dad was always very proud of the achievements of his people, but he always told us that the bush had been his school. He attended the local Purnim Primary School for just two days, leaving after seeing a teacher hit a child, and went back home to learn from the Old People instead. He lived and breathed his Aboriginal culture, never agreeing with the view that it was a thing of the past and irrelevant to the modern age: it was as relevant to him on the day he died as when he was a boy. Yet he never rejected modern culture, either, or its more positive advances. He believed that the old ways and the best of the new could co-exist in harmony, but that, for the sake of the earth and all the life it supports, the old must never be lost.

Above all, Dad embodied the spirit of reconciliation in its most generous and forgiving form. He espoused it long before it was even given a name, long before it became fashionable. He was fond of saying, 'There are good and bad people out there, no matter what colour they are.' Incredibly, despite all the hardships and racism he experienced in his life, he didn't feel comfortable with the notion of Sorry Day. 'You can't be sorry all your life,' he once said. 'Why don't they have a Happy Day for a change?'

When Dad laughed, the mountains trembled. People were healed by his laughter and his genuine, passionate universal love. He had the magic of a master storyteller, and there was never any bitterness apparent in him, though his life would have well justified it. As an Elder of the Kirrae Whurrong he had a moral authority which, like his reputation, spread well beyond the clan into the broader community – he had mates all over the planet. He owned virtually nothing, but was content with what he had. He was not a politician, or a movie star, or a rich man, or any of those things so many of us strive so emptily towards, yet by the time of his passing he had managed to reach thousands of people through what he regarded as the greatest employment of all – that of love, compassion and wisdom.

Camilla Chance recorded her interviews with Dad over more than two decades, many taking place beside a waterfall at Framlingham. It is appropriate that this book stems from an oral account rather than a written one, in accordance with Aboriginal custom. Aboriginal stories, legends and lessons have always been passed down from one generation to the next via the spoken word, and Dad wanted his story to be no different. The integrity of his speech and unique manner of expression have been preserved completely in this book, and his language has been unedited except for small points of clarity.

This would not be a true Aboriginal book if it were in perfect chronological order. When pressed to be clear about dates and times, Dad often became impatient. To a large extent, the spiritual life to an Aboriginal person means living in the eternal present, with the past, present and future all experienced as one and existing simultaneously. Dad would sometimes say, 'There is no past – everything is still happening.' Thus establishing precise dates and times were not always paramount to him. However, as much as possible has been done to verify all factual information in this book.

Dad frequently used the words 'old' and 'poor', and in his eyes they were a compliment, a term of respect; he used the word 'poor' to express empathy. Likewise, he meant no disrespect by his occasional use of the words 'half-caste' or 'full-blood', which many Aboriginal people understandably find offensive today. These terms were frequently used by Aboriginal people of Dad's generation with no emotive or disrespectful implications.

While our father did not live to see his book published, one of his greatest wishes was for the story of his life and vital message to be documented and preserved for future generations. We thank Camilla Chance for helping fulfil his dream and we are delighted to see this wish come true.

Helen, Patricia, Leonard, Elizabeth, Bernice and Fiona Clarke

Contents

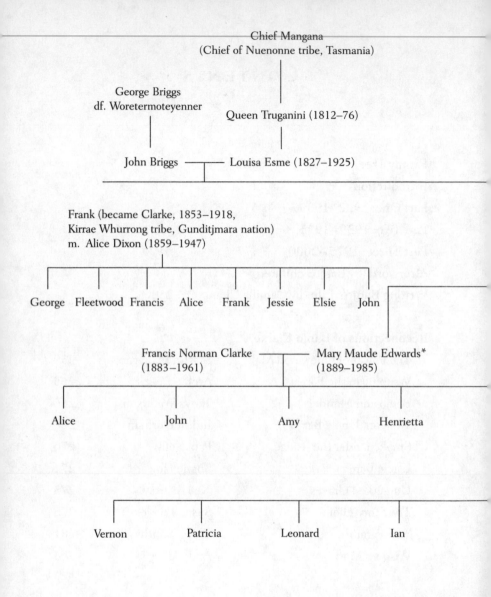

Chief Mangana
(Chief of Nuenonne tribe, Tasmania)

George Briggs
df. Woretermoteyenner

Queen Truganini (1812–76)

John Briggs ——— Louisa Esme (1827–1925)

Frank (became Clarke, 1853–1918,
Kirrae Whurrong tribe, Gunditjmara nation)
m. Alice Dixon (1859–1947)

George   Fleetwood   Francis   Alice   Frank   Jessie   Elsie   John

Francis Norman Clarke ——— Mary Maude Edwards*
(1883–1961)   (1889–1985)

Alice   John   Amy   Henrietta

Vernon   Patricia   Leonard   Ian

Family Tree

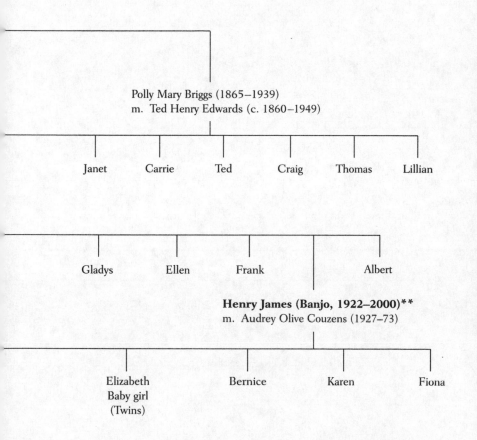

Polly Mary Briggs (1865–1939)
m. Ted Henry Edwards (c. 1860–1949)

Janet   Carrie   Ted   Craig   Thomas   Lillian

Gladys   Ellen   Frank   Albert

Henry James (Banjo, 1922–2000)**
m. Audrey Olive Couzens (1927–73)

Elizabeth   Bernice   Karen   Fiona
Baby girl
(Twins)

*Mary Edwards also had a daughter, Dolly (1903–80), by another relationship

**Banjo Clarke also had a daughter, Helen (b. 1943), to Agnes Adeline Gay;
and a daughter, Lee-Anne (b. 1966) to Gabrielle Leslie Hallowell

INTRODUCTION

I travelled a lot when I was a young fellah, looking for work, because I liked to be able to see into the distance. Aboriginals feel more safe that way, while Europeans feel safer surrounded by walls. I'd go to the pub in a new town, because that's where people know what work's available, and all the patrons would be grinning and snickering at me. So I'd pick up my swag and walk straight out again because I wasn't wanted, and all the men would come to the door laughing to watch me go. Us Aboriginals were used to these things happening, but we always wondered *why* – why were people angry at us and hated us? We'd done nothing wrong.

The police would follow me out of town, pull up beside me and ask what I was doing. When I'd say, 'Looking for work,' they'd say, 'You blacks don't bloody work! Come back to the police station with us.' Then they'd interrogate me for hours and lock me up on a made-up charge, like drunk and disorderly, and let me go the next morning without even a cup of tea.

I'd keep walking and then, as I came to another little town, I might see smoke under the bridge. I'd head for it and then be surrounded by Aboriginals saying, 'How you going, Bud? You looking for work? You had a feed? Hang on, and I'll cook you a feed.' We'd sit around the fire and laugh about all the obstacles in our paths, feeling sorry for the people who were refusing us work. We'd think they must lead very unhappy home lives to feel such hatred for people they didn't know.

I'd say to myself, Round the next bend, I'll meet good people, or,

This young policeman might learn something and be human when he gets older. I knew that good people would arrive one day, and times would slowly change.

They *had* to.

Then that day came. In July 1975 the biggest change of my life happened when I encountered the Baha'i religion. A small group of Baha'i people visited us Aboriginals at the Framlingham Mission. We saw them sitting in the grass outside the mission boundary, singing songs together and politely waiting to be invited in. A whole lot of us piled into a car and drove past to have a good look at them. All these people of different nationalities sitting there together looked like one happy family, real sincere, like *we* feel about people. I took this sight as a powerful sign that things everywhere were going to look up for us Aboriginals now. I was right. One of the Baha'is I met that day, Camilla, became my closest friend from that day on.

Very soon afterwards I was in Warrnambool Base Hospital. I get pneumonia regularly because I worked in the bluestone quarry – I think its proper name is basalt – for years and years. Another couple of Aboriginals, Lloyd and Albert, were in my hospital room too. While we were there, people got to speak with us who had never talked with Aboriginals before. And Camilla brought her little children to visit us, and sat with us giving us her presence.

The other patients and the nurses couldn't understand why Camilla – a respectable white woman with two little kids – was visiting Aboriginals. How could Aboriginals be so important? I could tell that was their attitude – they couldn't work it out. But in the end, when they understood that she was an upright lady with no feelings against anyone, they saw that they could be like that too. Camilla was teaching them how to get on with people. They started to treat us a bit differently then. You know, with respect.

And Camilla's little girl Ruth came to see us too and played her ukulele, and the staff thought that was great – they used to stand around and watch her play. Things like music, which the hospital people hadn't thought of before, draw people together. There was no question of black or white – a child was singing to make us better, make us feel well.

It was something different, meeting these Baha'i people. They didn't say much, but felt deeply. You was treated as more than equal. You was treated as somebody special – special because you was Aboriginal. We'd never heard them sort of words before. All we'd heard was that Aboriginals were no good. Yet here I was, listening to this little girl saying, 'You're special because you're Aboriginal. You've got a beautiful culture.' And I thought, What more could anyone want, when a little girl like that's speaking? I've been called all kinds of things before by white people, but never special. White Australians here always became suspicious of me if I wanted them to treat me as a true friend and help me get a job. They'd confine themselves to saying g'day and being friendly in the street. And whenever we're turned away from something today because we're Aboriginal, all our past treatment comes back to mind. Because it's the same prejudiced outlook that's causing it. But these Baha'i people were different.

On my last day in hospital Camilla turned up and I told her, 'They've just discharged me. I'm going home.'

She said, 'I know.' Then, when she was driving me, she turned off the main road. I said, 'Not that way – the mission.'

She said, 'My own place is going to be your home for a while.' I was confused, and exclaimed, 'But I'm better now!'

'No, you're not,' she told me. 'I asked the doctors to let you come here so we could nurse you back to health.'

3

And she and her family looked after me. I thought, There must be a lot of good white people around, and we hardly met them before! Where did they come from? Grown-ups and children with open hearts.

Camilla's little ones loved me being with them. Young David was just starting to walk, and he'd keep walking out of the door wanting me to follow him. He'd lead me straight to the woodpile, where I made a stool for him. I also made a tree house for him and Ruth. He liked doing things and helping me.

A lot of my friends came to see me while I was at Camilla's, Aboriginals who had lived a heartbreaking life trying to cope in the white man's world. Camilla invited them in and showed them her trust. She left the house open for them if she had to go out for the day.

All these events inspired me to want to write a book. I reckoned that the way these high-society people shared with me would tell something to the world about equality, and having love for people from different races. I reckon if people knew about true Aboriginal qualities – so similar to the Baha'i beliefs – then this would help the world do things from the heart. I think for people to learn about Aboriginality might even be the saving of the world.

I asked Camilla to help me write my book and she agreed. Twenty-five years later, we have still been working out everything that I want to say.

Part One
1922–1939

Chapter 1

The Hopkins River below my place is sacred. That's where we went as little kids. All around the valley there you'd hear children's happy laughter, all calling to one another. These days you don't hear that.

I was born in a bark hut on Framlingham Mission, right in the heart of my father's tribal country. There never was a time when our whole family left that land, and even as a child I was never away for long. They say I was born in 1922, or probably earlier – Aboriginal people often don't know when their birthdays are – but I don't know. They put a number on me, but it seems like a long time ago.

Most of my brothers and sisters were born the same way. My sister Ettie was born way up in the bush. There were four of us boys and five girls. Norman, Frank and Bert were my brothers; my sisters were Alice, Amy, Ettie, Gladys and Ellen. My older sister Alice was born on the Murray River, at Cummeragunja Mission. My mother came from there, so when my parents married they stayed for a while. Old Aboriginal ladies nursed all us babies in their own Aboriginal ways, and they done a good job too – I'm well over seventy now and they looked after me, so they must've knew their job all right. It's been sad to see them pass on, though. When they did they took a lot of customs and tribal ways with them.

Framlingham Mission was all more or less forest when I was a little fellah – just natural. The people was living in bark huts, but there were a few old houses here. More than a hundred of us lived on and around our mission then. All the Old People lived here – the people what were getting rations. They was all good Old People. As well as my Granny Alice, Granny Bessie and her husband Billy, many other families rented government-built weatherboard houses, with a rainwater tank outside each home: Henry Alberts, John Egan, the sisters Hilda and Mary Fary, and Emily Rose. Emily Rose was the daughter of Lionel Rose's great-grandfather – Lionel who became bantamweight boxing champion of the world. The rest of us lived in huts round about – the Couzenses, the McKinnons, lots of Austins, lots of Alberts, lots of Clarkes and Roses.

Later, all the old houses of that time were cleared away, except one my grandfather built. They shouldn't have cleared them away. They was good houses, full of memories. The Old People took great pride in their homes, lining the walls with tar paper against the damp. But government officials raised the rent if they made their houses too nice, or added a room. Paying to live on their own land made my people so mad that most refused to in the end. The rent collectors were met with such anger that they just gave up and left.

When I was no more than a little child, I learnt how to build a bark hut like the one I was born in. They were easy to make. They was warm in winter but kept the heat out in summer, and the draughts too. But I remember stormy nights when the roof bark of our hut would sometimes be blown off. I'd watch my dad climb up in the dark to put another bit of bark over the hole. He'd get it done so quickly that we'd hardly feel the rain.

There were other huts like ours in the forest, but some had been built the lazy way. They had old manure bags for walls, split and opened to double their size, hung overlapped with each other and waterproofed with tar. A heavy rug would cover the doorway. Some people still slept in the traditional mia-mias, or humpies – they were oval-shaped shelters made of bent boughs and bushes, with a place

8

for a little fire just outside the entrance. Other families used nothing more than a traditional brush-fence windbreak to sleep by. They did really well on hot summer nights.

We lived in several places – on Spring Hill, for instance. We used to get water from the spring. It's still there today, that same spring. But nobody goes there now.

I was only a baby when the ferret bit me. My family left me in the hut one day and went to do something. They came back in and heard me crying. My sister Alice grabbed the ferret and pulled it away. The ferret hung on and tore all the skin from my throat. Dad took the old horse and cart to Warrnambool with me tied up in it, and then poor old Dad got frightened that the doctors might do something wrong to my throat. He brought me home and he fixed me up himself with salt and a bush poultice, and things like that. He sewed me up with an ordinary needle and thread, dipped in kerosene. There are still scars where the ferret tore into my throat and chin. Dad done a lot of things like that. When people cut themselves with an axe, or had any accidents, they'd come to my old dad's place and he'd get the needle and sew them up.

One of my sisters sharpened every tooth of a cross-cut saw once, and she had it sticking out on the stump, the way they used to sharpen them. She led the horse to the stump where the saw was, and got on the stump to jump on the horse's back. The horse pulled away and she fell across the saw. From above her knee right up to the thigh the sharp saw went right in. Dad stitched her up – all those stitches. The doctor asked him who done it, and my dad said he done that. The doctor said, 'Well, I can't do any more. It's just what I would do.' So my dad drove home again.

I used to be always with the Old People. I think they liked having me because I used to listen to them. They taught me all the principles: how to go about life and how to share with other people. I used to share with them too. And if I had a pair of shoes, I didn't want to wear them if my mates had none – all sorts of things like that. That sharing still happens today in the older generation of Aboriginal people, but I can see a lot of those principles fading away from Aboriginal society now.

Every day I learnt a lot from helping the Old People, because they used to teach me all the reasons behind what we were doing. They taught me to hunt in a way which would make nature stronger, and that I must use every part of a tree or animal. They taught me never to eat in front of another human being or creature without sharing, and that all things must be respected for what they are. They taught me the secret names of the people buried in the cemetery, and which plants were used for healing and which ones I must be very careful with. All being well, they said, one day I would find a child or children to pass the story of our tribe on to.

It was the same with my dad. Among my people, the father has always been the Elder of the clan, the protector. Most days at sunset my dad used to take me walking in our cemetery on the cliff overlooking our river. He too would confide to me in secret the names of the earliest full-blood people buried there. He told me that when I became an Elder, I should wait to find someone worthy before I could pass the knowledge on.

It was tradition for our tribe that once a person died their name had to be dropped from our language forever, and from the English language as well. It was a sign of respect. So I would just tell people, 'My friend is buried here.' We wouldn't name them.

And at funeral after funeral we would keep our tribal customs despite the Christian service. Even the youngest little kid would come and cry at the grave. Everyone would cry and wail. We would sing the old American hymn: 'Yes! We'll gather at the river,/The beautiful, the beautiful river,/Gather with the saints at the river/That flows by the throne of God,' all the while eyeing whichever bush animal had come to watch us this time. The animal's presence would comfort us with the thought that it might contain the spirit of the departed one.

It's still traditional here that if you're buried on your tribal land, your spirit will be at peace and you'll affect the future development of the tribe. But if you're not buried on your land, your spirit will wander sadly forever. So everyone wants to come home to die.

There's a huge, lone pine tree that grows in the middle of our cemetery. It stands up there like a big monument, and you can see it for miles around. It was planted in 1886, I think. Up until recently, if one of our tribe deliberately and publicly stood and faced that giant pine, it was a message to all of us that he or she had come home to die, or knew she was about to die. No more needed be said or done. Everyone knew. Little children and all knew it – they lived through it, and remembered not to be scared of death.

CHAPTER 2

Down below this house, we used to help the Old People put the fish traps in. We had great fun helping the Old People. We spent hours along that river. We walked for miles across farmers' paddocks where we knew there was fruit trees and things like that. Sometimes we'd catch a rabbit or a possum and roast him on the coals in the bush, and cook him with potatoes.

We hardly ever went to Warrnambool when I was little. It was a big deal when we did – we couldn't get over the houses and people everywhere. Instead we had great fun all the time in the bush. Kids today don't do them things. They still can do them things together, but they don't. They don't walk along the river much, they don't go in the bush much. Usually it's only when they have a bit of a drinking party or something they'll go up the bush. But we used to love being in the bush – just to be there.

We used to play a game called Hands Up from the Ned Kelly days. That's how we learned to track. A lot of kids would take off in the scrub and hide, and leave one fellah to look for them. He'd have a lot of little balls of clay, and if he saw someone he'd put one on a switchy stick, like a woomera, and send it straight at them. If he hit that person, the person would have to join him to search for the rest. That game would go for hours in the scrub and we'd end up real good trackers. Everyone's got a different way of walking, and the one searching would put his foot in the other fellah's footsteps and do the action of that walk and identify who the fellah was.

We'd go fishing in the night – spearing, or put the fish traps in where there's rocks, before the rain comes and all the eels travel out to the sea. The Old People knew when it was time to put the fish traps in, and all the little children would be helping. And down along this big gully in front of the house I have now, near the river, you could hear the laughter of all the little children and Old People singing out, directing them where to put the stone, what to do. Great laughter! When I look down over that gully these days, there's no more laughter, and all them things are gone. But I like that place because that's a spiritual sort of place to me. That's where all the little children had their laughter. A lot of them passed on, some were taken away. As teenagers, many were told by police to go to Melbourne, or otherwise trumped-up charges would be laid against them. A lot got caught up with grog and gaol.

All the Old People had good principles about them, and the old culture they was hanging onto. They was hanging onto that culture very strongly, and I was happy to be with them. I was the lucky one to be with them all the time because I never went to school, except on days when there was a free feed. The first time I went, I only stayed two days because I didn't like how the teacher would hit the little kids. So I went back to the bush. The bush was my school. I camped with the Old People and walked the roads with them and got odd jobs with them in Warrnambool and different towns – camped with them in a shed somewhere – and all the time they was guiding me all through this life what they had to face. And I tell you what, it was pretty good things what they taught me – how to cope with things, with the racism and prejudice what was flying about everywhere.

'Learn how to cope with it,' they said. 'Don't hold any anger about anyone, just feel sorry for the people what was having a go at you. Them people what have a go at you and call you "black this and black that", *they* are the unhappy ones, because they've got unhappy homes. If they call you that, you still be their friend – maybe one day you'll help them.'

The Old People taught us that way, and I still do them sort of things today. I hold no grudge against anyone, no matter what they do to me. They make you a bit angry sometimes, but you look on the funny side and laugh about it after.

Them Old People, they're all gone now and there's no more left. And when they died, something sacred was taken away from us, something precious: the people what lived the traditional way, what still had Aboriginal principles. The young people today what I see, what never had that chance to associate with and meet them Old People, they never learnt these things. That's why I think they're angry young people today – because there's something there what they lost, like their culture and the principles, all the old Aboriginals' way of life. And if you lose your principles, you lose yourself.

I think that's why the young Aboriginals have got nothing to cling to, and have sort of lost their identity. They think, Now which tribe am I from? Who was my uncle? Who was my auntie? Where do my people come from? And they don't know these things, they're searching for their identity and there's no one here to tell them where they come from no more. They get on drugs and drink and things and get into trouble because they're angry with the world, and angry within themselves too because they lost their identity. They're lashing out everywhere trying to find their way back, and I don't think they'll find it now unless they get back into the bush and live like the Old People. Never mind about the money and the big motor cars and all that sort of thing. Get back and live! Go hunting! Get your own food – don't wait for the government to give you money to buy a loaf of bread. Go and cook damper or something. And be happy! Be children of nature again, instead of living in the big cities and being corrupted and going to gaol and seeing your mates dying there and in the parks, and the sort of things what I don't like.

The Old People picked me to tell me things for some reason. Everywhere they went, they told me a lot of things they wouldn't tell other people. And that's a funny thing, because all my mates what grew up with me, who they didn't tell, most of them have passed away now. It was like the Old People knew they would. A lot of my mates died because they never got any medical treatment, or didn't believe in or trust doctors. A few of them died in gaol. And I'm thinking, How come these poor Old People was telling *me*, and had *me* with them all the time, like as if they chose *me* to tell their story, and their principles, and now I'm telling that story today to the little kids I know who want to listen. I'm the only one that's left. And I hope the little children I tell will learn by that too.

It felt good to be with the Old People. And I tell you what, I learnt a lot off them what I would never have learnt in school. The things I tell people – they say they never heard things like that before. Most Aboriginal history is all oral, you know, it is talk and song, just like the white people have their ballet and operas.

I'm glad to pass on the ancient wisdom to anyone who likes to listen. And a lot of the young people *do* listen. They come along to see me – lost kids, little white kids, little Aboriginal kids on drugs. They come home and ask, 'Could I stay for a while?' 'Yeah!' I say. 'We've got lots of room here – have a feed, mate. If I'm ever not home, help yourself. Have a good rest, mate.' I treat them with kindness, you know, because they feel at this time in their life that they've got no friends. But some people say to me, 'Why do you have all these no-hopers coming here? Don't take them in. They're druggies, they're this, they're that – they're thieves to feed the habit they're on.'

'Listen, mate,' I say. 'This is a refuge for lost souls. My door's open for everyone, and they're all welcome. That's all I can do. You don't hunt them away, kick them in the gutter somewhere. You reach out a friendly hand and help them, mate.'

And they're crying out for help, too! They come and say, 'Can I stay for a couple of nights?' and I say, 'Yeah, stay here, mate, till you get yourself right again. Get yourself in order.' And they go away real strong, and some of them make good and some don't, and they come back again.

A young woman drove all the way from Western Australia to see me once. She was terrified, she said, because there was a spirit in the back of her car. She wanted me to make it go. So I got some branches and smoked and purified the car. Quite a few people have asked me to do things like that. And I'm always glad to.

If I wasn't following the Old People, I'd be away for many hours with my mates. In the mornings we'd have rabbit with damper or kangaroo meat for breakfast – whatever there was – then my brothers, my sisters and I would sit down outside and decide what to do that day. We were too young to go to school. Some of us boys would want to go hunting for rabbits or possums, and some would want to spear fish. On a typical day I might decide to go hunting. But we never killed anything that the tribe didn't need, and it was our responsibility to make sure that the animals had quick deaths.

My group would work with waddies [wooden clubs] and dogs. Like everybody else in the tribe, us kids made our contribution. If we had been careless, all the Aboriginal families in our area would have suffered a bit.

Our big dogs used to be hunters of hares, kangaroos and rabbits, and our little dogs were burrow dogs – to snuffle in the scrub and flush out game. The big dogs would wait outside the scrub. They all knew their job. The little ones would be snuffling and barking, and the big ones would be circling around waiting to give chase.

We'd go down below a hill, probably where the river was running, and then creep up through the bracken fern to where a bunch of rabbits would be feeding in a paddock. The dogs would be wide awake to what was going on, and we'd tell them to stay behind us. After a lot of crawling, we'd appear over the top of the hill, and the rabbits – that the white man kindly brought to our area – would stand on their hind legs to look at us. Then they'd squat down. We'd circle around them, and some would be game enough to make a dash for freedom. We'd throw our waddies and knock them out. We were all good shots and we'd have plenty of rabbits for our families to eat. The dogs would kill any that were only wounded.

We lived on rabbits and hares a lot because we never had much money. Way back in the late 1800s, when the full-bloods got rations, the government decided to cut back the meat rations and starve my people, with the purpose of forcing us to catch rabbits to eat in order to survive. This was a free way for the government to keep down the rabbits. But when it was Depression time, the farmers wouldn't let the Aboriginals go into their paddocks like before to get the rabbits because they wanted the rabbit skins for themselves. The result of that was that when good times came again for the farmers, and they didn't bother killing the rabbits, their country was overrun with them.

We could catch a possum at any time of day, whenever we wanted. Scratches on a tree would tell us his whereabouts, and the hollow where he went into his nest. But we'd only take one when we were very hungry, or it was time for our people to have a change of tucker.

At midday we'd need our own little feast, to keep us going. We'd make a fire and maybe cook our possum in the ashes, with the fur on and everything. They cook better that way. Taste better, too. Fire-making was in our blood. Not long ago, our people used fires to chase game into special parts of the forest. Then they would keep the birds and animals together by burning wide firebreaks around them. The idea was that when visitors came to us for a celebration – a corroboree – they would not need to waste time hunting. Their food was at hand.

By clearing the forests of undergrowth, fire helped our ancestors move around under the trees; they also used it to create pasture for kangaroos. Many Australian plants can only seed themselves during a fire.

When my mates and I made lunch after a morning's hunting, we occasionally discovered that no one had matches. But it was no problem for us to take turns rubbing a thin hard stick into a soft stick's hole. Just like the Old People. Soon the hole would get hot and start to smoke. Then we'd blow on it, add stringybark, and it would come into flame. Next we'd peel thick bark off the trees, add it to our fire and let it burn into red-hot coals, then really hot ashes. We'd dig a hole in these and put our food in – possum or rabbit and potatoes.

We knew where there were some potato paddocks. We always tried not to be seen by white farmers, although we were hunting where kids had always hunted for thousands of years. But our territory had also become white men's land, and we'd been taught about massacres.

We used to 'bandicoot' the potatoes – do the same as those little animals do with their long noses. We'd dig underneath the plants. The stalks would still be there, so until harvest time the farmers wouldn't know that their potatoes were gone. But we never took much, and we thought the white people would only laugh when they found out what we'd done. They'd know that Aboriginal kids was the culprits.

Occasionally a farmer would ride up on his horse and scare us. But we'd all stick together. He might say, 'If you go that way, you'll find an orchard. You can have some fruit, but don't take it all.' That would be what we were planning to do anyway!

We'd track kangaroos in the scrub – we always knew where they was. And we'd make a snare across their usual path, just enough to slow them. Because kangaroos always put their heads first through thick ferns, we'd weave the ferns together with rope made from young bark and stick a bit more bark behind. Then we'd surround the poor fellah.

We always gave animals like the kangaroos we hunted a swift, merciful death. We would never do otherwise because we believed that the kangaroo we speared was on some deep, mysterious level the kangaroo the spiritual world wanted us to catch. So we respected all the animals that gave themselves to us so that we could be nourished.

Before sunset, we'd head for home. We'd meet up with the kids who'd gone spearing fish. We'd talk about our day and show one another what we'd got. We might give a couple of kids from different families some rabbits and potatoes, and they'd give us a few eels and fish. I suppose it sounds like bartering, but my mates and I were really trying to make sure that all the families had enough food. We'd worry about everyone, and everything would be shared.

The kids who'd come back from fishing would have obeyed strict Aboriginal laws like us, to only take what we needed. It was our understanding of nature that we must throw the little fish back so they would grow up and breed more for the tribe. We looked forward to somebody having a proper feed when the fish had grown big.

If we couldn't catch a trout because it was hiding under a stone in the shallows, we'd lie down in the water and waggle our fingers near the tip of its belly. The trout would move backwards and roll happily on our fingers. We'd keep moving our hand back slowly and the trout would gradually come out. Then we could spear it.

Spears were handled carefully by all of us kids because every day was a hunting and fishing day. Spears were handed down from one generation to the next, and if a mate borrowed one it always had to be given back. They stayed sharp forever because we were not allowed to use them as walking sticks or drag them on stones. We'd always keep the tip pointing up.

The Old People would make spears by splitting ti-tree wood and hardening it over the fire. If they wanted a trident, they'd bind a couple more sharp wooden prongs on with kangaroo or emu sinew, using a little stick to keep the points apart. Often the Old People would also thread a whole bunch of worms, like a ball, on a string for us to drag through the water. A fish or eel would give a big gulp, and we would pull it in.

On weekdays the grown-ups depended on us children to bring home all the food because they would be working hard cutting fence posts for white farmers. But on weekends they'd hunt kangaroos. And when we met up with our mates on the hillside before going home, we'd talk all excited about what the grown-ups might teach us on their next free day. When we reached our huts, we would cover our day's catch with sacking to protect it from flies and hang it on long, forked sticks against the wall, or even from the roof, with bits of wire to keep it away from the dogs. Our fathers would clean and dress the meat as soon as they arrived home from work, and our mothers would start cooking.

In the right season, the Old People would take us for a day's expedition to Wangoom Lake to get duck and swan eggs. We'd always behave ourselves. We understood that we were keeping a custom alive which makes the bird families strong, and which had gone on in our area for thousands of years. Wangoom Lake used to be three and a half miles in circumference. The Government of Victoria sold it to some landowners whose properties reached its banks, and they have now drained it. That's sad, because in those days thousands of swans used to settle on the mud and shallow water. They would pull the reeds up to make nests.

Our elderly women would also pull up the reeds. They'd march along the Wangoom Road with huge bundles on their shoulders, bundles which we couldn't get our arms around. They'd weave sunhats with brims a foot wide, and giant baskets. These they'd sell to shops and outside hotels – wherever white people were.

When we arrived at Wangoom Lake we'd see nests everywhere, and we'd start collecting eggs for our tribe. We'd gently lift one or two from each nest of five, being careful not to leave human scent. We'd never even think of removing a whole clutch of eggs. After our visit, the mother could rear up the remaining four strong babies from the start, without wasting food on the weakest one, which soon gets thrown out of the nest anyway. Without our help, there would always be one baby what could not reach the food the mother brought. We were as kind as we could be to nature, and nature was kind to us.

So, when my mates and I met together after a normal day's hunting and fishing, we'd have done a lot of the same things that children had done on that spot for thousands of years. But it was extra hard having the white man around!

One way or another we'd always be talking about catching food. And we'd usually have good stories to tell about what had happened that day. There'd be girls with us, but not every time. Often they'd stay to clean up the camp, but they used to be good hunters too. They were especially good at climbing trees. They'd take one baby kookaburra at a time from a nest and rear it up until its feathers grew. The girls would have orders from white people in town who needed a kookaburra to keep the insects down in their gardens.

The sun would be nearly setting when we'd carry the food back to our camps. Our mothers would start cooking what was needed that night, and would try to save some for tomorrow. They'd make damper from pounding together nutty bulbs, seeds and yams, or even from flour.

Water would have been brought in during the late afternoon. The Old People kept a huge network of wells and dams. It was nothing for an old person to walk four miles for water, carrying two kerosene tins hanging from a yoke. Lots of moving of camp in the bush, to keep things clean, meant that the well with the best water was sometimes furthest away. But my family liked to live by the mineral spring. Many generations of my family were brought up on mineral water, mostly in cups of tea.

Sometimes we'd eat at home, and people from other houses would call in. They'd sing on their way to us, so we would know they were coming as friends, with a good heart and with good stories to tell. Everybody helped each other in those days. We were all in the same struggle. If somebody was sick way up in a bush camp and hadn't been seen for a while, someone would go look for him with a big billy-can full of nice soup. They'd boil it up and give him a feed – we all did things like that for each other. Everyone knew we had to stick together through the struggle and make life as easy for one another as we could.

The Aboriginal way was always *sharing*. Aboriginals believe that, rich or poor, black or white, yellow or red, we all suffer sorrow for situations we can't change. We all have the same *feelings*. An Aboriginal mother whose son is in trouble feels just the same as a white mother in that situation. Those two women would belong to each other in spirit. They might think that their feelings are different, because they would interpret them differently, according to their culture. Some people think if you have a different colour or a different nature, you feel tragedy in a different way. But it's the same. So sharing for Aboriginals is a way of expressing our inward knowing that we all belong to each other. We share sorrow, happiness, and food.

On special nights the young men from the camps would make a bonfire outside and we'd have a proper sing-song around it. We'd also have a sing-song every Wednesday night in the mission church. People would come from all around for it. The Old People was all good musicians. I remember that they could pick up any musical instrument and play it, even if they'd never seen it before. It was marvellous the way they were gifted in music. Old Uncle Billy Austin was great on the organ. And we would sit and sing around the campfire together, all helping each other by harmonising with each other's voices.

Looking into the bonfire, our mothers and fathers used to make up their own songs about recent history. And our grandparents would stand up to sing tribal songs what had been passed down, and explain to us kids what they meant.

When my mates and I started to get sleepy, we'd head for bed along the bush tracks to our huts. We never had a proper bedtime. Older kids would come with us to settle us in bed. From our bush huts we'd still hear the voices singing – secret songs. But after a while they'd quieten down. We knew then that the Old People would be telling stories, about great Aboriginal hunters and sportsmen. And about hardships and massacres.

They were wonderful singers, and their music filled our dreams. I miss them now. When at last they went through the night to their camps, we'd hear their voices in the distance, singing all the way.

CHAPTER 3

For generations we depended on our skills in catching fish when times were tough. The Old People would put in fish traps, teaching the children. Then, as we grew up, if we was hungry or somebody had expressed a desire for fish, we'd look along the river to see where big trout and eels was swimming. I knew this place we called the Spring when I was little, where water comes out of the ground a few yards from the river. Old Dad made a shower there when we used to go there as little kids. We used to get under the spring water. It was like ice! We used to have to jump in the river water afterwards, because it was warm.

Down where the spring is there's a lot of watercress and willows. In summertime, pools were left in the rivers, and you'd sneak down to the bank and stand on the rock above the water and watch, because you can see the fish better when you're up higher. You'd watch them, and sneak in when you thought you could catch them near the shallow. They'd always come from the spring, which runs into the river. The first thing you'd do when you'd go there is look where the water was running into the river. That's where the fish hang around, because they like the cold water.

I used to help the Old People make channels to trap fish half a mile upriver from where I lived. When the river creatures were really on the move, they wouldn't swim but would catch free rides where the water was rushing. I'd do the same if I was a fish. My Old People would tell me where to put a certain stone and where other stones needed to be taken away. They would explain where the water flow was strongest, and that's where I'd help build the trap.

While we worked, the Old People would talk about wonderful times long ago at Lake Bolac, on the western border of my tribal country. Eels would travel in huge numbers downriver from the lake there to the sea during autumn rains. The Buluk Bara tribe owned all the country around the lake, also land on both sides of the river for a very long way down. No other tribe was allowed in without permission, or there would be fighting. But every autumn they would welcome us to a huge gathering on the banks of Salt Creek, which would become like a big village.

Each tribe would be lent its own bit of the creek, which it returned to year after year. The families would camp for about two months beside their own stone rivermarks, where they would lay their eel traps. It was a time of celebration – wise talking, corroboree, making marriage arrangements and meeting old friends. Sometimes there'd be important talks and decisions to be made, like about a problem with food or a neighbouring tribe or whatever, and the Old People would get together and hold a council to seek spiritual guidance. They would always try to have everyone agree on whatever it was, helped by the spirits.

I was told that at the beginning of the 1860s a group of white men from Ararat took to arriving at the lake every year as soon as it began overflowing – the only time when eels can be caught there. They would place their nets across the whole of its only outlet and not allow any Aboriginal people near. This was the end of the great gatherings of the five south-western Victorian tribes which made up the Gunditjmara or Mara Nation. One of the most powerful tribes in the five, our coastal neighbours, also took the name Gunditjmara, which simply means 'belonging to Aboriginal people'. I would hear and

25

learn about all these things while helping my Old People below where my family lived.

I also heard about the special gatherings up at Mount Noorat too. All the clans with different dialects met together there at a full moon. They all gathered there, little children too, and the Old People told stories about everything what happened, where their land was being stolen, where their people was being murdered, how people rode into their camps with big horses and guns, how an Aboriginal man was dragged to his death behind a car, running and shouting about white people's lack of feeling while they laughed – all the stories was told around the campfires. All the different tribes came from everywhere, from the Grampians, up the north way, along the coast. Another place down here, Killarney, was a big meeting place along the beach – the shell middens are still there. All the children were there too, that's the way they learned their history. They *listened*. It mightn't mean nothing to them when they were children, but they still listened. And later on, as they grow up, all these things come to them. It didn't mean much at the time, but they knew it was something important for Aboriginals to know for later.

In every season there would be something else to do. Summer, when the river was low, was the right time to build a big dam with stones and branches. Soon the water would rise and then fall again, trapping the fish.

Learning to make eel traps, I would watch the Old People weave long, narrowing shapes out of grass, with a hoop and then a funnel, which the eels could get in but not out of. We'd build stones up around the finished nets and wait for the floods, which usually came in May, at the end of autumn.

Us kids used to love this time. We'd jump in, hunt the eels into their traps, and whip them or bite their necks to break them, stunning them first by tapping their tails. Or we'd splash a lot in the water to chase a number of fish into a corner, so they'd end up flapping on the rocks.

After the rainy season, we'd take the nets out and dry them in the scrub. The Old People would check them again before next autumn.

The flood season was special, a time for feasting. There'd be so much food. We'd invite our friends from town, and anyone else who wanted to come. That was the best part of Aboriginal life – sharing, and being kind to strangers who visited us. [Banjo's song 'The River Knows', on pages viii and ix, further describes the eel celebrations.]

When people were travelling through our area looking for work, or going to see a relation, we'd make them welcome and help out. They'd go on to tell others throughout the Aboriginal community where they'd been and who'd looked after them. Anyone who didn't know us would hear of us that way and plan to stay with us on their travels. When Aboriginals visited us from far away, they wouldn't walk straight on our land. They'd sit down half a mile away until somebody seen them. Then we'd tell somebody from our tribe, 'Go out and fetch 'em in.' And if they wasn't invited in, they wouldn't come in. Or they might in the night, and then trouble would start. Them rules were pretty strict. So the white person in turn would be punished for coming in without permission, we believed. If they overran the land, the land would one day destroy them.

Old Dad done all the woodcutting and fencing and various jobs for farmers around the district. When the farmers first came, they would give axes and lend cross-cut saws to willing Aboriginals for them to make five hundred fence posts at a time. The farmers were pretty good and understanding of the old Aboriginal people. They always kept them employed. Some of the old fences are still standing – some of the old posts what the Aboriginal people cut. That was important, because nobody got any rations or anything from the government then. [Rations had ceased in 1890, when the government tried to close the Framlingham Mission for the second time, taking all the staff, farm animals and equipment. The Aboriginal people were literally abandoned there as part of a plan to reduce the number of Aboriginal stations.]

Sometimes my dad used to take me into the bush on working days and make me a bed out of the soft, springy leaves. I could hear the wind singing in the trees, the beating of birds' wings and the strokes of my father's axe. That's the kind of happy childhood I had. Dad would chop down the special stringybark and messmate trees. One stringybark tree could supply four 6-foot posts for the farmers at its base, three in the next 6-foot cut, and two at the top. Sometimes one big strainer post could be chopped from the very end. Nothing would be wasted.

Our mothers used to clean the cut trunks of the bark by hitting them with a heavy implement. An axe would then be put in the crack they made to prise the bark off, and this bark, left over from the farmers' posts, we would use to build our huts. The bark sheets would have come off the tree semi-flat. Before we used them, they were turned upside down to dry over logs, which kept them from touching the ground. Lots of pieces were laid across each other, with posts dropped on the very top to keep the pile in shape. Once their material had dried, my people could build whatever they wanted.

To make a bush hut, the bark would be nailed in sheets onto a solid sapling frame with about six-inch gaps between. Nails were cheap in them days. A second set of sheets would then go over the gaps so no draughts could come through. And the bark of the roof, with its sapling skeleton, would overlap the walls on all four sides to let rainwater run clear.

My old dad was that proud, if he couldn't earn any money to feed his children he'd roll his swag and go somewhere else for work. He wouldn't ask a person for the crust off a loaf of bread. Most Aboriginals was reared up like that here. My parents were determined to look after us as best they could, and my dad worked hard for us kids, to keep us happy under the harsh conditions. To try to look after all us kids, my mother worked around different places too. All the older women done the same work, and looked after children around the district while their parents milked the cows and worked farming. Any little thing our parents was happy for us to get. But if our mates didn't have any toys, we'd give them half of ours. Nobody was left out of anything.

Late in the evening often used to be a worrying time for Mum. She would look out of the door to see if Dad was coming home from the bush. Then she'd send us little fellahs to go and search for him before dark came. We'd hunt about in the bush and call his name. We'd hear his voice answering us. Then we'd run to where his voice was coming from and see him lying on the ground. He couldn't move. Cramps would be all over his stomach. He used to drink water in the heat, but often had no food. During times when food was scarce, he'd leave what there was for his children in the camp. Many a time us kids used to find him fallen on the ground after a hard day's work. We'd cut a couple of saplings, take off our clothes, tie them to the sticks, roll him on the stretcher and carry him home.

He used to lie on the dirt floor – he couldn't be on the bed. When he moved, cramps would grab him. Mum would make a drink with a lot of salt in it, to put the salt back in his body. He'd lie there for a while, then gradually the cramps would leave him. She'd lift him on the bed then.

Next day he would be still weary from the cramps and the hard day's work in the bush. But he'd always go back again. That's what he had to do – he had to work to keep his children going because we had no assistance from the government or anything. If he didn't work, his children would starve.

My dad and other Old People used to sit around the campfires in the night, talking about how all the land was disappearing and there was no more hunting ground left. How they was put on the mission and not allowed to go anywhere. Talking about all the bad things what's going on, and the massacres.

I was taught about a massacre that happened not far from here. Some of my people had stolen a few sheep because they were hungry. The settlers would always come after any Aboriginals for revenge – it didn't matter to them if they'd done it or not. They had to show us 'who was boss'. This time they took some innocent Aboriginal children to the beach near Killarney, where they buried them up to their necks in the sand. Then the white men took it in turns to try to kick the little children's heads off. They tried to see who could kick the heads the furthest, while the little brothers and sisters of the victims watched and waited for their turn to die.

My dad and the rest of the Old People told me other stories too. How my Grandfather Frank as a young man went on walkabout with our tribe, and when they reached Killarney a white squatter invited them over into his paddock. This squatter was happy to see them and quickly organised a big feed for them. His servants made porridge in a big copper and plenty of meat was cooked on the coals. The whole mixture was poured into horse troughs and everyone had a good feed. The squatter seemed as though he was having a wonderful time, thrilled to bits about being surrounded by Aboriginals. He kept encouraging them to eat more. So my people all felt glad too.

When they was saying goodbye to the squatter, he told them, 'Why don't you tell all your friends to come here? I'll give them all a good feed because I love Aboriginals.'

Happy from full stomachs and memories of such a kind white man, my people continued their journey. But once they got away from the property, my grandfather warned his tribe, 'We must never go there again. Don't you fellahs go back there for any more food, because when you go back again it will be poisoned. White men have a history of making friends with Aboriginals and then poisoning them. Don't you tell no more Aboriginals about it.'

But some of the tribe didn't believe that this white man would do such a thing. They went back to the squatter's farm on another journey and took more Aboriginals. My grandfather went a different way, along with his family and everyone else who had listened to him. That included a twelve-year-old girl, Alice Dixon. When Alice grew up, this young girl became Grandfather Frank's wife, and my grandmother.

Later, the time came around for all the tribe to gather again, but many didn't come. So Grandfather Frank went searching for his people. He was accompanied by a few other tribal people, including the little girl Alice and her tribal grandfather, the end of whose name sounded a bit like 'gunja'. He was a true tribal man, with raised ornamental scars on his body and heavy eyes. He used to carry a skin bag slung over his right shoulder, joined at both ends with a reed thong.

They crept up to the squatter's property. The ground was very swampy then; it was something like mangrove swamps. They saw the partly cleared paddock, and horse troughs full of a porridge-like mixture similar to what the farmer had served them before. Everywhere around there were bodies. Bodies beside the trees and undergrowth, bodies among the grass tussocks. Dead babies lying on mothers. Mothers who had died clutching and comforting their children. They had all died in agony from strychnine poisoning.

This has not been told before, but as my people looked on in horror, a stripy wallaby appeared on the other side of the bodies. His black-, red- and white-masked face looked straight at my grandfather, grandmother and great-great-grandfather with heavy, soulful eyes, just like my great-great-grandfather's. Oh, that painted-up-looking animal with the mysterious face was such a comfort to the people to see! It was a message of kindness from the spiritual world, a message that life goes on, that my ancestors' spirits still live.

I guess the farmer wanted the land and we lived too close to it for him to feel safe. But we wanted our land too. And he saw us as vermin to be tricked, the way we trick a poor trout, a hare or an emu when our people are very hungry. That kind of madness – the madness of greed – should never take hold of people. Human beings must never feel that way about each other again.

Camilla wrote a song about it for me:

> Many Aboriginals would travel this road –
> Many Aboriginals, and that's a fact.
> The whites who heard them coming, the whites who heard them singing
> Wanted them to do their usual disappearing act.

> They invited my grandfather in for a rest
> They invited my grandfather in for a feed
> 'Tell the other tribes,' they said, 'tell all your friends'
> But my grandfather answered them, 'No indeed.'

They invited the other tribes in for a rest
They invited the other tribes in for a feed
Men, women and children lay dead on the ground –
Poisoned gruel in the horse troughs had done the deed.

Many Aboriginals would travel this road –
Many Aboriginals, and that's a fact.
The whites who heard them coming, the whites who heard them singing
Wanted them to do their usual disappearing act.

They invited the other tribes in for a rest
They invited the other tribes in for a feed
But, large as life, we are still here today
Because Grandfather answered them, 'No indeed.'

Camilla tried to research the massacre for me, but town officials withheld records from her about it, which is illegal. The only thing they were keen to do was deny that it ever happened.

Sometimes I have told little bits of this story to reporters. They have all printed the words my 'great-grandfather' instead of 'grand-father'. I suppose they couldn't believe that the massacre happened so recently. It would have been about 1861. They must have thought I got it wrong.

CHAPTER 4

My grandfather Frank, who survived the massacre, was born into the Killitmurer Gunditj – or Framlingham – clan of the Kirrae Whurrong tribe. His tribal name is secret. Kirrae Whurrong means 'blood speech', but our people were also sometimes known as Wirngill Gnatt Tallinanong or 'koala language speakers'.

When I'd ask my dad what life was like when he was a teenager, he'd reminisce about his father, my Grandfather Frank. How he wore a big moustache and would travel around to all the agricultural shows with his sons to watch the athletic events. Eventually they'd be asked to join in and they'd always end up beating the other competitors. Each would have their own speciality – one would run in the running races, one would enter the hurdles and another the high jump. Grandfather Frank used to be especially good at the Scottish game of tossing the caber – throwing a beam as a test of strength. My ancestors were all strong and tall men and women. They were proud Aboriginals, walked with their heads high and were respected wherever they went.

Grandfather built the old house that still stands by the bridge over the river – I think it might have been the first old mission house, way back in the 1860s. It's the only one left from those times. There were a few more before my time, over near the low paddock. There was a school there, in the old church – that church is restored back. They dragged it across from the low paddock and put it by the road.

My old dad and the Old People told me a lot about my grand-father's time on the mission. Life on other missions in those days was often very strict and harsh. Dormitories were built early on so that the little children could be stolen from their parents and brought up in a Christian atmosphere under white supervision. They were forbidden to speak their own language even. But on Framlingham we never had dormitories, which meant that we kept a lot of our tribal law well into the twentieth century, and a lot of our language too. You'd get in trouble if the missionaries heard you talking the lan-guage, though. So our Old People would teach it to me secretly when the missionaries weren't around. But they didn't teach everyone, so some of it was lost. So were a lot of the tribal names. The missionaries changed everyone's tribal name to an Anglo name and we were for-bidden to use them any more. But other parts of our culture was kept alive, mainly from neglect by the government, who just left us alone out there. And our culture is still blossoming and bearing fruit today.

In 1867 our reserve had fallen into financial difficulty as a Church of England mission, so the State government took over and closed it. This meant that my people were supposed to leave for other missions. Those who refused to go were threatened every day and sometimes starved a bit.

The government looked as if they expected – and probably wanted – us all to die out. They was certainly trying very hard to force all Victorian Aboriginals to live in one place. Because all those who were moved to Lake Condah (another mission, an hour's drive from here) later they got moved again to the big reserve at Lake Tyers in Gippsland. The plan was to have that as the only mission left open in Victoria.

Granny Bessie Rawlings – my grandmother-in-law – had been one of the leaders of the campaign to get our mission reopened after its first closure. She begged the government to find its heart. Inspired by Granny Bessie and others, my people travelled hundreds of miles to deliver letters and petitions to the government personally. And then, in 1869, they reopened it, with a rationing system. Ration day used to be an exciting time for the mission children, I heard. Mothers and fathers would stand in line, holding out their hands. Their children would line up beside them. The manager would hand out flour, sugar and tea. Anyone who had failed to obey an order that week would have his or her rations cut. And Aboriginals who received government rations were forbidden to work for wages. All over Australia, mission Aboriginals were taught to be dependent like that.

Grandfather Frank didn't like this system and asked the government to grant him forty acres for a farm instead. It did that, and helped him move his house across too. Grandfather knew he'd have a good chance of that happening because he had travelled with Daniel Clarke, our first missionary-manager, and been his right-hand man during the 1860s. The two men, Aboriginal and white, had explained to the Aboriginal people that they would be safe from massacres if they gathered in one place and helped start a mission there. Building the first houses on the mission was something that my Grandfather Frank did also. Eventually Daniel offered Grandfather his own surname, Clarke, as a way of showing appreciation. I am proud of that name.

Daniel was the son of a soldier and was born in Belfast. He was well educated, and left Ireland at the age of thirty-five in 1862 with his wife, Rachel. He took up work with the Anglican Church Missionary Society when he arrived in Melbourne and soon settled in Warrnambool. It was then that he gathered up the Aboriginal people of the district with my grandfather to start the mission.

Daniel was a talented artist and he understood the Aboriginal people pretty good. He loved the bush and the Hopkins River like they did. He did a lot of paintings of the district – one of the river was hung in the great Melbourne Exhibition of 1880, and another of nearby Tower Hill was sent to the Paris Exhibition. He thought Tower Hill was a real beautiful place and never stopped painting it.

But back to Grandfather Frank and my Grandmother Alice. They kept cows and milked them and sent their cream to a local dairy. They had them in a paddock by the bridge called Warrumyea. Warrumyea means 'left-handed woman' in our language. We have a traditional story that tells about a strong woman who had a lot to do with the creation of this part of the world.

Kids still swim in the river under that bridge but no one goes near the bridge after dark. A white workman is said to have been killed when he fell off that bridge, and some people have seen his headless ghost and went crazy afterwards. The ghost is said to follow people home from the bridge, but he never goes past a certain point on the mission.

Things was tough sometimes, they told me – big long winters. The Aboriginals always kept food back to make sure the little children had something to eat. The Old People also shared with the people out of work. That was the sort of thing that went on – everybody shared with one another. Anybody sick, they was all there to try and help, to give the medicine or cook the soup or whatever it was. Everybody cared for one another. Didn't matter who was sick – if a white man was there sick, they'd look after him too. Because that was the traditional way of life – to unite together and share with one another.

Then, over the years, all these changes came to mission life. In 1886 the government decided they was spending too much money on Aboriginals and passed the *Aborigines Protection Act*, which hunted the half-castes off the mission. Only full-bloods were allowed to stay. The half-castes were meant to go out and 'take their place' in white society. But they was reared up from little children as Aboriginals! They might have a bit of white blood in them, but they was still Aboriginals. They had Aboriginal traditions, Aboriginal ways of life, and they never fitted into the white man's community. The white man never accepted them anyway. Suppose they fitted in for a bit and managed to be treated equal as whites, the moment the whites found out they had Aboriginal blood, they was prejudiced against them and victimised them.

So, many of them went to camp in the forest around the area. They would sneak back, mainly at night, because the police would trap them during the day and arrest them or put them off the mission. They'd come in the dark to see their people, their own families, and because they needed food. Granny Bessie and her family were taken to Lake Condah Mission by force as punishment for feeding half-castes – their own family! Lots of the full-blooded people saved most of their food for them – they couldn't bear to eat while other family members were camped in the valley, starving.

Some of them tried to go out into the white man's world. They'd get jobs and never tell anyone they had Aboriginal blood, in fear that they'd get sacked, and it was a sad case for them because they were living in a false world and crying out for their culture.

A lot of sad things happened. Some young fair girls seen their Aboriginal mothers walking in the street and turned their back on them. They were frightened some white friends would see them talking to this Aboriginal lady. The mother knew it was her daughter but kept on walking. It must have been a terrible thing for that to happen – your own blood doing that.

Some other young girls what got married to white men would come back and visit their parents on the mission, and felt free again to talk the way they wanted to about Aboriginal problems and Aboriginal culture. And that's the only time they could speak like that. And they looked for the traditional food – damper, everything like that – and they liked to sit down and eat with their parents like when they were little.

In 1910 the Victorian Premier John Murray had managed to get the *Aborigines Protection Act* amended.* But nobody told us, and for years the police illegally continued to hound so-called half-castes off the land where they had been born and brought up.

I remember the day we found out that the Act had changed. I was about five. My dad and I had been cutting wood in the bush together and just turned towards home. We were feeling happy, sitting on top of a load of wood we had cut, driving our horse-drawn wagon. A big old-fashioned government car had pulled up at the corner of the mission. A man got out and called my dad over. Dad got off the wagon and went over and had a good talk with him.

'What's the reason for all those camps that are dotted about here and there around the bush?' the government head demanded.

_____

*John Murray was the State Member of Parliament for Warrnambool from 1878 to 1916, and Premier of Victoria from 1909 to 1912. During his early parliamentary career, he repeatedly petitioned the Aborigines Protection Board to allow Framlingham Mission to remain open, and for its residents to be better treated and provided for. When he died in 1916, Warrnambool's *Standard* newspaper wrote of his funeral that 'An interesting feature of the procession was a large drag containing a contingent of aboriginals from the "blacks" station at Framlingham, who gathered in full force to pay their last tribute of respect to one who had always been a stout champion of their rights, and to whom they were bound by strong ties of gratitude for the kindly and practical interest he had always taken in their welfare.'

'They're the homes of half-caste Aboriginals what have been put off the mission,' Dad said.

'The police can't put them off any longer,' the man exclaimed. 'It's been forbidden since way back in 1910. You tell me who ordered them off.'

Dad told him and he wrote down the name.

When my dad got back on the wagon, I asked, 'Who was that?'

'Government head, government head,' was all he said. But at home he repeated the conversation he'd had with him to everyone, and I listened in. The half-castes started coming back then, except those who preferred to live in the bush, and they was glad to be with their families again.

CHAPTER 5

During the late 1920s, my oldest sister Ettie went to Melbourne to look for work. Italian and Jewish cafe owners would often employ Aboriginal girls to clean up and wash the dishes, and clothing factories would also employ Aboriginal girls. My sister had no trouble getting a job.

We already had an uncle and an auntie living there in Melbourne, and Ettie stayed with them. There wasn't many Aboriginals in Melbourne then, only about one or two families. It was Depression time. Back in the bush we were all poor now too. The farmers were poor as well and they couldn't employ the Aboriginals any more. We were all starting to go hungry sometimes. It was also at this time that white shooters, with Aboriginal help, had caused our bush creatures to dwindle almost to nothing. There was good money in kangaroo, rabbit, wallaby and fox skins, so on weekends all of us kids used to get on horses and ride through the ferns, flushing out foxes for the white hunters. And white kangaroo-shooters used to take Aboriginal adults with them as trackers.

But we felt the bush was our soul. We belonged to its creatures and had to give them a chance to breed. We all knew where a few little wallabies fed and we wouldn't touch them. We hoped they would not die out, just as we didn't want to die out ourselves.

Some of the local churches raised money for Aboriginals camped in the bush, and that helped a bit. But otherwise it was mostly a case of 'out of sight, out of mind'. Aboriginals had just been left alone to live in poverty.

One evening in Melbourne my sister and her cousin went to the pictures, and when they was coming home a fight broke out in one of the houses they were walking past. A woman threw a bottle at a man, it smashed the window, and a piece of glass went in my sister's eye. She had to go to hospital.

My auntie sent word to my mum to come to Melbourne immediately, telling her that Ettie was in hospital with glass in her eye. And it was when my mum went to Melbourne to see her that we found out how the poor people were getting food there when they wasn't getting it in the bush. On certain nights of the week, different churches would take turns giving all the poor a feed, a big hot dinner in a great hall. The starving people would all line up against the wall in the cold and wait there for the door to open. There'd be weak little children with raggedy clothes on, old folks praying, and babies covered with sacking. And then when the door opened and everything was ready, they all walked inside – little children walking – nobody running or trying to get a seat first. They all took their turn and waited for everyone to get their share. They was all nationalities – Greek, Jewish, Chinese and part-Chinese, and a few Aboriginals.

Now that I'm grown older, when I look at the pictures from overseas of concentration camps and people sick and people hungry, I'm reminded of Depression days. The Depression people were free people, but they was still starving.

Anyway, Mum sent word to Dad: 'It might be better if you fetched the children to Melbourne, because at least they'll have a roof over their head and something to eat.'

So Dad got some money together from working harder than ever at woodcutting and gathered his little children round him and told a story to us how we was all going away from our bushland to try out the big city. But we'd never been in a big city before in our life. My oldest brother, some aunts and uncles and their children stayed behind, because we had a rule that the whole family would never, ever leave our tribal land.

Dad made arrangements for a transport driver to pick us up in a country town called Cudgee. We walked the six-mile journey from our bush hut through paddocks, all staying close to our dad. We climbed fences and crossed the Hopkins River at the top of the waterfall by leaping on stepping stones. It was a fine, mild day, and we was happy little kids on this big journey, going to a new place. I thought we was only going away for a few days, and my brother and sisters probably thought the same.

We reached the highway and waited and waited for the transport truck to arrive and give us a ride to Melbourne. But no truck came along. My old dad was desperate then. 'The truck must have broken down,' he said. 'He'd have come by now if he was going to.' Aboriginals believed that once you'd started on a journey you couldn't go back home, not then, because as Dad always said, 'If you go on a journey and turn back, it's bad luck.'

So we walked another few miles to the Cudgee railway station. Dad had a good yarn with the stationmaster and asked him, 'Have I got enough money for me and my children to catch the train to Melbourne?'

The stationmaster looked at Dad's money and he said, 'I'm sorry, mate, you haven't got enough. But if you can walk another eight miles to the next station, Panmure, you'll have just enough to go to Melbourne.'

Dad said, 'Come on, kids, we'll give it a go.' So away we went. We didn't follow the highway – we cut across country and followed the railway line to the next station. Us kids played all the way, jumping from sleeper to sleeper. We arrived at the station just in time before the big train pulled in.

The stationmaster came out to talk to our dad. He looked at our big suitcase on the ground and at us little kids. Then we saw him sell Dad a ticket. 'Now you have to wait for the train,' he said. 'It will be here any minute.'

We heard the train whistle away down the line. We hung onto our dad's trousers. We had never been close to a train before. Soon, with great amazement, we were watching the terrifying monster grind in, slowly, slowly. So much noise! And all the steam blowing.

Our dad helped us onto the train. He had trouble – we was all trying to hang onto him at once. During our first few minutes on the train we were scared, but then we got excited. 'Come here!' we called to each other. 'Come here, Dad! Look out the window! Look at all the motor cars!' We'd only seen one or two cars in the night, but no more. And there were so many lights! We'd never seen so many lights in our life. We thought all the lights was motor cars.

My dad said, 'That's not cars, that's lights above the street.' But we'd never seen anything like it in our lives. At home our lighting at night was usually candles made by filling an old tin with earth, burying a rag in the middle with its end sticking up like a wick, and pouring melted fat over the top.

Then we said to each other, 'Ah, it don't get dark down here. Look, there's lights like daytime all the time.'

When we got off the train in Melbourne at Spencer Street, we'd never seen so many white people in all our lives together. It was the greatest cultural shock we ever had. And we was frightened little kids. White people had a scary effect on us kids for all sorts of reasons. My dad made us hang onto one another in a chain to get through the crowd. A lot of people were looking and smiling at us – they probably realised we was little bush kids going to the big city for the first time.

Outside the station, there were cars and lights everywhere. We walked across the street, and a funny-looking old cable tram came along. Dad put us on the tram. He knew exactly what to do. He'd been to Melbourne before, passing through when looking for work all over the place. But we were scared stiff. The tram had two carriages, full of people. They made room and we sat at the back. Next thing we knew, the driver – a tall, raw-boned fellow – leaned over and tapped the shoulder of the man sitting in the front. He asked would he please find another seat, to let the little Aboriginal children sit up there. Everyone in front got up politely and we came to sit by the driver.

Now we could see the road coming at us and we were terrified! And we was ducking down as we went around corners and hanging onto one another, and the tram conductor was ringing his bell and singing and yelling out! He tried to make us laugh because he was giving these little bush kids a ride, and he knew we was scared. I think he was happy to have little children what never rode on his tram before. He entertained us all the way to Fitzroy, ringing the bell and singing he was, and it was all great excitement to us little bush kids.

We got off in Gertrude Street then, not far from our cousins' house. We watched our dad pull a paper out from his pocket and stare at it under the streetlight. We walked around the corner and found the old house straight away. We knocked on the door and went in. From then on, over the next few years, I would be back and forwards between Melbourne and the bush, living and working all over the place.

Our cousins' house was a ramshackle, two-storey terrace place joined onto others. A narrow lane ran beside it and that's where the family always went in and out, through the back door. The house looked all made of cement, but I suppose it was a stone house – just full of holes, some of which were filled up. It had small bedrooms, with cheap wallpaper in some of them. The bedrooms stunk of bugs. You could see the bugs scattering back into their holes in the walls when you turned the light on. My auntie used to fumigate the rooms by burning sulphur and pouring scalding water or kerosene over the bed-springs, which were full of eggs. But by the next day, a torch shone on a child's cheek at night would still show bugs crawling all over it.

On hot nights the bugs were torment and torture to us bush kids. At home we'd had bush fleas but they were nothing to the horrible insects of the city. In those Depression days, people would often move from house to house, always looking for a better place. But they couldn't find one because everybody was worse off than they used to be. So they just had to live in horrible conditions.

At night in bed I tried to imagine my old bush hut, and my dad making me a bed out of ferns and gum-tree tips when I was a little fellah, when he'd carry me into the forest where he worked. I'd try to remember all the Old People who held our community together, coming out of the bush after a hard day's work cutting fence posts for farmers – the men walking, carrying axes and sugarbags over their shoulders with left-over damper from their lunches, and the rum-bling old horses and carts whose drivers would pull up to have a yarn with my dad. But it was too difficult to concentrate on this when bugs was crawling all over me.

Soon I began to learn city ways, but I still longed for my home-land. All I wanted to do was get back in the bushland, go walkabout, walk along the gullies, look into the rivers, and find a fish and eels and make a spear. All these things kept coming back to me. We found the nearest we could get to real bush feeling was in the parks, but there the trees looked shaped, and the lawns were neat. We wanted to fill the parks up with wild bracken, dogwood and gum trees like we had at home.

But at night the city trees did watch over us. My family would go to the Exhibition or Fitzroy Gardens then. Someone would bring a guitar and we would start to sing and tell traditional stories, like back home. We would light just a small fire so the police wouldn't know, huddle around it together and look into our Dreamtime.

Months later, other Aboriginals began to come up to us in the dark, from all sorts of places. They'd be carrying wine bottles and musical instruments. Fitzroy was fast becoming an Aboriginal centre.

Often visitors from Cummeragunja and as far away as Dubbo would camp in our small backyard and light a fire in the evening. Everything felt better then. Us little kids would sit around their fire at night and they'd tell us bush stories. We'd hear the wind blowing in the trees and think of the water running through the gullies at home. In the dark, under the city's pretend moonlight, it was no trouble to think ourselves back in our bushland again.

We were scared of the little white kids in our neighbourhood because we were bush kids and we'd heard all sorts of things about white people in them days. Then one day a little white boy came up on a little billycart and gave us a bottle of milk he had, and he made friends with us. And then we got to know people better after that.

His name was Billy Paul. He and his brother Charlie spent most of their time in orphanages. Their father was an alcoholic and he would turn on them when he came home. When we later moved to Kerr Street, Fitzroy, we found we were living next door, so they used to jump over the fence and spend the night in our house.

Billy Paul became a criminal in the end because of his hard background, but his mother used to look after everybody. Charlie married an Aboriginal girl who later became sick, and he devoted his life to caring for her. He died soon after she did. My people wanted to honour him for having been our mate and so they buried him next to his wife.

With most of the other white boys, I had to fight or get kicked. My brother and I could have been kicked to death many times, but we always fought our way out of it. We accepted that this kind of thing was part of Fitzroy community life and never held any grudges. The kids we fought with ended up being our great mates. The white kids taught us to run past and grab an apple from the display boxes outside the Italian or Greek fruit shops. 'Don't you come here stealing my apple!' the man would say. 'If you want an apple, I'll give you one. I can get good money for that other apple. I have to eat too, and feed my own children.'

The fruit sellers soon got to know us and would come out to give us a bag of apples or vegetables that were going off a bit. And the fish man would call us in and roll up a big packet of fish and chips for us. 'You come round Sunday morning and knock on my back door,' he'd say, 'and I'll have all the fish and chips for you.' He'd pack up the stuff that he couldn't sell on Saturday night and give it to us little Aboriginal children to take home for Mum to cook. People all around were doing things like that to help one another.

In our street on a cold winter's afternoon, there might be a team of great draughthorses pulling the brewery wagon around to different pubs; a few square-shaped, yellow-topped taxis cruising along; and a police car with its big bell hanging down in front, racing through the slushy streets. Sometimes I used to go to the market, where all the people went to get food. People of all nationalities, but mostly white, used to hang around the stalls waiting for anything that the sellers had to reject. They'd be pushing and shoving to get the one good apple among the rotten ones. Sometimes a real fight would break out, over a pumpkin or something. That's the different environment we came to from the bush. None of them things happened in the bush, but in Melbourne we seen the other side of life, and how other people lived.

I never sort of took to school. My parents had thought I wasn't well enough to go to school anyway, because I had a weakness in the legs [rheumatism]. I sometimes turned up at the Church of England school on the days that they served free meals. But the lessons there sounded pretty useless compared with what the Old People had taught me, so I soon stopped going. All my sisters went to school properly, though. But my parents didn't think education was much use to an Aboriginal person. They thought that Aboriginals did not have much chance in life those days, and that education would make no difference. Keeping each other alive was about all we could do. And sitting still in class, for me, meant time wasted when I could be running errands. Every day my family desperately needed all the money and food I could help get. So when I was about eight, I started doing my bit.

I got a job in a shoe factory. The owner took a liking to me and wanted to train me for a more responsible position. But I had a headache all day from the chemicals there and eventually had to quit. I needed to be outside.

I helped an old lady clean her place out once, and I helped a shopkeeper – he was a good, kind man who treated me real good. That's the time I started to realise that all white people wasn't bad people. Because there's a lot of good people out there too, what are glad to help Aboriginals. That's the sort of thing that kept me whole, and kept me going without being racist or nasty. After all the stories you heard about them in the early days, there are still a lot of good white people out there what help Aboriginals to keep on going. Being your friend and treating you as equal to anyone else.

We'd go around collecting bottles from alleyways where drunk people had been and sell them to bottle-ohs for one penny each. Bottle-ohs were men with hand-carts who used to walk for miles collecting dirty bottles. They'd take them to the bottle yards to be washed and recycled.

An old baker's shop had its back on the street where we were living. The big flour bags used to be brought by a cart pulled by four beautiful Clydesdale horses. The bags would be hauled up to the loft by a block and tackle. I would keep a lookout for the truck and run to help the men. A horse would be hitched on, and when I made the horse lean forward, the bag would go away up to the loft. A man would pull it in and then I'd take the horse backwards again. When we finished the work, I'd be given a few shillings and extra bread to take home.

On wood days, when the poorest people got their susso money [sustenance payment], one-horse trucks used to cart their free wood from the railway sidings. Then there'd be great activity in town. All us little children would be pulling our homemade carts, bringing wood off the trucks to take to families. We'd get a few pennies for that.

Proper lorries would come in from out of town too, selling wood from the bush. And when the people bought it, they'd want a child to deliver it to their house. I enjoyed smelling gum-tree tips again while I was delivering them. It would take me back to my homeland.

I covered a lot of ground in the day, but playing in the street was another way of showing I was around for anyone who needed a job done. We'd hit a ball against the wall in the main street because the lane beside our house was too narrow. But we used to get told, 'Don't you play in this street. You go round and play in the next little street.'

We used to wonder why they said that. Smart young girls would be standing at their doors beside our house. They used to say g'day to us, and then, 'Now, run round the corner, love.' And away we'd go.

When we began to mix with little white boys who had been in the city all their lives, they told us, 'They're street women. They're prostitutes.' But we had no idea what prostitutes was. As we stayed longer in that street we learnt then, but we always had respect for them. Their boss-lady, Bessie, had a friend called Col, a big German fellah that she was always throwing out. He would arrive at her house drunk in the evening and they'd have a row, but we noticed that they always made up next time they met. He was always kind to us kids and would often lift handfuls of coins for us out of his pockets.

On cold winter's days we'd be running around the street trying to do messages for old folks, to get a penny so we could buy something. Pennies was good in them days. Often we wouldn't have much, and we'd be running home through all the water in the gutter – little kids going their way and the street ladies standing at their door with Bessie. And they'd see us little Aboriginal children running to our house in their street and Bessie would call us over. They'd have a big list for us of things to buy. They'd tell us to take it to the grocer, the greengrocer, the baker and the butcher – all sorts of things. And they'd say, 'Now, you run back and get us all these things and fetch it back here. You'll be doing a favour for us ladies. That'll be all.' And we'd be happy, thinking, We'll get a penny out of this.

We'd go to these shops and tell the man to read the list. Then me and my brother and sisters would run back with all these big parcels for the ladies. All the while we'd be out in the cold rain and the wind would be blowing.

We'd hand all the parcels over to the ladies, and they'd say, 'Oh, good, you've got everything. Have you got change?'

'Yeah, we've got change.'

Bessie would then say, 'Now, you put that change in your pocket and divide it up between your brothers and sisters. And you take everything, all this food, home and give it to your mum to cook.'

That's the sort of thing they'd do. A lot of times we would've gone to bed starving if not for those ladies.

And when I grew up and understood what they was doing, I always had great respect for them. As I got older and got jobs and all, I always thought about them and what they done for us little black kids in the city. Although it was cold stormy nights in the big city, and although we had nothing to eat, those ladies were like angels to us that came in the storm and gave us food.

I still think about it and I often wonder what happened to those poor women. Because things was that tough, a lot of young girls from good new homes went on the street and used themselves as prostitutes and everything else. They might have had a bad name, but to us they was our angels, and they was our friends.

It was twelve months before my brother came to fetch me home to our tribal land.

CHAPTER 6

For all the sweet month that I was home, everything seemed more real than before. Despite the hardships, the good Old People what held the community together were still there.

I went to church – all of us did, so we could meet together and sing together. I remember white visitors coming from near and far to hear us pour our hearts into their old hymns, weaving harmonies in and out as we always did. Our church stood on the banks of the Hopkins River, with only a horse-and-cart track leading to it. In winter the old-fashioned cars what they had then couldn't drive over there. Good cars, flash ones – they'd all get bogged. All the mission was boggy in the winter – you could only use a horse and cart. Cars were kept for summer.

I had a look at where the old slaughter yard used to be, down by the river, but it hadn't been used for years. I ran over to the ruins of our old pit sawmill and pictured in my mind one man standing above and one below, supervised by the missionary. They'd work a crosscut saw on a log balanced lengthwise between two planks. Our first mission houses were built of the slabs from them logs.

At Greasy Jack's Ford a few days later, I found my Grandmother Alice sitting in the doorway of my grandfather's old house, watching the bridge over the river and the hill. We'd had a wonderful reunion at the church. She was so happy I'd come back, and took me inside. She was known now around everywhere as Lady Clarke because of the proud way she had about her, and her beautifully kept home. Everybody loved and respected her. White people would even ask her over to their houses. Surrounded by a colourful garden which was famous all around, her house stood among hollyhocks, larkspurs and roses at a corner of the mission named way back after a white fencer who we called Greasy Jack because he used to smooth his hair down with grease. He liked to sit down on the riverbank and talk with Aboriginals, so we called that place Greasy Jack's Ford.

I visited Granny Bessie Rawlings, a very strong woman whose daughter Bella later became my mother-in-law. Granny Bessie was one of the leaders of the campaign to get our mission reopened after its first closure. She had brought me, my brothers and sisters into the world. A full-blood woman who hardly ever smiled, she would never allow any men near while she was doing women's business. Us kids used to weed her garden and the gardens of the other Old People. They would save us flour, sugar and tea to take to our families.

I went to see the old bark hut where I used to live. It was sunrise – our old breakfast time. Red parrots fluttered and landed on the ground beside my feet. Us kids used to share our breakfast with them and never try to catch them.

It was good to be back home, at the place where I was born. I was sad when it was time to go back to the city again.

Some time after my brother brought me back to Melbourne, my family moved to 76 Kerr Street, Fitzroy. Now we had a huge backyard where many, many visitors were welcome to camp, and so our two-storey house became famous throughout Australia. Aboriginal people from everywhere brought us news and enjoyed our hospitality. We had no trees in the garden, though, only well-worn dirt where no grass had a chance to grow.

The Aboriginals who came to visit would go on teaching me like the Old People had done at home. They'd stress the importance of keeping our people's principles – how life should be looked upon as a sacred thing, to be handled carefully and not ruined by anger or lashing out. 'If something terrible happens,' they said, 'you stop for a while and have a think, and then you work around the next big problem coming up. Like water around a rock. It's all part of the pattern of life; you keep on going. And you still help people when you can, even your worst enemy. The moment a person has a need, you forget what he has done to you.'

Our playmates across the road were Chinese, and we had many white friends. There was no other Aboriginal family in our street, but every few days I used to meet up with Aboriginal children from all over the district who were as thirsty for natural things as I was, and we'd spend the day out together. We'd walk for miles out of the city just to find a real river.

The Maribyrnong River was a favourite of ours. It ran through Footscray, a suburb to the west of Melbourne, but we'd join it further out where the trees were native and no houses could be seen. We liked looking in the water to see fish or eels swimming. That was very important to us. We'd walk back home towards the end of the day, or maybe hitch a ride in a horse-drawn cart.

One day me and two other Aboriginal kids headed off to the 1930 Melbourne Cup to see what it was all about. I can't stop laughing when I think of it now! I must have only been around seven or eight. There were all those people there dressed up in their good clothes and in their big cars, and then they spotted us little Aboriginal kids with no shoes on striding out in their midst. A motorbike policeman saw us and gave chase. When he caught us, he looked us up and down, then leant over and pulled out a bag of bananas he had stored in the side car and gave it to us.

All the young white teenage lads in our part of Melbourne used to stand on street corners at night. There was nothing else for them to do. We got to know them and they became our friends. Sometimes twenty lads would be together on the corner and they'd ask us Aboriginal kids to spy for them, to look out for police. You see, young people were not allowed to hang around in groups outside, especially at night. They might be scheming to rob a place, the police would think. The police used to jump out from nowhere, run at all the young fellahs, then grab a few and take them in for questioning.

But little Aboriginal kids were hard to see in the dark, and when we'd see the police coming, we'd yell, 'Look out! Joongai [police]!'

The young fellahs would all take off. The police would jump out of the lanes at them, but our mates would be running so fast they'd knock right into the policemen and their shiny hats would roll in the gutters. But our friends weren't doing any harm in the first place – only meeting to have a yarn. The police were locking people up just to keep them off the street, but that didn't solve any problems.

Some of the white lads that we'd spied for did grow up and join the gangsters, though. A lot of the crooks you heard about in the news came from Fitzroy. A few got shot, or did long times in gaol. But a lot did all right in life too. When they reached the age to start thinking about a career, it was interesting to see what they chose: to be poor, or to be a crook. Even for the crooks life was a struggle. They never robbed the poor, though, and they was always ready to help other battlers in time of need. Many died in other States. I used to hear what happened to them from people passing through and from the radio news.

My Aboriginal mates and I never resorted to that sort of thing. We could easily have carried guns like them, but we never did it. It was a dreadful thought to us, I suppose, to carry a gun. We had heard about guns from way back, and how they'd been used to murder our people. We didn't want to go near them.

Most days we used to pass the house where Squizzy Taylor, the famous gangster, was shot, and a real-life gangster leader called Walkerdine, who lived close by, would call out greetings to us. Mr Walkerdine had the nickname Scotland Yard because he knew about everything that was going on. His gang had an ongoing battle against another mob to run the illegal gambling clubs, where big money changed hands. One night the rival gang let the air out of his tyre. When Mr Walkerdine bent down to look at it, the rival men showed up and shot him dead.

One day my dad took us kids to the Melbourne Museum, where I saw a replica of the skeleton of my great-great-granny, Queen Truganini. Mind you, she was never a real Queen. In tribal life all over Australia, we respected each other equally. But white fellahs would call our natural leaders – those who spoke out for their tribe – 'Queen', 'King' or 'Chief'. It was a system they understood. White people said my ancestor Truganini was the last full-blood Aboriginal to die in Tasmania, the big island State, but we know that's not right. My father told us, 'That's your great-great-granny.' But what I remember most is my mother's fury that no respect had been shown to our heroic ancestor. There she stood in the museum, exhibited like an animal. And there's been a controversy raging anyway as to whether they kept the right body skeleton. Her skull was recognisable all right – Granny Truganini had distinctive features.

A lot of people think Granny Truganini never had any children, but my great-grandmother Louisa, who we call Granny Briggs, swore all her life that she was her daughter. 'Why on earth would she lie?' my mother would ask. 'She was famous for her good character, a true human being who spoke out fearlessly all her life on behalf of Aboriginals, as did her husband John, and she was a regular churchgoer.'

The night after we saw the skeleton of our famous ancestor, my mother felt it was time to tell us her tribal history.

'My ancestors came from over Bass Strait in the mid-1800s,' she said. 'For twenty thousand years before that the State of Tasmania had been separated from the rest of Australia by waters too stormy for Aboriginal people to cross, and so I suppose we would have become very different from the tribes here on the mainland.

'My great-great-grandfather was Chief Mangana of the Nuenone people. His tribal area included Bruny Island, off the south-east coast of Tasmania. He's gone down in history as strong and gentle, a loving family man with a good sense of humour. One night your ancestors, Chief Mangana and his family, were peacefully sitting around their small campfire when a party of armed white men from a ship crept very quietly up the beach and through the trees and jumped on them. They grabbed hold of little Truganini's mother, Chief Mangana's wife, and stabbed her for no good reason. She lay dying, poor woman; they finished her. A short while later, she died of her wounds.

'As you can all imagine, your ancestor Chief Mangana was in a terrible agony of mind. When Granny Truganini was old, she told people how he used to go off by himself every night and make a fire. Then he would feel her mother's spirit come to him.

'His young daughter, Granny Truganini, grew to be no taller than four feet three inches. They tell me she became known as the Beauty of Bruny. For better or worse, I say – because she got in trouble for it, of course, and was betrayed again and again – she tried all her life to create peace between the black and white races. More than that, she could feel the future in the depths of her being. I don't know whether I can make you feel the depth in her – her dedication and devotion to the cause of my people. She knew that time was running out. She could see far more than anyone around her, I think, and attracted people the way we attract an emu before catching it – she used the skills of a hunter. She stood up and fought – only a couple of times she bowed her head. I think I might be very forgiving, like her. But the white men disgraced us. They slaughtered our men so that they could get us poor women. It is due to the sins of white men that I have whitish skin. But I try to forgive them and make Granny Truganini proud of me. More than anything, she saw cruelty to women, and foresaw the near-annihilation of her people.

'But my story at the moment is about when she was just a little girl. In the end her father, our ancestor the so-called Chief, followed tribal custom and took another wife. They say that eighteen convicts who had mutinied aboard the brig *Cyprus* made a raid ashore and forced the new bride into their boat. She was never heard of again.

'Your great ancestor Chief Mangana was ruined by grief, as all my proud people have been. He made himself a kind of raft out of bundles of bark held together with grass ropes. He pushed himself out to sea and a big storm took him away. I think that everything in him wanted to be part of that storm. He happened to be rescued, poor man, but from then on the life was gone out of him. Those were terrible times, oh, unbelievable! The great man had no family left now except for Granny Truganini. All his family had died or been taken away.

'But our time of grief was only beginning. At the age of fifteen, your great-great-granny Queen Truganini, "the girl with the luminous eyes", they say, was being rowed home to Bruny Island with her promised husband, Paraweena, and his tribal friend. Suddenly, midway across the sea, the two white sawyers who had offered to row them jumped on the two Aboriginal fellahs and caught them off balance. They pushed them overboard. Those poor fellahs swam up and clung onto the boat, but you know what the Tasmanian white people would do when that happened? They hacked their hands off and left them to sink to their deaths. Then they rowed to a sheltered place and did everything they wanted to poor Granny Truganini.

'Oh, the white men will pay for what they have done! That is the law of nature. We don't have to do anything.

'When your great-great-Granny Truganini gave birth to a daughter, she kept quiet about it. She wanted her child to survive. In that century, all the full-blood Aboriginals in Tasmania were indeed wiped out, and very few others remained. There was little hope.

'So when a white man who had been rounding up Tasmanian Aboriginals left to take up a post in Victoria, Queen Truganini, who was in the party of Aboriginals who accompanied him, saw her chance to smuggle her daughter overseas – over the stormy ocean of Bass Strait, which none of us had been able to cross. This was in about 1839, and the man was called George Augustus Robinson. In accompanying him, Granny Truganini was continuing her mission to bring about peace between the black and white races. So poor little Louisa spent her early years with an Aboriginal family on the Victorian coast, but she wasn't left in peace. She got kidnapped by a white sealer, along with the woman named Marjorie who was minding her, and he carried them off to tiny Preservation Island in Bass Strait. It's important to remember that. There was a lot of slavery around in them days, but still nobody admits to it. Little Louisa would grow up there and become your great-granny, who you know as Granny Briggs.

'Her kidnapper is supposed to have had a thriving trade in

mutton-birding before the young Louisa came to live on his island. Mutton-birds got used for fuel – their oil and fat – and for eating, and their feathers got sold for pillows or mattresses. Aboriginal slave women used to carry a whole lot of mutton-birds in one go, strung on digging sticks which they would balance across their shoulders.

'But you must also be wondering what was happening to Granny Louisa's mother, Queen Truganini, whose tribal land was way down in the south. And you should be wondering about her, our respected ancestor. Well, of course Granny Truganini and her people ended up being political prisoners on their own land, Bruny Island. From there they were moved around from one island to another [including Swan Island, Gun Carriage Island and Flinders Island]. They used to sit on the beaches, looking across the ocean towards their holy native land. When they was almost all gone, the survivors were brought back to the south Tasmanian mainland [to Oyster Cove, near Hobart].

'In the Tasmanian town of Hobart, white people were beginning to think that all the Aboriginals were at last under their control, kept together on windy, frozen islands with no trees where we died of tuberculosis, pneumonia, starvation and misery. I suppose this was about the 1830s. They had been turning my people into pet food. But not all Aboriginals had been caught. The town people had forgotten all about what might be going on in their far north where the government had no control, among the brutal men – well, not all of them were without hearts – who came home for six months of every year to the slave women who they'd dumped. Dumped on this island or that in wild Bass Strait. These lawless men were pirates and sealers and whalers.'

Mum stopped then, saying, 'I need a cup of tea now, and a spell.' Us kids sat in total silence. We were always really interested in the stories my parents told us in the evenings. There wasn't much to do at night – we didn't like going up the street. And we knew that this story was special, probably never to be told again. We hadn't known there was such a big difference between the islands around Tasmania. After a while, Mum sat down again and went on.

'I was telling you how our modern history began. In them far northern islands, all kinds of things were happening. One of the white sealers, he was your ancestor too. That red-headed and hazel-eyed George Briggs is a hero, special to us, no matter what he's done. God has been very good to our tribe, very, very good to us through him. We have made a new beginning here on the Australian mainland. But our modern history began with terrible violence – George Briggs himself took away a young girl, the full-blood daughter of your ancestor Chief Lamanabungarrah of northern Tasmania's Leterremairrener tribe, your great-great-Granny Woretermoteyenner. George Briggs still talked with the Chief, and told him his daughter was well. To this the Chief replied that he knew exactly how she was because she sent him smoke signals every day from her lonely hut on Cape Barren Island.

'This George Briggs, the sealer, he soon became very famous throughout the islands. Although his moods were as changeable as the weather, he was supposed to be a good seaman, responsible and skilful. Their son – his and Granny Woretermoteyenner's – was called John, and he grew up to be a noble, tall, strong, handsome man with a weather-beaten face, they say. And in 1844 our Grandfather John married Queen Truganini's daughter, Louisa – our Granny Briggs, who had been kidnapped and taken to Preservation Island all those years before.

'All the spiritual world is wailing over what happened to our women, and their children too. But working hard was something Tasmanian Aboriginal women were used to. Their jobs for the sealers meant killing seals and kangaroos, drying and curing their skins, building huts, gathering firewood, diving for shellfish and kelp, and making baskets and necklaces.

'Like any animal, seals could be caught by tricking. Tricking animals was only women's work now, there was no Aboriginal men around any more. Our women used to wet themselves all over and pretend to be seals. They enjoyed being seals – those were good days for women. They would lie down where the wind was blowing away from a seal colony and keep the seals calm by scratching when they scratched, and looking around when the seals did that. The seals would be convinced that the women were other seals! Then, suddenly, everyone would shout out, jump up and each hit two seals on the head with the waddies that they'd kept hidden.

'The white men what carried on a trade around Bass Strait generally kept a few Aboriginal women working for them on various islands. But when they had children, the women and men would usually throw them away. [Some children, though the result of rape, were kept.] The men gave the women rough names, like Boatswain. And some men would hang their women slaves upside down and beat them if they hadn't prepared enough sealskins for them.'

Our mother paused here and looked at us hard to see how we was taking in her story. Then she drew a deep breath and went on. 'They took our tribe's food – the seals, that is – they took the women and in the end there was not enough seals left for the men to make money. So they began settling down to family life. The Bass Strait Islanders might still be haunted by their terrible beginnings, but now they were managing to build a strong community. You would see neat homes with gardens and farms, well-built whaleboats and good-looking children running around. The women, they became advisors in the community. And the women told their men to think about mutton-birding.

'You have seen the mutton-birds around the coast at home. Little charcoal-grey fellahs – they look like fat seagulls with long slender wings, and when they are near a shark's nose they will dip their heads in the water to have a look, then flutter to just above the shark's tail, fearless and friendly. And they bravely swim near boats, even though they make such good fishing bait.

'They arrive on the Bass Strait islands every October from places the other side of the world, and lay their eggs in burrows high above the ocean. Once the young birds are hatched, the parents work hard at sea all day and land beside the burrow in the dusk. They'll fly straight into anyone standing there.

'They hatch in February, the youngsters, and after nine weeks they're fat and oily, double the size and weight of full-grown birds. That is when the parents fly off, and that is the best time to collect the youngsters, before they lose condition. The babies stay in their burrows, starving, for up to eight weeks, missing their parents. They are much too heavy to fly. But in the end their fluffy down changes into flying feathers and the survivors all fly away together.

'This is Granny Louisa's story that was handed down to me and which I now pass on to you, my children. You must remember it all your lives, although you may never have the chance to tell anyone else.

'It was about this time a terrible massacre of Granny Louisa's people occurred. I think she might have been out mutton-birding at the time, with children and other women. A number of them was rounded up and herded towards a cliff by white sailors. They were yelling, "Jump or be shot!"

'I'm told lots of boats were anchored in the water below the cliff – it was all planned. Oh, the sailors were having a great day out, a great picnic. You could hear them laughing as the women and little children fell to their deaths. As usual, our people swam to the sides of the boats and held on, begging for mercy. But the sailors hacked off their hands and they drowned. The water turned red.

'Our ancestor George Briggs was working nearby with his son John when word of the massacre reached them from white people who wanted no part in it. They quickly brought their whaleboat around to see if they could save anyone. They pulled it around and around, picking all the people they could out of the water. They picked up Louisa and the other strong swimmers. Then George Briggs turned his boat and headed straight for the coast of mainland Australia, without stopping. Victoria, in fact. And that is how my side of our family began again here, through Granny Louisa and Grandfather John's daughter Polly.'

That is what my mum told us kids that night, and she was very tired when she finished. Mum was always very proud of being the great-granddaughter of Queen Truganini of Tasmania. I have kept this story secret all my life, and have only just spoken of it now.*

---

*It certainly used to be dangerous for Aboriginal people to talk about massacres, and the habit of secrecy has tended to continue.

Queen Truganini died at Oyster Cove in 1876. Her body was exhumed in 1878 and given to the Royal Society of Tasmania. From then until 1904 she was kept in a vault in the Museum of the Royal Society of Tasmania, but in 1904 she was taken to Melbourne where a plaster cast of her skeleton was made. She was then taken back to Tasmania and her skeleton displayed there until 1947, when she was returned to the vault as a result of complaints that she was being treated like a sideshow. During the 1970s, Tasmanian Aboriginal people campaigned to have her body returned to them. The government agreed and in 1976, one hundred years after her death, she was cremated and her ashes scattered in the D'Entrecasteaux Channel. Banjo Clarke's mother, Mrs Mary Clarke, and his children Leonard and Patricia went to Tasmania in an official party to supervise the scattering of the ashes.

CHAPTER 7

Granny Truganini's daughter Louisa, who we call Granny Briggs, was a strong-minded, hard-working and caring woman with deep, flashing eyes. Mum always had a big photograph on her sitting-room wall of her, holding Granny Polly, her daughter. All of us descendants from Granny Louisa and Grandfather John have a reddish tinge to our black hair, and when I visited Cummeragunja Mission I noticed the flaming red curly hair on some of my aunts and uncles.

Granny Polly, my mother's mother, already had grey hair when I knew her as a teenager. I remember her sitting and smoking a clay pipe on the ancient verandah at Cummeragunja Mission. I can still hear her saying hello to me and feel her taking my hand.

Granny Louisa and Grandfather John are supposed to have had ten children before they came to mainland Australia in 1853. They tried their luck on the Victorian goldfields for a while, and then went to work as shepherds near Beaufort. Granny Louisa even spent time in Warrnambool at some stage. They later moved to Coranderrk Aboriginal Station near Healesville, and Granny Louisa became a nurse and midwife there. In 1876 she was appointed matron, and then became spokesperson for all the residents and fought for everyone's rights. She was instrumental in getting the popular first manager, John Green, reappointed after he was sacked. He was a good man who believed that Aboriginal people should be allowed to manage all their own affairs. He even put all his own wages from the Aboriginal Protection Board back into the mission.

Coranderrk Station was founded by Mr Green and the tribal people of the Yarra Valley area in 1863. At the time only about two hundred and fifty of the local Kulin people had survived the white man's coming. Most of them agreed with John Green's suggestion to make their home at Coranderrk where they would be safer, and later fought to keep it because the reserve was the only land left to them.

John Green and Granny Louisa appealed and spoke to the board in the 1870s when the board decided to sell the mission and drive the residents away to other reserves. Granny Louisa gave evidence at an inquiry about that, but was removed to Ebenezer Station in Victoria's north-east because she spoke out. Then, after another inquiry, she moved back to Coranderrk in 1882. A few years later, in 1886, the government passed the *Aborigines Protection Act* that had caused such heartache on our own mission at Framlingham. It forced all the half-castes off the missions, and Granny Louisa's own sons were driven away.

Coranderrk had been a thriving, successful settlement until then. The people had built up a real little community there, with a school, a sawmill, a dairy, a bakery and a butcher's shop. They had planted many crops, had a thriving hops industry, and were pretty much self-sufficient. But when the Act came in, Coranderrk's population was halved, and with it its workforce. The farm fell into disuse then, and Granny Louisa moved to Maloga Mission and afterwards to my mother's childhood country, Cummeragunja Mission. So many families were completely broken up at this time.

Granny Louisa died at Cummeragunja when she was very old. This obituary for her appeared in the *Standard* newspaper on 29 September 1925:

Louisa Briggs, an Aboriginal half-caste died at Cummeragunja Aboriginal Station on September 8 . . . Being directly related to

King John and Queen Truganini, she was therefore the absolute last of the Tasmanians. [This is disputed today.] She was a fine type of half-caste Aboriginal, her hair being snow white. She had a constitution of iron, and was a very heavy smoker, but did not indulge in intoxicants. She was a prolific reader of good literature, but was happy as any child when able to see a comic paper. She was in possession of her faculties up till twelve months ago, and at short periods since. Louisa left Tasmania when in her teens, crossing to Victoria in an old sailing clipper. She . . . set out with her husband to the goldfields. From there she wandered to Warrnambool, thence to Maloga mission, where she for many years acted as baker to the whole camp. Finally she moved with the rest of her people to the present government station of Cummeragunja. She was buried in the station cemetery with full religious orders, the service being read by one of her relatives. The school children made a large wreath of violets which was laid on the grave.

A few full-bloods were allowed to stay on at Coranderrk, but half the remaining farmland was sold to surrounding white farmers in 1893. Then, in the 1920s, the board moved most of the remaining residents to Lake Tyers in Gippsland under police escort. The government planned to close all Aboriginal settlements except Tyers. Only a handful of elderly residents were allowed to stay at Coranderrk while the government waited, and probably hoped, for them to die out. Then, after World War II, all the Coranderrk land was sold for a token sum to returned soldiers, but not to any Aboriginal soldiers.

There was, and still is, so much anger and frustration over what happened at Coranderrk. It was probably the most happy and successful mission in the country and yet it was a constant battle just to be allowed to stay there. You see, as soon as the farm was going well and the land was all cultivated and fertile, most of the surrounding white farmers got jealous and wanted it for themselves. And yet they hadn't wanted it before it was successful farming land. No one had wanted it then. And the government wanted to keep them white farmers happy of course, because they could vote and the blackfellahs couldn't, so what they wanted didn't matter. That's what it came down to in the end.

Another famous crusader and leader of the Coranderrk community who would have been Granny Louisa's friend was William Barak, who they called 'the last king of the Yarra Yarra tribe', and the last king of any tribe in Victoria. Even white people called him a king, in both name and nature. But he's a bit forgotten now, and that's a sad thing. He was leader of the Woiworung people, and as a teenager in 1835 had witnessed the handing over of 600 000 acres of land around Melbourne to white people, at the signing of John Batman's 'treaty' with his father Bebejern and seven other so-called Aboriginal chieftains.

As the settlement around Melbourne grew in them early days, Barak went to school for a while and became a Christian. But then he went back to his beloved bush and lived with his tribe. He grew up strong and healthy, and was well known for his skills at fire-making, boomerang throwing and hunting. While still a young man, he joined the Native Police and became an excellent tracker. After he left them, he went to Gippsland where he got married, and then to Acheron where he and his wife lived with the Yarra Yarra tribe again. That's when John Green came into contact with them and they all moved to Coranderrk Station.

It was at Coranderrk that Barak succeeded his half-brother Wonga to become, in effect, the leader of his tribe. Everyone said that Barak always carried himself erect, and with real dignity. He had thick, wavy hair, fine features and piercing black eyes. A white woman, Anna Leuba [born Herr, whose family had migrated from Switzerland in 1857 and settled in the Yarra Valley area], befriended Barak and commissioned an oil painting of him by French artist John Mather. Anna's daughter Natalie Robarts, who was matron at Coranderrk for fourteen years with her husband Charles, later donated the painting to the Melbourne Museum.

Barak was a great campaigner for his people's rights and spoke for them at the same inquiries as Granny Louisa. Twice he marched with a group of supporters to Melbourne to protest against the board trying to close Coranderrk. He was very brave doing that, because when Aboriginals spoke out in them days, they were often moved off their missions as punishment.

Natalie and Charles Robarts' son Oswald, who grew up around Barak at Coranderrk and later became a journalist, wrote an article about Barak after he died, with Leo Kelly. They titled it 'Barak – Aboriginal Monarch', and wrote:

> One of the most memorable of Australian Aboriginal chieftains was King Barak, the distinguished leader of the Yarra Yarra tribe that at one time roamed southern Victoria.
>
> Barak was a king not only by name but by nature. He was a man of many parts . . . statesman, hunter, singer, artist and champion of his own people . . . He was a great statesman of the Aboriginal race. His dignity, intelligence and integrity of character also commanded the respect and admiration of governors, politicians and people of influence and position in all walks of Australian life.
>
> Barak felt deeply for the hard lot of his people in the early years of colonisation, and he spoke up bravely and eloquently on their behalf. He led many delegations of chieftains to those in

authority, and with the aid of two half-caste secretaries wrote on
these matters to the newspapers.

Due to his efforts, much was done to lighten the burdens of
many Aborigines.

Barak met with much personal sorrow in his life . . . He was
married four times, but each union was broken in turn by the
death of his partner. The death of a 16-year-old son from tuber-
culosis at the Melbourne Hospital dealt a severe blow to him in
his later years. Eventually all his children predeceased him.

The impact of a western mode of living . . . took its toll of his
own tribe, and as the years passed, their numbers dwindled. In
the end, King Barak was the only one left in his little kingdom.
He was sustained in the sadness of his old age by his deep reli-
gious beliefs.

He predicted his own departure in the words: 'When the wat-
tle trees come into blossom, I shall be going home.'

And so it was. Wattles commence to blossom in early August,
and it was on August 15, 1903 that he died, aged 85 years.

POSTSCRIPT TO CHAPTER 7

Before Banjo died, he asked for letters to be found that were written
by and about Louisa Briggs while she and her family were at Ebenezer
Station, in exile from Coranderrk. He had heard that some still existed
and were heartbreaking in their descriptions of the family being split
up, and their unhappiness at the mission station. A long search finally
led to the National Archives, where some of the letters were found.
They give a strong impression of the responsibility for others that
Louisa naturally took on herself; of the deliberate splitting up of the

Briggs family because they were so vocal about their rights when they were together; of the refusal of permission for Louisa to visit her dying son Jack at Coranderrk, as if it were a matter of no importance (and of the Aborigines Protection Board's initial failure to let her know about his condition); and of the family indeed starving. Louisa seems to have been too proud to mention the starvation herself (her daughter wrote this letter on her behalf), and too proud to request to go back to Coranderrk until she had been away for four years and her request had some chance of meeting with success. She obviously knew that she and her family had been exiled as punishment.

Excerpts from these letters follow, some written by Louisa (in painstaking and beseeching politeness), and some by the manager of Ebenezer Station, Reverend C. W. Kramer, to Captain Page, an official at the Aborigines Protection Board.

Rev. C. W. Kramer to Captain Page, 23 June 1879

The other day he [Louisa's son Mooney] *asked permission to go away to Swan Hill, Gannawarra and Echuca . . . When I refused permission he commenced to lecture me as to what he considered to be my duty and what not . . . Of course I took exception to this . . . If you would kindly inform him that he has to submit to the mild rules of the station, you would most assuredly do a good and desirable thing, otherwise a bad precedent will be established and you will be constantly pestered with worthless complaints by these blacks whenever they are crossed. Mrs Briggs would* [not] *be long following suit with a grievance. I refused to advance her the money for a trip to Coranderrk to see her son who according to accounts that reached her from there is in a dying condition. Meanwhile, of course, she would leave the girls with their fits here for me to mind, I suppose.*

Rev. C. W. Kramer to Captain Page, 29 June 1879

*Mrs Briggs having received another letter to say that her son
[Jack] is dangerously ill and is being taken to the Melbourne hospital wonders whether the information is correct. It is puzzling to
her, that you should not have mentioned Jack, when writing
to her about Mrs Charles. Maggie* [Louisa's daughter] *is in the
hospital in Horsham.*

Rev. C. W. Kramer to Captain Page, 1 July 1879

Our people were not a little amused when he [Louisa's son
Mooney] *told me in their presence that he had been told I was
managing this station for the German Government, a thing
that ought not to be.* [The German Government had the
reputation of being particularly strict.] *Another thing that
causes him much perplexity is that we call this place a Mission
Station and not a Government Station on which point Mrs
Briggs is much exercised in her mind. You will have to settle a
great deal.* [Louisa was known to be a devout Christian and
she could see the disparity between how the station was run
by the Protestant missionary body and the mission of true
Christians.]

*I am glad you do not take any notice of Mrs Briggs's applica-
tion for this, that and the other thing. If her big daughter Sarah
would do some work they would have money enough to buy their
necessaries.*

Rev. C. W. Kramer to Captain Page, 13 August 1879

*I am sure you are deeply grieved to hear about Maggie Briggs's
bad behaviour while in the Horsham Hospital. I was going to
trouble you with a long account of the three eldest Briggs's*

children's further misdeeds which led to the turn-over I had with Mrs Briggs on Monday, but shall forbear, Mrs Briggs and the two girls having promised submission to the rules of the place and the boy, I believe will do the same shortly. I may however, just mention what their objectionable behaviour consisted in, viz, going without my knowledge and consent after nightfall to evening parties and dancing with unprincipled young white and black fellows, at a neighbouring station . . . You may fancy how much shocked we all were when these goings on of theirs came to our knowledge which might not have happened for some time . . . had I not descried them dancing in the bush one day when they did not suspect me to be about.

And now I have one request to make even at the risk of being considered fickle and given to change in my views and that is not to send Jack Briggs and his family here, they being, apparently, strong and healthy, but only Mrs Briggs's daughter who, she says, is delicate. As the Briggs party from their large number must necessarily have a great deal of influence in a place and as that influence of those here manifests itself in the wrong direction I am decidedly of opinion that in the interests of this station it is desirable to keep the party split as individuals.

Louisa Briggs to Captain Page, 25 August 1879
Please Mr Page will you be so kind enough to send a pass for me to go down to see my Daughter [at Coranderrk] as you promised that I could go down to be with her at her confinement, please could you send me up some money for to pay the coach affair, and to buy a pair of boots and stocking and a hat. I want some boots for the children they are nearly barefooted I sent down once before but I never got an answer but if you would send them up I

would be very thankful. My daughter wrote up twice for me to go
down at the end of this month . . .

 So I must conclude with my best regards to you . . .
Your ever dearest Friend
Mrs Louisa Briggs
Write soon

Rev. C. W. Kramer to Captain Page, 8 October 1879

Would you kindly inform me whether I may expect some more
help from the Board through you as regards the supply of meat
for the blacks, and whether the Board would approve of, or
object to, my soliciting donations in sheep from some of the
squatters in the district. These last two weeks I have been
killing off our own sheep and shall be able to do so for some
more weeks, when, I'm afraid, all wethers fit for killing shall
have been drafted off and I shall find myself in a dilemma
again.

Louisa Briggs to Captain Page, 22 October 1881

Dear Sir, I am writing these few lines to you asking you to go back
to Coranderrk Stat again. I have now been here about four years.
So I would like to go back again to see my friends and my family
again. Please would you let me know by Wednesday. I will thank
you for your kindness. My kind regards to you.

Louisa Briggs to Captain Page, 15 February 1882
(penned by Louisa's daughter, Maggie)

I now takes this hurry opportunity of Writing these few lines to
you; I was expecting you up since I got your letter; Please will
your finds me a pass up; So I'll could go to Coranderrk; and if you

did sends me a pass let me know . . . and I will know to know; let
me know by Tuesday or Saturday
the place is too hot: and we are starving
So I must conclude this short note with the conclusion
with my best regards to you
I am dear Sir your truly
Mrs Briggs
Write the return of mail

Rev. C. W. Kramer to Captain Page, 13 March 1882

Mrs Briggs left about 10 days ago and is camping near Dimboola
where Jack and her son-in-law Allan are working at the railway
to earn some money to pay their fare to Melbourne . . . she will
probably leave for Melbourne on Thursday. [Louisa and her
family had finally been given permission to return to Coranderrk after six years in exile.] Ask her for an explanation re her
starving here when she passes through Melbourne as I shall not
see her again. She told me that Maggie wrote it without the
mother's knowledge and consent. When here she got rations
according to the scale given in the official letter. I must say, however, in regard to her son-in-law, who is a strong able bodied
half-caste, that I stopped his ration and very probably they would
run short if she fed him out of their allowance . . . After having
cautioned him a number of times [about coming home drunk]
without the desired effect I was at last compelled to take the step
indicated above, and the place is much more quiet. He will probably come to Corranderrk too, although you told him some time
ago you did not want him there.

CHAPTER 8

One day this newspaper boy told me that a couple of girls had a ballroom-dancing school in the city centre and they wanted an Aboriginal lad. I didn't know what they wanted an Aboriginal for, but I went along to find out.

They gave me a big cane and a uniform. From 6.30 p.m. to 8.30 p.m. I had to stand outside a big building, all lit up, and sing out, 'Miss Nancy Lee's Dance on second floor! Miss Nancy Lee's Dance on second floor!'

I suppose I was about ten at the time. I had a little cap on, and gold buttons all over me. I pointed my cane towards the door, letting people know there was a dancing school there. People had never seen an Aboriginal boy singing out like that in the city. They used to stop and ask me what was I doing there, and what it was all about. A lot of them went on upstairs after that to have a look in the big hall at the lessons being given. In the end they'd often sign up for dancing classes. 'Miss Nancy Lee!' I'd call, and point the way.

I only did it a few times – I got itchy feet and wanted to get out of the city. The girls said I brought them a lot of customers, though, so they were disappointed when I left.

My dad went to help build the big reservoir at Sylvan and I decided to go with him. There had been no work for the fathers of families to do, so the government created jobs. People would work at something for a fortnight, then give someone else a go. They done a lot of good jobs – built reservoirs, cleaned logs out of the Gippsland rivers. Wonderful jobs they did, although they probably didn't get much pay for it. But they was proud to be working. They was hard-working people from all walks of life. No matter where the job was, they'd go. My dad had constant employment that way.

Not like today – you get given money without working. And some of the young people today, they've been out of work so long, it's like getting an invalid pension. In the end they believe they can't work. When work is mentioned, they get scared, because they're frightened they won't be able to do it. And they're depending on this dole money. It's ruined the young people's lives, I think, because they've got to depend so much on government handouts. White people, I'm speaking about now. And that's what destroyed the Aboriginal people too. The handouts from white governments and mission stations. Now the governments are doing the same thing to their own young unemployed people. You can get cut off from your independence very quickly.

On mission stations like Lake Tyers, the big white manager handed out flour, sugar and tea and a bit of baccy if you worked. And the little children followed their parents along to the good big white manager. Then when they went to the big city looking for work, they'd be shunned and hang around on a street corner. A good white man would come up and say, 'Hey, you boys, where do you come from?' They'd answer, 'Oh, such-and-such a place. You got two bob on you?' The white bloke would give it to them and everyone would turn around and say, 'Them lazy blackfellahs, hanging around the street cadging.' And that's what they were taught to do on the mission, hold out the hand to the missionary. The kids grew up believing you gotta hold your hand out to the white man, otherwise you get nothing. They gave out supplies for a while on Framlingham in the early days, but never in my time. Even in the early days our people were independent workers, fighters for our rights.

It was good to work alongside my dad at Sylvan. We would talk about all sorts of things. I'd wonder aloud how the Old People back at the mission were getting on. I'd ask my dad what life was like when he was young, and he'd reminisce about things. Dad would tell me about tribal wars, which were mainly over the stealing of women from other tribes and ended as soon as blood was drawn. And about the clever-man he watched healing people when he was young but who would break out with a terrible cry if there was no hope and someone was going to die. And about the custom of operating on weak men so that they couldn't have children. He'd tell me about the nett-netts – mysterious little short fellahs who used to live in our valley among the rocks, feeding on bush tucker and fish, before white people came. As we talked, my homeland would come alive for me again.

Other Aboriginals would pass through where Dad and I were working on the Sylvan dam. They'd be carrying an axe in their swags, on their way to a fruit-picking or woodcutting job. From time to time they'd take me with them.

My dad ended up having a permanent job in Melbourne on the Board of Works when the dole job was just about finished. But I soon got sick of the city. You couldn't walk up the street without the police having a go at you. Even if you was stone cold sober, they'd say you was drunk and lock you up.

There was nowhere to go. My mates used to sleep in the parks, and most would go to gaol. But all I wanted to do was get back in the bush and walk along the gullies, look into the rivers, find fish and eels and make a spear. So I got out of the city. I was just twelve years old when I first rolled my swag and left Melbourne. From then on, I would be back and forwards between the city and the bush, working all over the place. I worked in factories, as a builder's labourer, and at men's pick-and-shovel work when I was older. I done a lot of woodcutting – that was in my blood because my dad used to take me in the bush cutting with him when I was just big enough to walk.

Early on in my travels, I headed towards Bendigo and got a job up there cutting wood – my sister Amy was living there. I'd be there for a while and come back for a while. Then I went fruit-picking. I used to jump trains to get around. I'd wait near the grading for a train to come with a lot of trucks on – a big load. The engine would slow down and I'd run beside it and jump on. My cousin, another mate and I would go together. We'd hide in one of the trucks where they were carting all sorts of things. When we came to a station, we'd duck right down until the train pulled out again.

Occasionally our truck would get shunted off to a siding. When everything was quiet again we'd get out, ask someone the name of the place and work out where we had to go. Then we might hike across paddocks. One time we were walking in the night and it was all dry. There was hardly any grass. We asked a farmer at a farmhouse miles from anywhere could we have some water. He held out half a bottle of water to be shared between the three of us. We thought he was pretty mingy until we realised – no rain! He probably had no water himself.

So we kept on going till we found a dam. We was glad for a big drink of water. We camped there that night. And in the morning we got up and looked at the dam where we had drunk the water. It had dead sheep in it! But the water never made us sick.

On the outskirts of Echuca once we seen this white family outside an old decrepit farmhouse. They waved their hands to us – a lady with a lot of little children. We were hungry but we didn't know whether to go and ask for something to eat. But we had been taught that it was always best to ask from poor people, because they'd be more likely to share their food with us, knowing the feeling of hunger themselves. So we went across to the weatherboard farmhouse. The lady there was very kind to us. She did understand what it meant to go hungry.

But I often asked rich people for a feed too on my travels. I'd go up to well-to-do houses. Sometimes the owners wouldn't come out for a long time, and I thought they were scared of me. Plenty of times I was about to walk away, then someone would sing out, 'Hello! Are you all right?'

I'd say, 'I'm carrying my swag, searching for work, and I've had nothing to eat for a while. Do you want any work done around the house?' And some of them were good people and would fetch a feed out to me. But there was one little boy who fed me once that I've never forgotten.

One day I was crossing Melbourne on the Bendigo line when I seen this old squatter's house way back in the paddock. I thought, I'd better get a feed here, don't know how far the next house is. I left my swag on the highway and walked up the big tree-covered drive to the house. And when I was getting there I seen a tower, an old fortress tower. I was thinking, It might have been built in the early days, when the Aboriginals were travelling around and the squatters were scared. I'd heard that they used to take their guns and get together in towers and shoot Aboriginals like rabbits. It looked just like that to me, and I started thinking, Well, I'm Aboriginal but I'm hungry, so I'm going to ask these people for food anyway.

All them things were going through my head, but I wasn't going to turn back because I was nearly at the house. I knocked on the kitchen door.

A little boy came out. He said, 'Hello, mister. Can I help you?'

I asked him, 'Are your mum and dad home?'

'No, they've gone to Melbourne.'

'Well, is anybody in charge of the house?'

He said, 'No, only me. But my sister's down in the paddock rounding up sheep.'

'Never mind, mate.'

But he asked, 'What is it you want?'

'I'm carrying my swag and I'm feeling hungry for something to eat.'

'Oh,' he said. 'I can do that!'

The little boy left the kitchen door open and went and opened a security door to the larder where they kept bread and meat. He got a chair and stood up and reached down a can of pork. Then he took down homemade scones and cake and he pulled out a big leg of mutton. He was cutting it with a proper carving knife, putting it in a clean bag, and I was watching and thinking, I wish he'd hurry up. His people will come and see this Aboriginal, and their little boy giving all their tucker away!

I said, 'Thank you very much – that'll do.'

'No, no,' he said. 'I'll give you some more. There's plenty here. We've got lots of tucker.' And there he was, cutting away.

'That'll do, mate,' I said again, nervous. 'I'd better go.'

'All right,' he said. He wrapped the tucker up nicely, poor little fellah. He came out with me into the backyard.

I said, 'My swag's up on the highway.'

He asked, 'Could I walk with you a bit, mister?'

'Yes, mate,' I told him. 'You can walk with me any time you want to.'

So off we went. He walked beside me, and I'd catch him looking at me every now and then. So then I'd look sideways at him and smile at him.

'Excuse me, mister,' he finally said. 'Are you Aboriginal?'

'Yes, mate.' I said. 'I'm an Aboriginal.'

'Ah! Beauty!' he said. 'Beauty! You wait till my mum and dad come home. I'll tell them I met an Aboriginal and I gave him all the food.'

He was that glad! After a while, he was still walking with me and we was getting further and further from his farm. In the end I told him to turn back home, but he wouldn't. Getting desperate, I made him stand there still and I walked on.

When I looked back minutes later, the poor little bloke was still standing way back there watching me. I never forgot that little fellah.

During my visits home to Framlingham every now and then, I used to be with Cyril Austin all the time. We all called him Uncle Pompey. I camped with him in the wood yards where he was wood-cutting, walked the streets with him, hitchhiked to Warrnambool, and we went to the Warrnambool races together. He was a great man for betting. He was also the main person to provide eels and fish for the Aboriginal community from the traps he set. All the little children would help him. I stuck with Uncle Pompey when I was little, and also when I was a teenager.

It was because of him that I came by the name of Banjo, because I was born with a different name – Henry James. In Aboriginal law, around the age of fourteen years is the traditional age at which young men are initiated. And that is always done by an uncle. We adapt our Aboriginality to totally different circumstances today, but we always keep it; we always find an Aboriginal kind of answer to things. So when I reached fourteen, I had now become worthy to be initiated, to be given a new name. But when people ask me, 'Why "Banjo"?', I'm a bit cunning. I don't tell them the secrets behind the secrets.

I answer, 'I don't know why. I was always quoting Banjo Paterson, though.' But it was really because, throughout the day, I was always making up rhymes and poems describing every situation I found myself in, or we found ourselves in. And Uncle Pompey was the one who called me after Australia's most famous poet. And I grew to be more worthy of the name, and became a storyteller.

Anyway, this is how it all happened. One day when I was about fourteen, we was walking up the street in Warrnambool together and Pompey met a couple of his old white mates. They said, 'How're you going, Pompey?' and he said, 'All right.'

Then his friend said, 'You got a little mate here. What's his bloody name?'

Old Pompey replied, 'That's my young cousin, his name is Banjo Clarke.' But I'd never heard that name in my life.

And they said 'How're you going, Banjo? You stick with old Pompey, he'll look after you. He's a good old mate.'

I said, 'Yes, he always looks after me.' And from that day on I had that name, Banjo Clarke. And that's over sixty years ago. Old Pompey was the fellah that gave me that name and I'm proud he did, because I'm well known all over now as Banjo Clarke.

Pompey to us was a good worker and he was kind to children, and all the children loved him. But when he came to town, people looked on him and thought he was a no-hoper and a man hanging around the street cadging, and they were nasty to him. He found it hard to fight his way into the white man's society with his Aboriginal way of life because he still hung onto that. When there was wood-cutting in the bush, he'd be hired by all the farmers and he'd do all his honest work, and harvesting, and even milk cows for people and help them for nothing. But when he came to Warrnambool and couldn't get a job, he'd stand around the street and people would say, 'There's that

Aboriginal again, he's hanging around town. He's a no-hoper, he ought to go back out to the mission where he come from, all he do is cadge around the street.' But that wasn't the way it was at all. People used to come up and speak to him what knew him, and they looked on him as an old friend.

Pompey used to tell us the story of how his father, who we called Old Pompey, was locked up in the Melbourne Gaol once. The police gave him the job of cleaning out the death cell, where they hanged people. He saw the trapdoor and he cleaned the cell. Angus Murray had just been hanged. That man said he was innocent right to the end. Pompey said he had carved a hymn on the wall before he died. 'Sweet Hour Of Prayer', it was. The chorus went:

> All my petitions I shall bear
> Farewell, farewell, sweet hour of prayer
> And I'll shout while passing through the air
> Farewell, farewell, sweet hour of prayer.

Those were Angus's last words. Pompey used to get us to sing that hymn with him. Everyone would join in. It was real soul-singing, you know. Everyone singing from the heart, all different voices. It was beautiful – you could hear it for miles. Pompey loved hymns. He even died singing one.

His cousins used to get into trouble. They used to steal rabbit skins and sell the skins for money to get a bit of tucker, and the police couldn't catch them. They used to go in the middle of the night when everyone was sleeping and sell the skins next day. One day the police seen them with money and arrested them, and locked them up. Pompey got locked up there too, for questioning. They were all waiting in gaol for their trials, and his cousins were worried about it, but Pompey was walking up and down in the gaol singing, singing away all these gospel songs as usual and being happy as he used to be. Most of all, he was singing his old favourite hymn, 'Throw Out The Lifeline'. It goes:

Throw out the lifeline
Someone is sinking today
Throw out the lifeline
With an arm quick and strong
There is a brother whom someone should save . . .

And he said to his cousins, 'I feel so happy today that I don't like being that happy, because after happiness there is always sadness.' And he kept on singing the hymn and then he fell down. When the police came in, he was dead. He had died of a heart attack. He was only in his forties.

Everyone was sad over that. We took him back out to the mission and had a funeral, and everyone turned up what knew him – his cousins were allowed to come from gaol – and some of his white bosses turned up, because they had great respect for him. But most of all, all the little children missed him, because they loved their uncle. He used to help them put in the fish traps and do kind things for them. He was real kind-hearted to children. And I don't think he stole anything real bad or anything, though he done things to survive in this world what was hard to get on in.

CHAPTER 9

Back to Fitzroy, in Melbourne. I was just drifting around there when an old friend of my father's, Jacky Green, who had been working in the bush to the east, was about to return to his job. He said to my parents, 'I'll take young Banjo up for work. He'll be with good people.'

He took me with him to Tynong, and that's how I met the Weatherhead family. I helped Jacky Green fell timber for their sawmill. I stayed on for a long time after Jacky left, and the family treated me, a teenager, like one of their own. It was a new experience to be working for white people what treated me as an equal of anybody else.

I remember the early mornings when the boss's daughter Muriel and I would round up the working bullocks for the sawmill. It was all scrub country then. We'd wait to hear the leader's bell and hunt him out. The other bullocks would hear their leader going towards the yoke-up yard and they'd all follow.

One strong-looking Aboriginal from Lake Tyers Mission used to come regularly to see his old uncle there, who worked with me. He would come with his wife and little son. I'd say he was about twenty-five. And he started to embarrass me, because he wouldn't work. The Weatherheads were still kind to him, though. He liked to sleep in the big shed where they stacked the hay.

One day the whole lot of us workmen just hung around, doing odd jobs close to the house, because it was raining. This mission fellah from Lake Tyers was over in the shed with his wife. And I think it was Muriel who went to see him first. She invited him to the family kitchen for lunch, because when we ate we sat at the table with the family. But I think the man was a bit like me, not used to being at the same table as white people. He didn't want to come.

Old Mr Weatherhead said, 'Well, we can't let the poor fellah starve.' So he made a big plate of food and Muriel took it to the shed.

A few hours later, the weather fined up a bit, though there were still showers, and old Mr Weatherhead started thinking about a stump on the side of the track. He wanted to give our visitor something to do. So he said to me, 'Go and get your mate over there to help you grub out that stump.'

I said, 'Okay,' and went to the shed. 'Mr Weatherhead wants you to come up here, mate, to grub this stump out.'

'What?' the mission fellah said. 'I didn't come here to work. I came for a rest.'

I didn't know what to say. I thought he'd be glad to do something for his food. I went back to Mr Weatherhead.

'Well, is your mate all right? Is he going with you?'

'No,' I said. 'He's crook. But I'll go up anyway.'

Muriel was listening and she said, 'I'll go with Henry.' She often called me by my Christian name. She was my friend. Every chance she had, she'd help me. We had become like a real brother and sister. In no time she had the hoe and was digging around the stump. And I kept thinking about the man over there in the shed, probably having a sleep after his big feed, while this young girl worked hard.

The Weatherheads never mentioned working to that man again. They probably understood some of the effects mission life had had on Aboriginals. Mission Aboriginals was reared to be dependent – they couldn't have responsibility.

The Weatherheads used to take me to social dances. The first time they asked me, I said, 'Ah, I'm not going.'

'Why?' they demanded.

'Because I'm Aboriginal. They won't allow me in.'

'Don't talk stupid. You're our mate.'

'I might be all right with you fellahs, but not with other people.'

We went together anyway. Muriel and her brothers would protect me from any racist remarks. They was there to be moral support. That way a lot of young white people got to know me, and I learnt about them. And they treated me with respect.

While I was staying with the Weatherheads, Muriel kept asking me, 'When are you going to write home to your family?' And I would keep worrying about her questions and make excuses, saying, 'I never have time.'

'Your parents will be wondering where you are,' she'd say.

'They know where I am.'

'Well, you ought to tell them how you're getting on up here.'

Most days she said something like that. One Sunday, I was sitting under a big shady tree when I saw Muriel and her girlfriends coming towards me. There was a paper in Muriel's hand. Oh, God, I thought. Don't tell me she's going to make me write. She had a pen and ink too, and she said, 'Right-oh, Clarkey. No more excuses. You're going to write home to your mother today.'

'Ah,' I protested. 'Today? On a beautiful day like this?'

'Yes, this is the best day for you to write home. I was just telling my girlfriends while we were coming to see you that you'll make every excuse you can think of. You'll even tell us that you don't know how to write, won't you? Isn't that what you're going to do?'

I answered, 'Well, I can't.'

She turned to the other girls. 'See? I told you he'd say that, just to get out of it.'

I was silent, coming to the conclusion that I'd better tell the truth.

At last I said, 'No, I can't write. If I could write, I'd have written home long ago.'

'Really?'

'Yep. You might as well know the truth now.'

And the girls went sad. Before, they was all laughing.

Muriel asked me, 'You're my friend, aren't you? You don't tell me any lies.'

'No, you're like my sister. There's no way I would tell lies to my own people.'

'You know what?' she said. 'I believe you now. I didn't know that. I'm sorry, I wouldn't have come worrying you with my girlfriends.'

The girls had turned their backs, looking away. One girl was wiping her eyes. All these poor girls, I thought, they're real upset for me!

They put their arms around me, and said, 'Don't worry, mate. We'll look after you.'

And so they did. Every night from then on, after the day's work, Muriel and her sister would take me to where their father did the books and give me a lesson in reading and writing. They taught me all sorts of words, like 'hospital' and 'injury'.

'Why are you giving me all these big words?' I complained. 'They're pretty hard to do.'

'That's in case you get hurt,' Muriel said. 'You can write home and tell your people.'

I was only doing it to please Muriel and her sister, to go along with them, because I didn't understand the point of reading and writing. After all, I could work, I could make money. Knowing how to work was very important to me, but not reading and writing. As long as I could work, I was happy.

But they kept on teaching me, and in the end I got to like learning. 'Come on, it's lesson time. Hurry up!' I'd say. 'I'll help you wash the dishes so we can get started.' They were glad that I was keen to learn.

Muriel later said how surprised she was at how quickly I learnt to read, starting with letters of the alphabet, then graduating to the names of nearby towns. In no time, it seemed, I was reading her a poem from one of her schoolbooks. I even remember which one – Henry Kendall's 'The Last of His Tribe'.

Then, finally, I wrote home, a broken-English letter. But it was a good letter, right from the heart. My mum was surprised. When I went back to my parents for a holiday, I explained what had happened. Everybody was pleased about these good people who were looking after me. Muriel and I became the best of friends, and we still are today, over sixty years later. [When Banjo passed away, Muriel attended his funeral, and she died herself just a few months after him.] She became a schoolteacher and writer when she grew up, and always said I had been her first pupil.

And I love reading now, both books and newspapers. I've read a lot of things written from the white point of view. And that inspires me to tell people how I see things, through Aboriginal eyes.

When I left Muriel's family, I went back to Melbourne for a while. I used to hang around the boxing gymnasium in Russell Street a lot while my white friends were in school. My brother Frank and his mates were training there, so I'd tag along and watch them. But then Frank left and went up to Queensland to travel with the boxing troupes. After Frank had left and his mates all settled down in different places, I still hung around the gym on my own.

One day the trainer said to me, 'Can you box?'

'Um,' I said, 'I don't know.'

'Well, fetch a pair of shorts and a pair of sandshoes with you next time.'

The next day, I brought my shorts and borrowed the sandshoes, and he let me skip and punch the bag. I done all right. Afterwards, the trainer taught me to punch the speedball. I felt at home on that and learnt pretty quickly because I was always sparring with my mates. I done pretty good too, for a lad. I trained hard and had some good wins in the stadium – some losses too, but I was never hurt.

When I was fifteen, the Harry Johns boxing team snapped me up. He lived just up the road from us in Fitzroy. There were a lot of such teams around. I didn't join Jimmy Sharman's famous troupe until I was seventeen. It was easy for Aboriginals to get in the troupes – the managers knew we was better drawcards than the white blokes, because people in the audience were more interested to see us wild, black-looking men fight. Some people in the audience would be pretty racist. You'd hear them shout out, 'Kill the nigger!' sometimes. But that only made me more determined to win.

In all, I fought on and off with the troupes for about twenty-five years. I fought under the name of Henry Armstrong a lot of the time. I didn't want to be rich or a champion at it or anything. I just did it for the fun of it most of the time, but the few bob we made did come in handy. My cousin Henry Alberts travelled with me a lot.

People used to come to boxing tournaments in buses from miles around. It must have been pretty well their only form of entertainment. We in the troupes would follow the circuit of the agricultural shows around Victoria. In whatever town we journeyed to, we used to pitch the tent and put on a boxing show. There'd be bells ringing and drums going and the spruikers singing out and all the Aboriginals up in a line with their pretty robes on. All the groups' managers were showmen. They'd come up with every kind of idea to bring in the crowds and get money. They'd invite members of the audience to take us on. They'd say, 'Come and see your local champ fight the big Aborigine! Your local champ – I'll give him twenty pounds if he can stand up to him in three rounds.' They would also plant what we called 'gees' in the audience before a fight. They were mostly our blokes, posing as locals to get the crowd going and offer to take the troupe boxers on. The gees would get the crowd real fired up, giving us boxers real cheek. Then the crowd would pay to see the fight.

Then there would be the true locals who really wanted to fight you and knock you out. We called them 'takes'. Everyone would come in to see their local hero take us on. Some of them couldn't even fight, but it was part of our job to pretend that the local man had managed to knock us down. If we didn't, the crowd would be liable to burn the bloody tent down! We'd let a man hit us on the chin and we'd swiftly thump our own chests at the same time so the audience would think that a big punch had knocked us down. We boxers were great actors.

Just after my eighteenth birthday, I was in the open back of a truck travelling from the Port Fairy agricultural show to Maryborough with Jimmy Sharman's troupe, when we sped past an old weatherboard farmhouse that I recognised straight away. I hadn't seen it for years. I'd been boxing a lot in Melbourne by then, and it was my job to teach Jimmy Sharman's other young boxers. We were all piled in the back of his truck, seven or eight of us boxers and tent hands, along with tarpaulins and swags of bedding in case we needed to sleep. When I recognised the farmhouse it was about one o'clock in the afternoon on a blazing hot day.

Then further along the road I saw the flat roof and wide open doors of the old blacksmith's shop where we used to hang about as kids, watching the horses being shod. And I shouted, 'This is my own place!' So I knocked on the truck's cabin and told the driver to pull up. I yelled out, 'This is where I come from!'

The driver understood, all right. He said, 'If you get to the Maryborough show you can join up with us again.' But I don't think he really expected to see me there.

I got off the truck and I walked back a few hundred yards to Purnim store, where I saw a young shy girl, Audrey Couzens, and her brother Ozzie delivering cream. I didn't know it then, but here was the woman I was later going to marry! I hadn't really noticed her before, even though we were from the same place. She would have only been a baby when we first left the mission.

They offered me a lift home. Ozzie had a horse and cart with milk cans in the back. Audrey sat between us as we drove, and Ozzie and I talked. In those days girls usually didn't speak when two boys were together. I noticed Audrey looking straight ahead, her hair in two very long black plaits. I thought, All the little kids at home are growing up, and I felt real glad to be back.

They let me off at the corner of the mission and went on to their dairy. I was amazed to see so many new weatherboard houses. My people had mostly lived in huts before. The Couzens family had a new house, and so did my older half-sister Dolly. They were built by Aboriginal people and a new local board of management. I think the whitefellahs living near us had started to worry about us, and made donations. I walked along the track to Dolly's house, and stayed for many months before heading back to the city.

Us Aboriginals in Melbourne only joined the boxing teams every so often, in between working at other things. Because I didn't like the city, I rolled my swag and headed for the country whenever I could – any part of the country, as long as it was out of town. I used to come back home when I could to Framlingham because I still loved my old home, the place where I was born. And in the end I came back home for good after years travelling with boxing troupes, working in sideshows, being a builder's labourer, just carrying my swag searching for work.

Many times I went to country towns and people looked at me like they didn't want me there. I'd be laughed at and would walk away. But I never had any anger for people. I just felt sorry for them because I thought, They must be unhappy people and they're taking it out on me. I've never done anything to them. And often the police would arrest me and lock me up because they didn't believe I was just looking for honest work.

All them things happened in the 1930s and '40s, you know – it was terrible, but it was a part of life you had to live. I never felt anger over it though, I just felt sorry about how people was looking on us Aboriginals. But I got a lot of good jobs too and met a lot of good white people prepared to give me a go, and that's what kept me going. They'd come up to you and accept you from the goodness of their heart. They wouldn't go along with the official policy on us. And some of them are still my friends today, and their children.

Part Two
1939–1975

CHAPTER 10

I remember 1939 as the year Cummeragunja Mission residents declared war on their manager, and the year Britain declared war on Germany.

I was visiting my relations at Cummeragunja when the famous walk-off happened, looked upon as the first Aboriginal strike. Cummeragunja Mission, New South Wales, where my mother came from, is just across the Murray River from Victoria. As on most government reserves, people were not allowed to leave, and if they did, their cottages were pulled down to prevent their returning. Their rations were so pitiful that big numbers were dying of everyday illnesses. Children were being stolen from parents too, and so the residents decided to take action and launch a protest against all them things.

The great Aboriginal leader Jack Patten came to speak with us and lend support. I was impressed by his courage and honesty, and the power of his words. But the police came and arrested him.

Next day, the manager drove past us with a big gun sticking out of his car window. My aunt lifted a waddy high in the air and shook it at him. 'You can't kill us now, the way you did before!' she yelled. I just stood there, taking it all in.

Next thing I knew, about a hundred and seventy mission residents disappeared over the Murray River, so quick! They went in boats. Some went the long way round with bedding. They swam over – children too, as fast as fish. And a canvas village was raised the other side of the river, in Victoria. I joined them as soon as I'd caught my breath. This protest was a success as it helped bring about changes to the *Aborigines Protection Act* afterwards.

When World War II broke out later that year, I was in Mount Gambier, South Australia, with the Harry Johns boxing troupe. Our cook went shopping for breakfast supplies. He came back saying, 'Right-oh, you fighters, you'll get plenty of fight now! I just heard that Britain has declared war on Germany.'

Shortly after this, I had a break from boxing troupes and went home again to Framlingham Mission, working on the way as a wood-cutter. Boxing tournaments were being held all the time in various towns, and we'd hear of them in advance and get there to participate. The boxers who challenged us had gymnasiums and sparring part-ners, but us Aboriginals just used to spar among ourselves with towels around our fists.

All kinds of funny things happen when you're boxing. One time I travelled a long distance with every kind of hardship to face the champ, what never turned up! When the audience found out about it, they all threw coins at me. One night I was supposed to box in Colac, halfway along the highway to Melbourne, and I just missed the bus that was taking a number of us local lads there to fight. But I caught up with the others all right, by wading through a flooded creek with my smart clothes tied in a bundle on my head. Then I hitchhiked along the highway to Colac. A good fighter was sched-uled to box me that night – he had a big reputation. But my friends and I had fought all sorts of people what was supposed to have good reputations, and we had confidence in ourselves.

As soon as I reached Colac, I ran into this big fighter's mate. I knew him quite well, but to him all Aboriginals must have looked much the same. And I probably looked a bit different because I had my old bush clothes on instead of the clean, pressed shirt and trousers he'd always seen me in before.

'How're you going, mate?' I yelled out.

'Hello,' he said.

I asked him, 'Who's this Gerry Brown?' That's not his real name, but I don't like to talk about them poor fellahs.

'Oh, he's the best we've got around. He's fighting Banjo tonight.'

I thought, This bloke doesn't know me – that's good.

'Yeah?' I said. 'Well, how d'you reckon Banjo will go?'

'Banjo's not bad,' he answered. 'But this fellah will beat him. He's much too good for the fighters around here. He beats top fellahs in Melbourne and Geelong.'

'What does he win his fights by? On points or knockouts?'

'Oh, both,' he told me. 'But he wins most of them by knockouts.'

'Jeez!' I said. 'It looks like I've got a tough fight tonight.'

'Are you Banjo?' he said, shocked.

He took off then, and I followed him. I peered in through the doorway as he ran into my opponent's dressing room. He shouted to him, 'Where's all the boys? Get all their money. I just spoke to the nigger. The nigger's already beat!'

Gerry Brown asked, 'Where'd you see him?'

'Out there.' He pointed through the doorway, and when they looked they saw me standing there.

'Okay, mate,' I said to them. 'I just heard what you said. So get in the ring and see if you can beat this nigger.'

But when the time came for our fight, he didn't last five minutes! I knocked the poor fellah out because I was especially determined to win. And I didn't even have boots on. I used to share a pair of boots with my cousin Henry Alberts. He had a fight right before me and wore our boots, but he didn't realise I was going on straight after him and went off into the toilet with them. I was running around before the fight looking for him, saying, 'Where's my boots? Where's my boots?' because I had to go on straight away. So I had to fight without any boots, but I won the fight all the same.

Years afterwards, I saw Gerry Brown in the pub, and when he realised who I was he took off. He must have been thinking about that night years ago.

Later, I met him again and said, 'How're you going, mate?' and shook his hand. He ended up being my best friend then.

It wasn't long after World War II had broken out when I first met the Alabama Kid, the great black American boxer, in Melbourne. The uncrowned boxing champion of the world, they called him. His real name was Clarence Olin Reeves, and he'd come to Australia in 1939.

He took me to his gym. No one was there to spar with him, so he asked me to. I thought, Oh, I might give him one punch.

We put on the gloves and he said, 'Hit as hard as you want.'

I was hitting him hard because I knew I couldn't hurt him, this great big black American.

'Hey, listen here, son,' he said eventually. 'You've got a mighty punch there. You rocked me a bit, and you're not even half as big as me.'

And from then on he took a liking to me. He was at my parents' place every night for two weeks, begging them to sign the papers for him to take me to America.

'You listen here,' he said to me. 'If you come to America you'll be a top fighter. You'll be the first Aboriginal to be a top fighter in the United States.'

But my mum and dad wouldn't sign the papers. They kept saying, 'He's too young. He's too young.'

In the end the Alabama Kid decided to stay in Australia too. He joined the Harry Johns boxing team I was in, and he always insisted on riding in the back of the big van with the rest of us blackfellahs. He could have gone in the owner's car, but he preferred to be in the back and sing with us. He was a good singer too. Going along the road, we'd all take turns to sing different songs.

He married a white girl here and they had two children, a girl and a boy. He worked in a boot factory when he wasn't boxing. He tried to get naturalisation here so he could stay permanently but the government refused. He couldn't take his family back to America because there was too much racial strife there. Clarence tried to appeal to the government and the public to allow him to stay, through the newspapers:

I'm black, but I've done nothing wrong. I love Australia almost as much as I love my wife and baby, but you can't love long distance. If I take my wife back her only friends will be Negroes. She would probably enjoy it until the glamour wore off, and then the memory of her mother and white friends here would bring heartaches. I want my wife to be happy always. If I leave here I'd travel back and forth every year to see her and the babies, but that takes money, and I'm no millionaire. I respect the White Australia policy, but if Mr Calwell [the then Minister for Immigration] *was in my place he would understand.*

But the Immigration Department grabbed him after a fight at Moss Vale and deported him. He never saw his wife and kids again.

Years after, I met his daughter. And when I told her my name, she put her arms around me and said, 'My dad talked about you. I remember you from when I was a little girl.' She was so happy to see me, she took me all over the place. She said she was planning to go to America to find her dad.

But I don't think she ever did. She joined a dancing troupe and they went to Tel Aviv, but I don't think she had the chance to go to America. Then she came home and got married. They had two children. Then one day she was in the kitchen and the poor girl collapsed and died.

My son Ian met the Alabama Kid's other child once, his son, and Ian was telling him about me. The son wanted to come and see me because I'd known his dad. So I might get the chance to meet him one day. I'll tell him all about how his dad and I both joined a travelling boxing troupe together. How he'd ride in the back of the big van with us so he could join in the singing. I'll tell him what a good singer his dad was.

Early on during World War II, they were recruiting soldiers for the army. A mate of mine, Herb, and I decided, 'Oh well, we'll join the army too. We'll go and see something.' We were only about nineteen.

So we went to the office in Fitzroy, where we met some army men. I told them, 'Me and my mate want to join the army.'

The young officer in charge demanded, 'What do you want to join the army for?'

We said, 'Everybody seems to be joining the army. Things over there are getting serious. We want to fight for our country.'

'What's the good of you Aboriginals fighting for this place,' he asked us, 'when you're not even treated as citizens here?'

The young officer seemed to understand our plight – being the first Australians, and yet denied citizenship in our own land. But we thought them was strange words for wartime.

'You could do something else useful without going to war,' he told us. 'Why don't you join the Allied Works Council?'

'What's that?' we asked.

'Building roads and aerodromes for the army in the far north. Making a highway through to Darwin.'

So we joined the Allied work camps on the spot, and three days later Herb and me left to join them up north. The first place they sent us to was a staging camp in Brisbane. A Maltese mate of mine in the camp there showed me my brother's photo in the newspaper one day and said, 'His name's Clarke. Any relation?' 'Yes,' I said, 'he's my brother!' So we went to South Brisbane, where all the Aboriginals lived, and asked around, and were told that my brother always came along a certain street in the evening after his boxing training. So I stood against a verandah post to wait for him and eventually my brother came past. I recognised him all right, and I said, 'G'day, brother.'

He said, 'G'day,' and I thought, Gee, this bloke doesn't know me. So I said, 'How are you doing?' and I went up and shook his hand.

He said, 'I know you from somewhere. Could it be Sydney, New South Wales?'

'No, Victoria.' And then he realised who I was and he couldn't have been happier to see me, and he took my Maltese friend and me out for a big meal. Later, when I had a fortnight's leave, I went to find him again and I stayed with him. He couldn't have made me more welcome.

Brisbane was full of soldiers that fortnight. It seemed like soldiers had come from all countries – Indian, American, every nationality. Naval ships were in, and all the black Americans gave big dances in the hall where they were stationed and they invited all the people around and were really, really happy to see Aboriginal people.

Aboriginal people were happy to see them because they put on big dances. There were whole bands that had come from America and played for us – really top bands. Black Americans that I'd met in Melbourne I met again then, because when the ship docked in Melbourne they used to seek out Aboriginal areas and put on big dances too. A lot of them were really young fellahs who missed their mothers, and meeting Aboriginal families made up for that in many ways. They were really well-educated people, a lot of them, officers and everything, with top responsibilities.

After the staging camp in Brisbane, we were sent to Eidsvold to work on the Banana Road. Men from all over Australia was working there, building a bitumen road through to Darwin. Some had been rejected by the army, but they still wanted to do their bit. But some fellahs were just there to hide from their wives and other problems!

It was a tough job, but being a country bloke I was used to country work – it was just part of our life. It was good heat for working in, there – clear heat. When it's hot down here, it burns you. I got a lot blacker there, but I didn't get burnt, and most whitefellahs didn't either. Only some with really fair skin. We worked for twenty-four hours a day, right round the clock. I've never seen so much machinery in one place. There were graders, big bulldozers, big trucks – a lot of truck companies closed down, I think, because the army took them over. I think the Americans brought the bulldozers, because I hadn't seen any on farms. The bulldozers mostly had caterpillar wheels – a metal band that went right around all the wheels one side, and another one the other side – and they would crawl up rocks, crawl up mountains, crawl over anything. Explosions would be flattening the hills in the daytime so that the road could go through; there was all this earth-moving equipment, night and day, day and night, and eventually we sealed the road. There were lots and lots of camps of work gangs, and we'd meet them when the roads we were building met.

We used to go to town on our time off, but we always came back sober on a Sunday evening. We'd be exhausted from visiting the Aboriginal camps around Eidsvold, and watching other people play cards and two-up until the early hours of the morning. We boarded in a hotel when we went to town.

One time we took some bottles of beer back with us, but we didn't even feel like drinking one bottle because we were fed up with our weekend. Our white mates came over what didn't go to town, and we said, 'There's some beer there, mate. Get into it.'

'Don't you fellahs want any?'

'No.'

They drank the beer, about six bottles between them. But before they left our camp we were sound asleep.

Next day, we heard that at about two or three o'clock in the morning a truckload of blokes came home and they put on the biggest disturbance you could ever hear, fighting and yelling all night. And most of the men in our camp had to get up early to go on shift work.

We went over to the big kitchen and were just sitting down to have breakfast – we were the only two Aboriginals in this big camp – when the overseer marched straight up to me and Herb. He said, 'Right-oh! You two blackfellahs, I've got something to say to you. Next time you get drunk in town, don't come home and keep the camp awake all night. There's men here that need to work.'

I knew we hadn't done it. 'No, we never,' we said.

'Yes, you did. Don't argue with me!'

There were six hundred men in our camp and it seemed like they all stopped eating to listen. The overseer offered to fight us over it. I sized him up. He wore glasses, but he had a broken nose and a cauliflower ear. I said, 'Right. We'll get outside and have it out. But Herb and I never did what you said we done.'

He walked out behind me, then he suddenly ran off, yelling, 'I'll sack you!' I knew you couldn't be sacked in them days, though, because you was working for the army. They had to transfer you instead.

The Chinese cook was walking past at this time, holding up a big knife. I grabbed the knife from the cook and chased the overseer with it through the scrub, just to give him a fright. I couldn't catch him anyway.

Later that morning, the foreman of our gang came up to me while I was working. 'You're going to another job, Banjo,' he said.

'Yeah? How come?'

'They need another bloke way down near Woolooga.'

'What about me mate Herb? We joined up together on this job. We work together all the time. Is he coming with me?'

'Yes, in a fortnight's time. They want a bloke like you to help them out. You can have your dinner and collect your things.'

I thought, Well, I might have been here too long. It's time I saw a few other places. But I was disappointed that Herb wasn't coming with me straight away. He was a good sticker in times of trouble. Now I'd be on my own, I thought, in a strange gubbah [white] place.

Later, I was sitting down waiting for the transport truck to take me to this other job, and looking out through the cookhouse, when I saw thirty or forty men coming towards my camp.

I thought, Cripes! What have I done wrong now?

And they came up to me. The leader was the union representative. He shouted, 'We hear you're going on another job, Banjo.'

'Yes,' I said.

'Do you want to go?'

'I suppose I'll go,' I said. 'I might have been here too long.'

But the union rep told me, 'They're sending you away for nothing at all. You didn't put on that fight the other night. We know who did – a truckload of white men.'

'Yeah?' I said. 'Me and Herb were sound asleep. We didn't hear a thing.'

'Yes, that's what your other mates say, that you fellahs were sleeping. The blokes who did it, they're well known for their rowdiness and fights when they come back from town.'

Then the union rep said to me, 'If you want to go, you can. But there are over three thousand men working along this road. If you don't want to go, I'll pull them all out on strike today. Because you're being wrongfully dismissed from this job.'

For a while I thought about it, but then I decided I wouldn't stay. I thanked them anyway – I really appreciated what they done for me, sticking by me like that.

That sort of thing never happened before, I think. Two young Aboriginals working for a white gang accused by the white boss of something we didn't do, and the representative of the union took our side. At that moment I didn't realise how momentous it was. But now, remembering how all those working men came up to me, I think I should have stayed. Because I reckon that it would have made history – so many white men going out on strike for me, the Aboriginal worker.

Men from every corner of Australia was working in the north. And they was powerful too, with their working-man principles. I could still have said, 'Oh well, I'll go now,' when the strike was over and everything had been cleared up. It might have taught the people of Australia not to do whatever they liked to someone just because they was Aboriginal.

Herb never turned up in Woolooga – that was a lie they told me to separate us. I stayed there for about six months, but I was a stranger among other workers – they weren't very friendly to me. But one old white bloke I'd met in Melbourne was working there, Frank Kavanagh. He was a nice fellah. He had knocked around a good bit and he knew how to look after himself.

It rained a bit there off and on, but it was usually quite warm rain and mostly very good clear weather for working. The gang of workers used to call in at a pub for the weekend on their way to our place of work. The first time I was with them, they left me in the back of the truck in the teeming rain. Sitting there wet and cold, I was attracted to a light across the road, and it turned out to be the pub. The men were all in there drinking and laughing.

So I walked in and went up to the bar. The publican ignored me. I was standing there for a good while. Then I went and sat on a stool against the wall. I knew then that they didn't serve Aboriginals there.

The publican must have said something to the white men at the end of the bar, and old Frank Kavanagh must have told him, 'Oh, that's Banjo Clarke. He's with us, he's Victorian.'

The publican called out then, 'What are you having, mate?'

I said, 'I'll have a beer.'

He went on talking with the truckies. I had one beer, then went back and sat down. I didn't want anything in an atmosphere like that. When the time came to go, I walked out and jumped in the back of the big truck again. There was room in the front for another passenger, but they wouldn't let me sit with them. So I went back to the job in the driving rain, only five miles from there. We was making a road from Maryborough in Queensland.

When payday came, I didn't want to go to the town, because of that first experience. It was a one-horse town. But the men kept coming and going all Saturday, and in the end I decided to walk to town to have a bit of a stroll and explore the countryside.

When I arrived at the pub, the publican came up and said, 'How are you going, Banjo?'

'All right.'

'I'm sorry about the night you came in here,' he said.

'Why, what's wrong?' I asked.

'I thought you were off Murgon Mission, about thirty miles from here. We're not allowed to serve Aboriginals off that mission.'

I said, 'Well, I'm Aboriginal, but I'm from Victoria.'

'Yes, the men told me. You're all right. You can drink, you're working.'

That publican and his missus ended up being really good to me – they looked after me. They'd take me everywhere. I used to go to see them every weekend after that.

There were a lot of dances in them days, to raise money for charity. The publican and his missus used to take me along with them. One night there was a dance at Woolooga and a young white American soldier was there with two girls. He walked up to me saying, 'Come here, man. I wanna see you.'

I thought he'd spotted the bottle I had in my pocket and was going to ask for a drink. I walked to the door with him – the dance hall was built on stilts – and offered for him to go through.

But he said, 'You go first, man.'

So I did, and when we reached the landing he pushed me in the back and I rolled down the stairs. I was a bit embarrassed then and told myself, You can't go walking into white people's dance halls. This is what happens to you! So I sat against the wall and thought about it for a while. Them two young white girls came to the door, calling out, 'Are you all right, Banjo?'

I was too embarrassed to call back but I said quietly, 'Yes, I'm all right. I'm down here.'

Then their voices started getting urgent, so I had to yell back, 'I'm okay! I'm all right!'

'You're not hurt, are you?'

'No.'

They came down the stairs and said, 'We saw what that Yankee did to you. Now, you go round to the front door and we'll tell him that someone wants to see him. Then when he goes outside, you punch him in the bloody nose.'

'Ah,' I said, 'that'll be good.'

So I went around near the front door and pushed it open a bit. I was peeping through at the girls in the middle of the dancefloor. The place was packed. They went up to the young soldier, who was laughing away, probably about what he'd done to me, and having great fun. I saw them point towards the door at me, and he came over.

But I opened the door too quickly and he stopped. I said, 'Come here, mate. I want to see you.'

He turned his back, laughing like anything. And he walked back laughing to the two girls. But one of the girls slapped him in the face, and the other took off her shoe and hit him across his eyebrow.

Suddenly all the bulldozer drivers and all the tall navvies were standing around asking, 'What's wrong? What's wrong?' Because he was the only American there, and they normally treated them with great respect, as people did everywhere.

And I heard one of the young girls say, 'This dirty Yank threw our Aboriginal friend out down the stairs, and he could have been hurt. He might get away with doing that in America, but he can't in Australia.'

Immediately all the men left the walls and they took the young

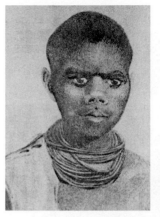  

LEFT This portrait of Queen Truganini, Banjo's ancestor, is considered to be the best likeness of her in existence. It was painted in 1832 when she was 20 and is attributed to Thomas Bock
CENTRE Banjo's mother, Mary Clarke
RIGHT Banjo's father, Norman Clarke, with daughter Alice

Banjo's father, Norman Clarke, with his brothers and sister.
(L TO R) John, Norman, Fleetwood holding Frank, Jesse

LEFT Banjo in his boxing days
RIGHT Private Reginald Rawlings, Audrey Clarke's uncle, in his army uniform

LEFT Herbert Clarke, with whom Banjo spent his war years, and his wife Maisie
RIGHT Banjo with 'Grandfather' Terrick

LEFT Banjo on horseback with baby Vernon and dog Sandy
RIGHT Audrey Couzens, who became Banjo's wife, aged 16

LEFT Banjo and Audrey, dressed for an outing
RIGHT (L TO R) Ian, Patricia, Leonard, Elizabeth

(L TO R) Banjo, Bernice, Elizabeth, Audrey, Ian

Banjo and Ian visiting the Weatherhead family

LEFT Muriel Clampett (née Weatherhead), who taught Banjo to read and write
RIGHT (L TO R) Banjo, Fiona, Audrey, Elizabeth

Camilla Chance with her daughter Ruth and the group of Baha'is who went to meet
Banjo in 1975. Barwoo is second from the right

The Clarke family at the blockade of the Framlingham forest, 1980. Frank Wilkes, then leader of the Victorian ALP, is second from the left

Banjo, Ian and Lloyd Clark (left) waiting to meet the Victorian Minister for Crown Lands and Survey, 1980

Banjo's first-born daughter Helen with her
husband Keith Morgan

Bernice Clarke, 1982

Filming *The Fighting Gunditjmara* in the Framlingham Forest, 1984. Banjo is on the left

Banjo by the Hopkins River, Framlingham, 1990

Banjo hugs his adoptive granddaughter Kirby outside his burnt-down house, 1992

Banjo with Cathy Freeman and friend Clayton Collyer at the 1993 national Baha'i conference in Melbourne

Banjo in a pensive mood, 1994

Banjo opening the Tarerer festival, 1998

Banjo belatedly receiving his medal for war service, 1998

Banjo and his granddaughter hold a Sorry Book, signed by local citizens apologising to the stolen generations, on National Sorry Day, 1998. (L TO R) Karana Morgan; Warrnambool's mayor, David Atkinson; Banjo; Kirrae Clarke; Henry Alberts; Aidan Stewart; Moyne's mayor, David Miller

LEFT Patricia at her graduation ceremony, 1999
RIGHT Elizabeth Clarke in Framlingham Forest

Banjo at Camilla's house with Baha'i dancers from Thursday Island, 1999

Banjo with his nephew Archie Roach at Tarerer, 1999

The Hopkins Falls, where Banjo dictated much of this book

LEFT Banjo at Framlingham with a nulla-nulla he made
TOP Fiona Clarke with writer Martin Flanagan at the opening of one of her exhibitions

Banjo's new house – with punching bag

Inside the marquee at Banjo's funeral, 2000

soldier by the back of his trousers and threw him outside, saying, 'Do it to him, Banjo! See how good he is.' So me and the American squared up outside and we had a good old knuckle-up. He wasn't bad either, but he kept wanting to wrestle. He tore the shirt off my back.

All the people had left the dance hall and they were barracking for me. When I look back, it seems strange that so many white people were supporting the young Aboriginal from their community, and not the poor American soldier.

The young soldier eventually threw the towel in, and my publican friend told the people what brought him, 'You get this Yankee out of our town, and we never want to see you or him again.' Then he invited me back to his pub and put someone else's shirt on me.

But I don't think I ever went back to the dance hall. I was too confused that night. And imagine how confused the young American soldier would be. Perhaps he went over to the islands and got killed. I didn't want to be his enemy, it was just one of those things. He probably had a mother and father at home what cared about him. If he lived, he would have had a good story to tell them when he went back home.

You hear about so much racism in Queensland. Yet I was there in the 1940s, when racial strife was bad, and I experienced the good side too. There's no way that I can say all those people are cruel to Aboriginals. There must be racism about, but there are other people what will side with you if you do the same work they do.

CHAPTER 11

While I was busy helping build roads all over the country during the war, some of my people had been allowed to join the army, unlike me. Many of them went to war, and some died for the country they loved. Same with World War I. Lots of them became heroes, even though they weren't even official citizens here. Becoming citizens didn't happen until 1967.

My people proved to be good fighters in the front line, against all odds. About fourteen Aboriginal men from Framlingham and Lake Condah joined the army. After the war, five Lovett brothers came home to Lake Condah, and they had been in the thick of it overseas, in France, Gallipoli and Palestine. When they came home they wasn't given land or anything like so many white soldiers, just treated like another Aboriginal – you know, 'You're not wanted.' That's the attitude, that was the attitude throughout your life. The returning white soldiers were given land, but not them. And then after World War II, the rest of Lake Condah Mission was divided up and given to returned white soldiers, and the black soldiers who'd been born and bred on that very same piece of land got nothing and were pushed off it.

One hero from my tribe in World War I was Private William Alex Egan. He was killed near the village of Villers-Bretonneux in northern France on 25 April 1918. After his death, his sisters got this letter from the commanding officer of his company, a fellah called Lieutenant Dyke:

I cannot help writing to you respecting your late brother. He was in my company on the night of his death. We were about to make a second attack on the enemy line.

I would like you to know something of what we all thought of him. He was esteemed by officers and men and a jolly chap who seldom grumbled. Unfortunately, we were knocked about a good deal after his death.

I am speaking for the whole company when I say how much we feel for and sympathise with you in your trouble.

I can only offer consolation, and that is that he died like a brave man and the true soldier he was.

Years after William was killed, when I was in hospital one time, I met a local white bloke who had known him. He told me how one day Bill had refused to remain in the trench when they were being attacked, and ran out shooting. He came back later, shell-shocked, pulled off his hat and said, 'Look! It's full of the blood of my mates,' and then ran out shooting again.

Reggie Rawlings was my wife's uncle and he was a full-blood Aboriginal. He enlisted in Warrnambool in 1916, giving his trade as a horse-breaker. A lot of people don't even know how he got into the army, because at that stage of the war they didn't take full-blood Aboriginals, or even part-Aboriginals. For some reason they wasn't classed as citizens. And yet they existed here for thousands and thousands of years. That seemed to be a stupid attitude. But the soldiers what did go over there died for the country they loved, just like the white men. And those that came back was treated just like a no-hoping Aboriginal again.

Anyway, Reggie fought in World War I too, and they made him a special soldier to go out and destroy enemy positions. He would go in first, with the bayonet. He was killed only a few weeks after William Egan, and after his death he was awarded the Military Medal for bravery. I'm real proud of him for that, because only one other Victorian Aboriginal was ever awarded that medal. The recommendation for the medal read:

During the attack [on the] enemy system this soldier had the responsible position of first bayonet man in the bombing team which worked down the enemy communication trench, routed the enemy and established a block in the trenches. Private Rawlings displayed rare bravery in the performance of his duty, killing many of the enemy, brushing aside all opposition and cleared the way effectively for the bombers of his team. His irresistible dash and courage set a wonderful example to the remainder of the team. On 9 August 1918 the 29th Battalion was involved in the successful assault on and capture of Vauvillers. The soldiers, however, faced extremely heavy machine gun fire. Rawlings was among those killed. Only 27 years of age at the time, he was buried in the Heath Cemetery, Harbonnieres, France. His outstanding bravery is remembered with pride by the local community.

Two others of my tribe, Reg and Harry Saunders, were soldiers in World War II. Harry died in New Guinea on the Kokoda Trail at the age of twenty-one. One of his commanders later wrote that he had been like a brother to them all, and that the other soldiers had loved him. His brother Reg was promoted to sergeant just three months after enlisting, and later became Australia's first Aboriginal army officer. Afterwards he served in the Korean War as well, as a captain.

Another fighter in that war was young Wally Alberts. He and his mates got pinned down by the Japanese over there in Malaysia, and when there was a bit of an ease-off he'd go out of his trench for a walk. Then the guns would open up and he'd jump back in the trench again. They sat there for days. I don't know whether it was before he died or after he was killed when his mum got this letter from him [Banjo recited this letter from heart]:

There's a lot of rabbits at home, Mum, where I used to wait for them to come out of their burrows and shoot them to take home to eat. In the position where I am now, when I hear the guns I run back and get in the trench. It reminds me of the rabbits at home, and how they must feel when they hear the guns going. When I come home, Mum, I'll never, never shoot another rabbit again.

After I'd been in Woolooga for nearly six months, we all got examined by a doctor to see who was fit enough to go further north. We might end up in Darwin, in the war zone, we were told, and only people fit enough could go. On being examined, I passed the test and we got two weeks' holiday in case we wanted to visit our loved ones at home. So I went to stay with my brother in Brisbane.

After our holiday, on a certain date, at a certain time of night, all of us fit fellahs had to catch the train north. There was nobody in charge and none of us knew where we were going – that was a big secret. But at two or three o'clock in the morning, when our train stopped at a station out in the never-never somewhere, I heard my mate Herb singing out. It was great to meet up with him again. We ended up working together once more until we left Darwin for home months later.

After the train trip, we ended up near Mount Isa. We was camping between Mount Isa and Camooweal, at Split Rock. There was always beautiful water there, in a hole in the dry creek bed. The old bullock wagons and drovers used to cross there in the early days.

It was a big camp, tents everywhere. It was run properly, super-efficiently. They had a big cookhouse, it was a big affair. They would bring a hot meal out to us, wherever we happened to be working, at lunchtime. That was something we really appreciated, having a hot meal brought to us. It was carried in a 'hotbox', and it was still hot. Even so, some people grumbled and said, 'This food is no good, give it to the blacks.' But it was good food! We said, 'Why grumble about good food? The people would have gone to a lot of trouble to make it for us, and they did it out of caring.' We were all volunteers and so were they. There was food shortage at the time – you couldn't get everything. But they made what they could out of what they could get.

I can still see the big American convoys coming through out of all the dust up there, because the road wasn't sealed yet. Lots of African-American soldiers and lots of equipment. They was all dressed fine, with shiny buttons. They almost had their own army. And those soldiers always used to pull up for a rest when they saw us working on the road. They'd give us tinned fruit and smokes like we'd never had, and they'd ask us about Australia and our way of life. We used to be glad to see them coming along. They always treated us with respect.

Herb and I were there for some months – I lost track of how long – working in shifts around the clock, all night and all day. And the convoys kept coming through, taking guns and rations to Darwin to send over to the soldiers on the islands. All roads led to Darwin. All the bush tracks had to be done up with bitumen. And transport vehicles would be racing through.

If we had half a day off or something, we'd go to Camooweal.

There were a lot of big cattle stations round about, and a lot of stockmen hung around the pubs. There'd be big dinners and dances in a hall in Camooweal, and Aboriginal children and Old People would hang around and even sleep on the verandah outside the hall. Girls from the stations would bring lots of food, like homemade cakes and sandwiches, out from the hall to them and make them welcome too. Whatever the rich people had, Aboriginal people had too. We'd watch the dancing because there was nothing else to do, and talk with the Aboriginals outside.

Next, we were sent to Darwin. Herb and I worked together for a few months more. There, we were mostly cleaning up after air raids – the post office and other buildings. There'd be big bomb craters along the road where enemy planes tried to hit the big pipe carrying water to Darwin. They'd be trying to blow up the road we were making also – everything. We were cleaning up the harbour too, where all the ships were sunk. You could see some of them when the tide went out. A big tunnel was being dug in the harbour, and storage space for food and guns was being dug out in the cliffs for the soldiers over on the islands.

Big Catalina planes – transport planes that go on water – used to wait in Darwin harbour and take off late in the evening. They'd drop food or whatever in parachutes on the islands and come back early in the morning. Soldiers were still stationed in Darwin, and big ack-ack guns were everywhere on vantage points, ready to shoot at planes when they came, like near the harbour and over near the gulf. I used to hear the Japanese planes in the daytime but couldn't see them, they were that far up, and the soldiers told me they were reconnaissance planes taking photos. The soldiers turned their guns to point at them, and I'd see shells bursting in the sky but couldn't see the plane. They must take the photos back and develop them and give them to the pilots.

Every moonlit night we expected a raid from the Japanese. They'd fly straight over our camp heading for an aerodrome hidden in the bush, I think. Ack-ack guns would be going and shells bursting. The Japanese knew where they was. They didn't let news out much, so we didn't know if planes were shot down. There was a lot of things going on, but we used to have to put our steel hats on and lie in a trench what we dug. When Herb and I first arrived, and it was going to be a full moon, the men would say, 'See you tonight,' to each other. And I thought there was going to be a party till I realised what they meant. We'd get a warning the Japanese was coming, and we'd put all the lights out and they'd fly straight over our camp. We had no guns, and the Japanese seemed to know that.

The weather was hot and sticky in Darwin – you sweated all the time. But you got used to it. I mean, we volunteered, we wanted to do our bit for our country, so what's the use of complaining? You can't go up north and expect it to be cool like down south. We accepted it. Aboriginals always accepted the way the weather was. Once we got used to the conditions, it was no more difficult to work in them than to work down south. We worked just as long hours too – no trouble. You just got used to that as well. When we were working in Darwin, a lot of Aboriginals were in the nightsoil business, because there was no sewerage. That was good – you can't see Aboriginals in the dark, so they had a certain kind of freedom. In the day we stand out like a sore thumb in the cities.

There was an Aboriginal working with us from Queensland. He was a nice bloke, but when I first met him he was having a go at a young whitefellah with a lot of scars. I thought, He's pretty game.

The Aboriginal, Pete, called out, 'How are you, mate?' when I walked past. Then he turned back and told the whitefellah, 'Never, ever do that again. If you do, I'll get back into you with knuckles.'

'It's all right, Pete,' said the white bloke. 'It's all right. It won't happen again.' The white bloke was just listening. But he certainly didn't look stupid, and I thought the Aboriginal was pretty game to be bossing him. It might have been a quarrel over a gambling deal.

Pete lived next to us and he was a great gambler. He'd win a lot of money – hundreds or thousands of pounds sometimes. Later, he'd come and ask me and Herb for money. And we'd think, What did he do with all that money? He must have lost it gambling. So we'd give him fifty or a hundred pounds each, and forget about it. We didn't care because we had nowhere to spend it. We were making big money working on the roads.

That went on for ages. Then he got drunk on whiskey one night. He didn't usually drink, but that night we had a bit of an argument. He said, 'I'll fight you in the morning.'

I told him, 'Don't be silly, mate. There's no reason for us to fight. We're mates.'

'All the same,' he said, 'you wait and see. When I say I'm going to fight someone, I never go back on my word.'

I thought, That whitefellah must have been in the position I'm in now. I expect this Queenslander's a good fighter, but he's a lot older than me. I took no more notice, and went for a shower early in the morning as usual. But when I came back, I found him clearing away the sticks in front of my tent.

My mate Herb was sleeping, and I said to myself, That Pete is fair dinkum. I went up to him and asked, 'What's wrong?'

'I said last night I'd fight you today, and so I am.'

'That was just drunken talk.'

'Yes, but I never go back on my word.'

'Okay then. We'll have it out.'

There was about six hundred men in that camp and only the cooks were up. No one had known the fight was going to be on. We had to wake Herb up to referee the fight. He was surprised too. He jumped out of bed wondering what was going on, but he agreed to referee.

Pete and I squared off there, in the bush in Darwin, out in front of my tent. We shaped up to one another. And he hit me with the best right cross I ever had in my life. He sent me about five yards backwards, but I didn't fall because I moved my feet real fast. If I hadn't I'd have been knocked right onto my back. I thought to myself, This fellah really knows how to fight. I walked in again and he hit me again in the body with a right cross.

Now I knew that I would have to plan how to fight him. He was a straight-back fighter, from before the Queensberry rules – before referees – when fighters stood up straight. They didn't duck and weave like present-day boxers. Back in the olden days, when fights was illegal, all the people would gather in a back paddock to watch the fight. And the men would fight with bare knuckles.

I had to watch how Pete threw his big punches, let the punches start and then beat him to it, using his momentum to make my punches heavier. Because if any man catches you with a big hit the first time and knows he hurt you, he's going to try that punch again. That's the punch he'll knock you down with if he does. So I had to move pretty fast to back-move and punch him while the main punch was still coming my way. All sorts of things like that I had to work out, though I really didn't like fighting. Even in the ring, I didn't like fighting. But we had to do it, because many times we'd have starved unless we got in that ring.

Well, I wore Pete down in the end. And I got sorry for him, poor old fellah, because he just wouldn't give in. He lay down a few times when I hit him, but he got up again. And I was getting weary too.

This man was like a tribal warrior – he fought to win. I mean, he intended to fight to the death. It was the toughest fight I ever had. If I'd been inexperienced, Pete would have won easily. He must have been reared up as a leader of his tribe, and a great fighter and a hunter. He fought as if his whole tribe was watching and depending on the outcome. But because I am Aboriginal, I was very experienced too. You had to be, even when you didn't like fighting. If you travelled around, as I did, you often had to defend yourself against all kinds of odds. Because if a whitefellah fought you and you won, the onlookers would usually mob you. They didn't like seeing their mate being beaten by a blackfellah. Then you'd get arrested afterwards, because it was always the blackfellah who was seen as the aggressor, looking for trouble.

But Pete liked to fight. Before the fight was finished, all the men in the camp were well up. They were hanging out of trees, putting money on our fight. Then a big man from South Australia – Hank Williams, the union representative – came up and stopped the fight. I was glad, because I was getting the better of the poor old bloke and I felt that I shouldn't be doing it.

But Pete didn't want to stop. 'You're too good with the knuckles,' he said, and walked into his tent. Then he came out with two cut-throat razors! 'Here you are, mate,' he said. 'You have this one and I'll have the other.'

'No way in the world, mate!' I said.

'But when I fight, I fight to the death,' Pete replied. Yet he was my best mate.

'There'll be no razor fights here,' the union man said, intervening.

'Okay, then,' said Pete. 'I'll fight you tonight.'

But that fight never eventuated. Everyday life resumed, and our mate would still ask us for money to gamble.

After working in Darwin, we ended up with a timber gang in the bush. We was cutting beams for food-storage tunnels in the cliffs around the coast. We were practically in rainforest country then. There were lagoons, and Aboriginals would come along that had been spearing fish and they'd have a good yarn with us. A lot had run away and gone bush, but a lot were still attached to the nearest mission or had gone to other missions. Yes, there were mosquitoes. Sometimes we slept under mosquito nets, but mostly we made fires and slept between them. We kept the mosquitoes away with smoke. You just adapt to the conditions.

At last the time came when Herb and I were preparing to leave and go home to Victoria. Pete said, 'I'll never, ever fight you fellahs again. I'll tell you something, Banjo, that's the first time ever I was beat with bare knuckles.'

'Well, you're getting old, mate,' I said. 'You must have been a great fighter in your time. But I'm at least ten years younger than you, and that was the toughest fight I ever had.'

'I don't see it that way,' he said. 'If you've got a fighting heart – a good fighting spirit – you fight to the death, like I said.'

'Well, I don't want to fight to the death, mate,' I told him. 'I want to live a bit longer. I've got plenty more things to see in life.'

'I owe you a lot of money,' he said next. 'You and your mate.'

'How come?'

'All the money I was asking you for when I was gambling. I'd win stuff on it and put it in the bank. I owe you hundreds.'

I said, 'Yeah? I never even thought about it, mate.'

'Before you go, I'll have all the money for you.'

And a couple of days before we left, he came and paid us back everything that we'd lent him. It was over six hundred pounds.

It turned out that when Pete gambled, he almost always won a great deal. Then he'd put the money in the bank, but keep a little bit out for his gambling. And if he lost that little bit, he'd borrow some more from me and Herb. He wouldn't take it from the bank. And he wrote down every single transaction in a book he kept. He was methodical all right.

CHAPTER 12

So Herb and I came back to Fitzroy after over a year spent working up north. [In February 1998 Banjo and Herb were belatedly awarded the World War II Civilian Service Medal for the fourteen months they spent working with the Allied Works Council.] We found that Aboriginal people were still coming to Fitzroy from all over Australia, looking to stay with my family and with a few other families where they heard they'd get hospitality and a good feed and a bed. Because all of us Aboriginals never knew how we'd be treated by whitefellahs in the next place we went to.

Herb and I went on taking whatever jobs we could get in the city: builder's labourer, pick-and-shovel work, digging trenches, or delivering briquettes around town from the Fitzroy railway yard. A lot of old battlers was still there in the city with their horse and cart. Old bottle-ohs, and people moving furniture. We'd help them because it was something to do – if you didn't do that, you'd get on the grog with your mates.

Aboriginals would be in and out of gaol all the time for things like drunk and disorderly. The police was locking people up just to keep them off the street. But that didn't solve any problems. Police would pull you backward, then pull you all over the street, making out that you were drunk and staggering.

At first, Aboriginals used to say 'not guilty' straight away when their case came to court. It was simple because they knew they were not guilty. But they realised in the end that it was no good saying that. The magistrate's attitude would be: 'Not guilty! How dare you say you're not guilty! You're Aboriginal – of course you're guilty.' And he'd give you a heavier sentence for trying to be smart. So a lot of Aboriginals just ended up pleading guilty to things they hadn't done, to get a lighter sentence. But you felt like defending yourself because you were innocent. You weren't given a lawyer in them days.

At that time, one old Christian lady was a great help to us Aboriginals in any sort of trouble like that. Her name was Helen Baillie, but we always called her Miss Baillie. She was a nurse from a well-to-do family who had once been farmers in the Western District, and she devoted her life to helping Aboriginals in every way possible. I don't think her family really approved. She used to pay lawyers out of her own pension to act for us if we was in trouble with the law. If black children were sick, she'd take them to hospital. She even went as a delegate to a government convention in Canberra to speak up for better conditions for Aboriginal people. She was an unsung hero for us blackfellahs. She loved everyone.

Miss Baillie bought a big old house on Punt Road in South Yarra during the 1940s. It was number 462, I remember, just over the top of the hill, near where it meets Toorak Road. She opened it up to all Aboriginal people, and made everyone in need welcome. It was a lovely old house, built of grey stone, with roses growing all over one side. There was a lot of fruit trees in the garden, and some people would lie under the apricot tree and eat the fruit. Many Aboriginals lived there with her, and any whitefellahs that needed help too. Many were drunks, but she put up with all of them and was kind to everyone. She'd often have the police banging at her door because the neighbours would complain about all the drunks and the noise. Eventually that was why everyone had to move from that house in the 1950s. But Miss Baillie put up with a lot because she had such a good heart, and she loved all Aboriginals.

Miss Baillie always kept her money in a little purse that was tied around her waist and hidden underneath her skirt. She always wore long, old-fashioned dresses that had been her mother's, and some of the blackfellahs would wonder how she managed to get her money in and out of that purse without getting undressed. Sometimes the drunks would try to get at her purse from underneath her skirts and she would slap their hands and say in her very educated way of talking, 'Don't you do that!' Sometimes she couldn't help laughing at them. She had a great sense of humour and when she laughed she'd always put her hand over her mouth. We often had a joke with her, especially whenever she drove us anywhere. She wasn't a very good driver and had some near misses in that car. So we weren't allowed to talk to her when she was driving because she had trouble concentrating. But she'd always drive all the blackfellahs to government elections and things like that, because although they couldn't vote she wanted them to have their say.

She could be strict with the blackfellahs living with her too. She would remind everyone of their Aboriginal principles and duties to each other, and once, when one of the blackfellahs was in hospital, she made all the blackfellahs that was staying with her go and sit on the lawn outside the hospital, the Aboriginal way, so that the sick person could feel their spirit.

Although Miss Baillie's family was very rich, she didn't always have money herself. Sometimes her money would run out, and when it did she would stay in her room for a few days. Everyone in the house would know why she didn't come out and wouldn't bother her. And when she reappeared, all the blackfellahs knew the money had come through again.

Miss Baillie did more than anyone I knew of at that time for Aboriginal people, never stopping to think about herself. And yet she has been so much forgotten. In the 1930s she began the Aboriginal

Fellowship Group and spent a lot of time visiting Aboriginal missions all over the country. One time she got a chauffeur to drive her around for months through the north of Australia and through Western Australia, meeting blackfellahs and trying to understand the problems they was facing.

Then, in the 1940s, Miss Baillie met some other good leaders – Pastor Sir Doug Nicholls, Mrs Margaret Tucker, Mr Burdeu and Mr William Cooper from Cummeragunja way – and those people got together and formed a small group to fight for equal rights for Aboriginals. They called it the Aborigines Advancement League. They'd hold talks and concerts, and protest about the conditions on mission stations, and things like that. They started off with no money, but what they did have Miss Baillie would often spend on clothes for blackfellahs and then get in trouble with the others.

In them days, they all became the great leaders of the Aboriginal community. George and Jack Patten were two others – they was all honest people. But only a few of us remember Helen Baillie, who was the 'power behind the throne' in so many helpful things. Just in case I don't manage to do it myself, I have asked a local family I know to build a memorial to her when I'm gone. Unsung heroes like her should always be remembered for the good they done.

Herb and I didn't like being in the city, but in them tough days it was almost impossible to get work outside it. All Aboriginals would try to hang onto a job, but they mightn't like it because they didn't get on with the boss, or because of racist remarks. Then once they'd got enough money, they'd hit the track again. Same with me – if I heard of a job on a farm, I'd leave the city for a while. Sometimes a young Aboriginal friend wanted to get out of town and he'd say to me,

'Come with me, mate.' So I'd roll my swag and we'd wait by a grading till a big train came along, and jump in an empty truck.

After I'd been on one farm clearing scrub for about six months, the boss asked me where I came from.

'Down in the Western District,' I answered.

'No,' he said, 'I meant before you came out to Australia.'

I looked at him and said, 'I belong to Australia. I'm Aboriginal.'

That's how much he knew about Aboriginals. But he was a decent bloke all the same.

When in Melbourne, sometimes we'd hear that one of the boxing troupes was looking for Aboriginals and we'd join up again for a while. Around 1942 I met a young girl from Gippsland called Agnes who seemed to know almost nobody. I told her it might be better if she went home, because Melbourne was a tough place.

I took her out for a feed. We kept each other company for a while, and made love a couple of times. Then I went away on my travels with the Harry Johns boxing troupe for two weeks, and when I came back she was gone. Just a few days later, I was sent up north to build roads and do my bit for the war.

But a couple of years after, I got news that Agnes had a baby girl, and that I was the father. I tried to get in touch with her, to do something for the little girl, because I knew she was my responsibility. I found an Aboriginal man called Edgar Murray who did seasonal agricultural work around Bairnsdale. He'd arrive in Melbourne and be gone in five minutes. At that time, huge groups of Aboriginals would be travelling from farm to farm, picking beans, maize and fruit, whatever work they could get. The instant they heard of a job, they'd be gone.

Pretty soon Edgar Murray was taking messages back and forth between me and my little daughter. I heard she was called Helen, like my sister Ellen. The resemblance in the names pleased me, you know. And every time Edgar passed through Melbourne, he told me how my little girl was growing up. The girl's aunt, Edna Solomon (her mother's older sister), and her husband Alby Solomon was looking after her, and one day my mate brought me news that they had gone travelling round the south coast, picking beans. They'd taken the little girl with them.

My daughter seemed to go further and further away from me after that. I kept making inquiries, but people would always say, 'They were in my area but they've left now.' Apparently Helen's aunt and uncle felt they had to keep on the move all the time, or the welfare might try to take Helen away from them if they stayed in one place for too long. Wherever they were, her aunt used to keep everything sparkling clean in case the authorities would come to inspect the house and take the children.

So Helen only ever went to school for short periods of time. Too long in school – they'd know about you. Too long in one place without going to school – they'd know about you too. But Helen loved school and being with other children. Sometimes, though, she'd burst out crying in the middle of class for no apparent reason, and no one knew why. She later realised it was the pain of not knowing where her father was, but the schoolteachers didn't understand.

Helen's foster parents loved her very much and treated her as their own child. They didn't take their eyes off their children for a minute – they knew it wasn't safe. Helen's foster sister Eileen was five days younger than Helen and they were great mates – like twins they was. They even dressed the same.

On their constant travels, the family would stay in Aboriginal camps along the way, and at night the little girl would listen to the men and women talking. Sometimes she heard my name mentioned.

She knew from her aunt that her dad's name was Henry Clarke. She half expected that one of the men would come up to her and say, 'Ah, little girl, I'm your dad.'

But that never happened, although she went right around all the camps with these two Old People what looked after her. And although she felt very loved, she used to cry herself to sleep because she couldn't find her dad.

The family travelled for years, picking peas, beans, tomatoes and pumpkins. It was very hard and thirsty work, but there was nothing else for them to do. During their breaks, Helen and her brothers and sisters would slide off branches into a river to cool down. They all slept in a tent in a row at night, unless it rained and the tent got blown over. Then they'd all have to pile into the car and sleep sitting up in there together.

This went on for years, until my son Lenny came across her when she was already an adult. But I'll tell you later the beautiful story about how we finally found each other.

World War II was beginning to draw to a close when at last I managed to leave the city and get back to the Framlingham Mission where I was born. There I ran into my young friend Audrey Couzens again, who I'd known since she was a small girl. She was a true mission girl, very strictly reared. I remained on the mission as much as I could, and we got to know each other really well. Then we fell in love and I decided I wanted to marry her.

First I had to prove to her parents that I was good enough to be her husband. I had to show that I would work hard and would be able to support a wife and children. They didn't accept me for some time. We had a lot of trouble, but two young people in love overcome all them things, no matter what, and so did we. Audrey was pregnant with our first child, Vernon, when we eventually married two years later. She wanted him to have my last name when he was born. We thought that much of the baby, and that much of each other.

It was a good wedding, very legal but without too much rigmarole. The date was 10 December 1945, and I think the minister would have been Methodist. We married in his home on the mission. My son Lenny lived in that same house for many years.

After we were married, life seemed to be hard on us for a long time. I often had to go hundreds of miles away for work and we missed each other. My parents-in-law resented me not having a house of my own to take my wife and little Vernon to. But it would have had to be next door to them. I wanted to build us a hut where I was working, mostly woodcutting, but they wouldn't allow me to take their daughter and Vernon away. I understood how they felt – she was their only daughter and they loved her too much. They were angry about losing her even a little bit to me. So until I got a house for us near them, I lived with my in-laws.

Little Vernon had to go to the hospital a few times. He had throat trouble but they didn't keep him in, just examined him and sent him back home. His old granny did what she could to fix him up, because there were no medical people on the mission. The little boy got better for a while.

Then on 7 June 1947, when he was about sixteen months old, a strange thing happened. He spent the whole day standing by the window. Whenever anybody passed on the road, he asked us to open the door for him. Then he'd run the sixty yards or so to the road, say something in his childish way and shake the person's hand.

We'd be standing at the door watching, and he would come straight back home each time. The people would walk over and tell us, 'Your little fellah ran up and shook our hands, then he just turned his back and ran away again.'

My old father-in-law, who was there, answered, 'He's been doing that *all* day! Nobody can pass our house without him running out to them. We don't know what's going on.'

Vernon looked for all the kids to come past on their way home from school, about twenty children in all, then he ran over to the gate and shook hands with every single one. They all loved this little boy and they loved him for doing it. Those kids went home happy because our little boy was glad to see them and shook their hands.

My father-in-law said to Bella, his wife, 'Something's wrong, something's going to happen. He makes me uneasy, watching at the window like that. He's treating everybody as if he's not going to see them again. It's as if he's saying goodbye.'

People on bikes, people driving their horse and cart – he ran out to them all. Everybody had to stop and get out to shake hands with him.

Then, later that evening, little Vernon got sick and found it hard to breathe. The missionary man, Mr Matherson, drove the three of us – him and me and Audrey – to the hospital. The doctors asked all sorts of questions, and we told them about his throat and how he kept being sent home from hospital. So they said, 'You'd better leave him with us this time.'

Then, at three o'clock in the morning, a car pulled up at the house we shared with my in-laws, and the schoolteacher got out and told us, 'You're wanted at the hospital. I got the phone call in Purnim.'

So we drove into the hospital, not knowing what we was going to find out. When we got there the nurse came up and said they'd done all they could but our little boy had passed away peacefully and they couldn't understand why.

She took us into his room. There he was, lying in his cot with a beautiful flower in his hand. I took particular notice of that flower because old Uncle Terrick, Lionel Rose's great-grandfather, used to pick wildflowers out on the mission and bring them to Vernon. He was his little friend. And our little boy used to ask to go looking for wildflowers, and he'd come home and put them in a special place. Wildflowers had a lot to do with his life, and he used to love picking them.

It looked unreal to me that when I saw him, lying so still in his hospital bed, he still had a flower in his hand. I said to the nurse, wanting to find out how they understood him so well, 'He looks real peaceful with the beautiful flower in his hand.'

'Yes,' the nurse answered. 'He looked so beautiful and peaceful that I thought somehow he needed a flower to be complete.'

She hadn't known about his love for flowers. His spirit must have told her, 'I want a flower now, so that when my people come, I'll have the flower they've always seen me with.' In the hospital it was a magnificent rose.

Towards the evening of that same day, Vernon's old mate Uncle Terrick came across the paddock to where we was living. We saw him stand still about twenty-five yards away in the paddock. That's what Aboriginals normally do, out of respect, they wait around some distance from your house for you to come and invite them in. Usually when old Uncle Terrick came, he'd have a bunch of flowers for Vernon, and Vernon would run out to him.

But then we saw him take his hat off. I thought, This poor old fellah must have got the bad news already. Though we knew it was unlikely. He'd been away in town shopping and catching up with people. And on the days when he did that, he normally stayed at an old friend's house halfway home. He'd go home next day, where he lived alone. Then he'd put away the food he'd bought and come straight to see Vernon, his little mate.

He remained standing for a while with his hat in his hand. I went out to see him. He walked a little way towards me, close enough to hear me speak.

I said, 'I've got some bad news for you, Uncle.'

'Yeah,' he said. 'I know.'

'Did somebody tell you?' I asked.

'It's the little boy, eh?'

'Yes,' I said. 'Our little boy passed away at three o'clock this morning.'

'I know.'

I asked him again if he'd run into someone who told him.

'No. I went straight home. I didn't see anybody.'

And I never asked any more questions.

Then, three months after we buried the little fellah, old Uncle Terrick said, 'Now I'll tell you about your little boy and how I knew he passed away that night.'

I was very curious to hear the explanation.

'As usual, my friends put me up overnight when I was halfway home. But at about three o'clock in the morning I was woken by something pressing at my feet. I thought a dog had come into the old bungalow and jumped on the foot of my bed. I wanted to hunt him off. I yelled at him but the weight stayed just the same.

'So I reached across and found the matches,' he continued, 'so I could sit up in bed to look at the weight on my feet. I struck a match, and I saw that on the foot of my bed lay a little white coffin. Straight away I thought about my little mate Vernon, as if he had put the idea into my head. Like he was telling me something. So I wasted no time at all hanging around in the morning. I packed up and headed for home. I had to come over to you as soon as possible.'

CHAPTER 13

Well, it was now the 1950s and I was a married man after drifting around all over the place for so long, and family life started to work out, although we felt little Vernon as a big loss. More children started coming along and I had many responsibilities. After Vernon we had Patricia, Leonard, Ian, Elizabeth, whose twin sister died at birth, Bernice, Karen, who lived only six hours, and Fiona.

When Audrey and I finally set up house on our own, away from her parents, life was tough but good. My old mother-in-law Bella turned out to be the best friend I ever had. If anybody said one thing against me she'd order them out of her house. I thought that was great, because you always hear complaints about mothers-in-law. My own mother-in-law was the best in the world, I think.

I got a job five miles away in the local stone quarry, Coleman's, which I liked all right. I used to work the big crusher — there was things banging together, big wheels spinning, noise everywhere. There were a lot of different-sized screens, made of metal, for different-sized stones.

When I worked there, or in any big groups of white people, lunchtime would come and I'd sit down with them and eat. Some of the blokes would be talking about women, saying nasty, demoralising things about them, sexually and every other way. I couldn't under- stand that. Why were they talking like that about their own people?

One day I went away on my own and they all called out, 'Why don't you come and have dinner with us? Aren't we good enough for you?'

'Ah yeah,' I said. 'You're good enough, but I don't like the way you speak about women.'

'What about the women?'

'You talk about women as if they're nothing. Yet they're your own colour. I wouldn't like anyone to talk in that demoralising way about my womenfolk. Most of you have wives, and daughters too. Why do you say things like that about other people's daughters? That's the sort of thing I don't like. That's why I don't sit down with you at lunchtime.'

And after that, they stopped talking that way when I was with them. I think they realised that they'd been saying the wrong thing. Before that, they'd thought they were saying the right things what everyone liked hearing. It was sad that they thought like that. To me, they were talking about their own mothers, their daughters, their sisters, and every other female in their family. They couldn't talk nastily about women outside without doubting the ones they loved too.

Although I worked hard, I was drinking hard too. I drank with my mates after work, and a lot of times we went to gaol for being drunk. But we never resented that – we thought it was part of the life that Aboriginals had to live. We were aware that we lived in the white man's world, and the Aboriginal part of our life looked as if it would disappear. The law was down on us, barring us from hotels.

We met a lot of good white people who were hard battlers too and knew what we was going through. After a life of trouble and strife with their own society, they found friendship with Aboriginals. Many came to live with us. They understood that life was hard enough for the white battler, but it was twice as hard for Aboriginals. So we befriended each other. A lot of everlasting friendships was formed. And when the people who lived with Aboriginals became better off and bought farms or businesses – because they had the opportunity to do them things what was forbidden to Aboriginals – they would write to us saying they learned a lot from living with Aboriginals, and thanking us. From my family they said they learnt not to resort to anger or lash out. You forget what your enemy done to you – them things leave you in a flash if you see someone destitute or crying out for help.

We'd meet other fellahs who only used us and manipulated us when they had nowhere else to turn. We could see what they were doing, and that when they got a better footing they wouldn't want to know us any more. But we looked after them too, just the same.

Aboriginals were very good at understanding what was going on in the minds of other people. You hear all sorts of nasty things about Aboriginal people – that we're no good and lazy. We hear that all the time. Aboriginals what never smoked or drank in their life get classed with the rest. That still goes on today, but not very openly. We know it goes on, but we don't even think about it. We'd be in gaol every five minutes if we thought about all the bad things what were done to us.

We feel uneasy if we meet someone who is friendly to our face but going to say bad things behind our back. We always know. But if you meet everybody openly, expecting to be friends for life, you're stronger than *all* the liars – easy.

About lying – you know, once one lie is told, people try to get back on the truth and they can't. Then they tell more lies to try to get back on the truth. Everything's gone astray then, there's no truth at all in what they say. They can't get to the truth because they told a lie in the first place, and then more lies. See? That's how it works. Then they just forget it, hoping it will go away.

One day I was drinking in the bar in the middle of an afternoon. A white, middle-aged man came in. Soon he started to yell racist remarks at me. I kept ignoring him but he kept at me. The fact that

I didn't let his words bother me eventually made the man so angry that he came up and threw a punch at me. The security fellah immediately threw me out, even though I hadn't said or done nothing. I had my boxing skills of course, but I chose not to use them and just went on my way.

Late one night, during a storm, about two years later, someone knocked on the door of my house at the mission. When I opened it, I immediately recognised the same man who had been racist towards me in the bar that time. I didn't say anything, though. The fellah said his car had broken down nearby and he'd walked in the rain to my house so that he could use the telephone.

'Come in, mate,' I said to him. 'You're wet. Come in and get dry.'

He came in and I gave him a good cup of tea and a bit of a feed. I dried his clothes by the fire. The fellah was real quiet the whole time, and I wondered if he recognised me and was nervous.

A bit later, he told me he'd been driving around the bush trying to find the place he was meant to go woodcutting, but had got lost. So I offered to drive the fellah there. We got in my car together and headed off into the bush. It was pitch-black and the fellah was still real quiet. I could feel he was frightened.

Eventually he said, 'Do you recognise me?'

'Oh, yes,' I said.

Silence. I think he expected I was going to do something terrible to him for revenge. Then he said, 'You could kill me here, you know.'

'I know,' I told him.

'Why don't you?' the white man asked. 'Why are you being so kind to me and helping me out tonight?'

I told him, 'Because I want you to realise that Aboriginal people are the same as many others and we have a lot of kindness. I want to treat you the way I would like you to treat me.'

The whitefellah seemed bowled over by this. He was real quiet for a minute, then he said, 'From now on, I'm going to tell my children and my grandchildren that Aboriginals must be respected like other people.'

I dropped him off in the bush. I was glad I'd had the opportunity to show him us Aboriginals were good people too.

My wife Audrey got a job as a teacher's assistant and worked at the mission school for quite a few years. She taught a great many little children to read and write.

It took a lot of courage to go to school in them days. The police and welfare people used to arrive there regularly in the 1950s and '60s and pick out children to be taken away. I'll never forget seeing those little kids crying and calling out for their parents. The welfare people would wind up the windows of the cars and the children couldn't get out and were taken away and put into homes. Some of them kids never came back again, and we don't know what happened to them.

Many days, my own kids would see their little mates being driven off in police cars and they would be scared, not knowing whether next time they'd be picked to be taken. If Audrey or I saw a government car pull up, we'd tell our kids to run and hide down by the river till we came to get them, just in case.

The little kids that were picked were terrified when they were pointed at, pulled out of the school, put in the motor cars and driven away. Their screams for their parents were to haunt many of the Old People until their dying day. One old lady, Granny Bella, told me, 'I can still hear the voices of them children screaming.' She was haunted by that, but she also saved a lot of little children from going to orphanages or white foster homes – her daughter's kids, and others from Melbourne and on the mission that she took under her wing.

She died suddenly of a stroke, which was devastating to everybody left behind. The children were flung into turmoil, expecting to be taken away. But the lady's relations obeyed traditional law. They took them in and did the best they could.

The mother of my nephew, Archie Roach, was that old lady's stepdaughter. The poor old lady was looking after Archie and his brothers and sisters one day because his parents had gone to town. They came home, only to be told by the lady that some of their children were gone. People had taken them away.

'What people?' they said.

'Gubbahs – white people come in motor cars.'

The parents went around everywhere then, trying to find out what had happened and why. Aboriginals didn't understand the white man's law about taking children away, or white man's ways. Archie's parents lived, like many other Aboriginals, in a tin shanty in the scrub with a dirt floor and no cupboards. They lived in the true Aboriginal style, the way Aboriginals had lived for thousands of years. But some laws had recently been passed saying, 'You've got to live like a white man now.' White people would come into the huts and see no sheets on the bed, no food stored, and would think the little children were being neglected. But we were living off the land. We didn't need to store food – it was all around us outside, all the time. Our ways made no sense in the white man's world, and a lot of little children were taken away just because of that.

Archie's parents never saw their children again. They split up in the end, after many years of searching, when they had finally given up hope. Archie grew up in foster homes and found out along the line that his mother had died. Till then he had not known who he was. That made him angry, and he joined up with other Aboriginals who had been kicked from pillar to post. His little sister ended up in Sydney and she was killed in a motor car accident. Everyone was sad for them things, you know, because when they was taken away, everything went wrong for the children what were lost and left to search for their people and their homeland again. Archie saw all these things; he lived with the Aboriginals around the cities and seen the corruption there. There was no hope for them there. But Archie often thought home of his bushland and how good the Old People was to him. They've directed him to how he is now, and he sings them songs and tells the stories about what happened to them as children, and many other Aboriginal children.

Archie's a sad person now, though he's a great singer and composer. He missed the best things in life – sharing with his mum and dad. He's still got sisters left, though he lost his last young brother not long ago. His happy days in the little humpy in the scrub are forgotten now. He was stripped of all that when he was pushed into the white man's world.

It was hard for him to get the feeling again of being Aboriginal. But no matter how many years an Aboriginal child is reared up as white, he'll always have a yearning for something that's not there. No matter how kind and gentle the white people are to him, there'll be something missing. He'll know deep down that he doesn't belong. Archie knew that.

People with Aboriginal blood who don't know that they're Aboriginal have an uncanny way of somehow searching back to where they came from. It's truly uncanny – often they'll choose Aboriginal children for their mates. They have a feeling that they belong to their Aboriginal friends. There's something there which they can't explain.

One Aboriginal welfare lady was telling me about a fair-skinned bloke in his fifties who went to her crying. He was reared up as a fully white person all his life, but he had recently found out that he was Aboriginal. All his friends had been Aboriginal and he hadn't known that he belonged to them. He was sad at having wasted all them years.

Even if our children went to white man's school, our traditions was still going on. The children came home to it. And many of us are still living the Aboriginal way today. For example, we won't ever leave our land. That's our spirit-land. That's where our ancient ancestors and our grannies and uncles were all born. They walked and hunted on it. It's our spiritual home and we silently protest that we do not want to leave it. If we go away for a holiday to look around other parts of Australia, we find that our black brothers and sisters are all much the same. Up north, over the west, anywhere, you'll find Aboriginals talking about the same things, on the same level. Urban Aboriginals are specially glad to see us. They've lost touch with their land, but the spiritual yearning is still there in their hearts. They are searching for something that they can't practise in the cities.

When you're visiting a city house, Aboriginals arrive from everywhere to meet you because you've come from the bush, their homeland. You might have some good stories to tell about what's happening. 'Is it still there, the old place where we used to play?' 'Does the river still have that big fishing hole?' Although they might have been living in the city for years, they can't stop thinking about their childhood days in the bush. And about the country where they roamed, catching food along the river and carrying it home for their parents to cook. Home to their little humpies. All them things are still alive in their memory.

They are living in the white man's world, though, still fighting for respect and equal rights. And white people say, 'But you're the same as us. You're living among us – there's no prejudice, no racism. We talk the same way, do the same work, go to the same shops.'

But apart from them things, there's a big difference. There's a big gap what white people will never understand till they've lived with Aboriginals. Then, when they hear Aboriginals talking so-called English truly among themselves, they'll think we are talking in a strange tongue. They'll think that the people they thought they knew have different, strange ideas, yet those ideas are part of Aboriginal traditions.

They'll hear people speaking from the heart about things what happened, the things they was taught. When Aboriginals speak, it's not just their mouths moving. Everything is sincere, everything has depth and really means something. That way the memory of little children dying or being taken away is a living one, always present. Whatever happens to us at any time is there forever.

Although none of my own children were taken away, one of my grandsons was. In 1969 my son Lenny and his girlfriend had a baby boy called Lyndon. When he was only a few months old, the police took him away to Melbourne, believing they were doing the right thing. He was one of the last Aboriginal kids to be taken like that. We didn't know what had happened to him for years, apart from that someone adopted him. My daughter Elizabeth, Camilla and our friend Adèle Howard researched and tried to trace him for a very long time. Finally, in 1998, we found out that he'd moved to England with his adoptive parents and had been killed in a motorcycle accident in 1986. He was only seventeen. It was a terrible shock to find him, only to lose him again.

Not long after we located his adoptive parents, Elizabeth met

Betty, his adoptive mother, over the phone. She then wrote Elizabeth the most beautiful letter:

What can I tell you about Lyndon? He was a lovely boy, quiet and thoughtful but with a good sense of humour. He loved children and animals and was very artistic . . . As he grew older, all the children in our street would come to Lyndon to get their bikes fixed and he never turned them away.

Of course, he was not an angel, and would get up to mischief as every child does. But I can honestly say that he never gave me a moment's trouble . . . [Lyndon] was determined to be a car mechanic. He was never happier than when he was taking an engine apart and putting it together again. When he left school he managed to get a year's YTS training with Clover Leaf Cars. The only drawback was that it was difficult to get there by public transport. So he persuaded me to buy him a small motor bike. He was a good, careful driver, but I did worry about him . . . I cannot dwell too much on the night of the accident, as it is far too painful. It had been raining and there were wet leaves on the road. He skidded as he went around a bend and hit a lamp post. They were wonderful at the hospital and tried their hardest to save him, but his injuries were too bad and they could not revive him.

How I got through that terrible time I will never know. He was buried on November 6, 1986, four months from his eighteenth birthday . . . there were over two hundred people there . . . The procession to the cemetery was almost a mile long . . . The flowers stretched to the end of the cemetery, but I could hardly see them through my tears. . . . It must have come as a dreadful shock to you all when you found out that Lyndon had died . . . He knew he was adopted and had no problems with that. Had he lived, and had he shown a desire to contact his family in Australia I would have backed him all the way. It would have given him a sense of identity. I had no fear of losing his love, for love has no limits and can encompass everyone.

A couple of years ago, Betty and her husband Eddie came over from England to visit and meet all of our family. They stayed with Elizabeth, and brought all sorts of photos and mementoes of Lyndon with them. It was wonderful to have them here and to get to know Lyndon better through them. They said they had let Lyndon know he was Aboriginal while he was growing up, and Elizabeth gave them an Aboriginal flag to take home with them, to put next to his photo. Betty and Elizabeth still write to each other today, and Betty shares her memories of my lost grandson.

Chapter 14

I once brought home a tiny little possum for the kids. I used to fetch these creatures home for them to rear up, to learn them with animals. We called him Son. He grew up to be a big possum and he'd go out in the night to roam around. But the other possums would chase him – they must've smelt human on him – and he'd grab the doorknob outside and be swinging on it in a real panic, shaking it to get our attention, singing out to get let in.

We'd open the door and he'd jump on our shoulders and stand straight up, looking out of the door at the others. He was a big shot now that he'd got inside, and he'd be growling and challenging everything that had chased him. But he wouldn't go back out again.

When we were having tea, he would look in every cup, trying and tasting them all – he'd go back and forth between them, deciding which tasted nicest. He must have been after the ones with sugar in them. We gave him his own special tea to drink too, and his own special food to eat.

In the evening we'd all sit at the fire having yarns. Ian, aged four or five, would draw pictures and hold out the paper saying, 'Mum, look what I drawed.' The little possum would be between us, sitting there. One time Audrey never took any notice of Ian, and we just said, 'Oh yeah, oh yeah,' to him. Suddenly the little possum grabbed the drawing with his hand and threw it straight in the fire. Just like a kid would do, and it burnt up and Ian just looked. It was a sort of shock to him that the possum done it. The possum was saying,

'Look, take notice of me, not that bit of paper. I'm the possum here, I'm the big shot.' And he threw it real hard. It was a straight shot too, it went straight into the flames.

When you rear little creatures up from babies, they get real cunning, and real lovable. They know they're loved. That old possum used to lean up lopsided against the wall on a hot day with his leg stretched out – he used to look like an old drunken man. His belly would be sticking out, we used to look at him and laugh.

Then one day the poor old fellah licked a paint tin out and got lead poisoning. We didn't know about that then, or we wouldn't have left it around. He used to try everything out.

I've had some great animals over the years. Nipper was one of them, he was Ian's dog. He had him as a pup, but Ian grew up while Nipper was a proper dog. Nipper used to bring in all the logs of wood until you finished cutting. And he couldn't stand the kids swimming – he got real worried and dragged them out of the water every time. Audrey's brother Hector used to work with Nipper rounding up cattle. And when poor Hector passed away, the undertaker brought Hector's old clothes after the funeral and put them on the fence post. Nipper ran up real happy because he smelt his old friend's scent. But when he sniffed the clothes he got a fright and sneaked away with his tail between his legs, because he smelt death. And everybody seen it. 'See that? See that?' 'Yeah, that old dog smelt death,' I said. 'Come on, let's go, let's go,' everyone said, and I had to drive them down the mission. Yeah, they had all seen it and they felt funny. The dog was real cowering, like somebody had hit him. Nobody felt like doing anything after that.

I'll never forget my big dog Sandy. He used to jump fences chasing hares. That's how he gained on them. Just like a steeplechaser he was, straight over he'd go. And he was a great big heavy dog, you wouldn't think he could run. I don't know what he was, a cross between an Alsatian and a staghound maybe. The kids were little when I had him. Fiona might've been just born. Sandy would never hurt the hares – he'd bring them back to my feet for me to kill.

I got a job as caretaker of the Warrnambool Surf Club in the late 1970s. While I was working there I met a bloke in the Victoria Hotel who I'd known years ago. He told me he had a German shepherd dog and was selling her pups. I had a look at them and there was only one black one, like a big Labrador – all the others looked like German shepherds. I took the black one for twenty-five dollars, and he grew up to be the biggest dog I ever had. Jet-black he was. When he stood up, he was well over my head. His mother was real savage, but he was the gentlest dog you'd ever see. I called him Goola.

When the people at the surf club had showers, he used to bring me all their belongings that they'd left outside the showers – their shoes, watches and keys – anything. He'd drop them on my floor in my bunkhouse. Goola seemed to think it was his job to take them. It used to embarrass me. People would get out of the shower and ask me if I'd seen their things, and I'd ask if they'd seen a dog around when their things went missing. 'Yeah,' they'd say, 'the biggest and blackest that ever I've seen.'

'Well, that's the culprit,' I'd say. 'He takes everything and fetches it back to me like as if he'd been taught to do it.'

He loved swimming. He used to go out to sea and swim back – I was frightened that a shark would get him. He liked to travel in Camilla's car too, sitting upright on the passenger seat beside her. One day he wouldn't do something I'd asked, so I teased him and said that Camilla had just driven up outside. Goola rushed out to see her. Then he rushed back in looking confused, and bit me on the ankle.

One day, out at the mission, I missed him and a bloke said, 'I seen a dog dead in the paddock.'

'What sort?' I said.

'A big black one.'

Oh! It was like a knife went through me. 'Was he really dead?'

'Yep,' he said, 'he's dead.'

I went over, and poor old Goola was dead all right. Poisoned. Lenny's dogs were poisoned too but they survived. Ian took them to the vet and he said it was snail poison. Goola must have had a lot. It was done on purpose – cut-up meat was put near the house for them. And all Goola had done was go in the bush. He liked jumping straight in the river from the bank – big splash! – and come back. You wouldn't see him for a while, and then you'd see him swimming across. You'd think, He's gone. He's drowned. Then you'd see him swimming against the current – he used to like that, to see how strong he was. That must have made him strong too. He was power-ful and he loved that water. I had a few good dogs but I never had none as good as him. He wasn't trained or anything, he was a natural sort of dog who'd *listen* to you, and seemed to understand what you were saying. So many good dogs I had.

One winter's night, while I was still looking after the surf club, this mate of mine came with a collie dog and a little kitten what fol-lowed him. The animals stayed with me while we advertised on the radio about them. Somebody claimed the collie dog but nobody wanted the kitten – the miserablest-looking kitten you'd ever see. But she grew up to be a beautiful, good, faithful cat, and a Persian cat breed. I called her Bushy-Tail. She had lots of beautiful kittens, all with big bushy tails and long fur, the most beautiful kittens you ever saw, and she was a great mother to them. She was always kind to other animals, except if a dog came near her kittens. Then she'd turn into a raving monster. She'd jump on their heads and still attack them while they were running. She'd jump at their eyes and scratch. The wildest dog out was terrified of her. Except for Goola – she let him pick them up and take them in his gentle mouth to the beach. He would play with them and watch over them there like a nanny, and Bushy-Tail didn't mind. She trusted him completely. Tourists took all her kittens, except for one – a giant sandy cat, and she used to feed him. I called him Sookie. At two years old he'd still drink like a little kitten from her, with his paws going. Kids loved to see a big cat like that being fed by his mum. But one man who came here used to kick him away when he did that.

I used to go for walks at Naringal, crossing the creek. Bushy-Tail used to come with me and she wasn't frightened of water. Cats are frightened of water, eh? She must have jumped logs in the water, but she always got across that creek. I'd turn around in the far paddock and ask, 'How did you get here?' And at home she was like a dog with me, crossing the Hopkins River, keeping up with me by jumping from stone to stone. I had her for a good many years.

My bull terriers that I recently kept had a big sense of responsibility. Jesse was blind and too old to walk – she couldn't go anywhere. A young dog I had, called Mulga, became like a son to her. Mulga used to go up to old Mr McCullogh's farm and fetch bones back to his old mum. He made a big track across the paddock where the old dog used to lie and wait for him. I'd say, 'Where did you get all these bones, Jesse? You can't go anywhere.' Then I watched and seen her son Mulga walking up there and coming back with the bones. That's why there were bones all around the old dog where she lied in a special place. And when Mulga had puppies, he brought food to the little pups, and to their mother as well.

There was this wild, black, baby razorback pig that a bloke

brought to me and I reared him up. Mulga used to fight with him and you'd hear the pig squealing. I'd be up in the paddock and think the dog was killing the pig, because bull terriers are their natural enemies. But the pig would have Mulga in the corner. I'd run down and pick him up and brush him. But they got to be good mates, and sleep together even. It used to be real comical, these two enemies sleeping with one another. The wild pig and the bull terrier. But they got sick of fighting one another and ended up real mates.

When we used to come in from up the paddock, if there was no food out for that pig he'd stand up on his hind legs and pull the clothes off the washing line and rub them in the dirt. And when my daughters-in-law, Jocelyn or Ange, came out with the broom, he'd take off. He knew what to do. He was a funny old fellah, but he used to love the kids scratching him. He'd roll over on his back. But he went down the other end of the mission and somebody shot him. All these animals were real precious to us, but other people didn't see it that way.

Another animal I brought home for the kids to rear up once was a little baby rabbit. I'd found it in its burrow after our dogs had killed its mother. He didn't have any fur and his eyes were still closed. I put him in my pocket and fetched him home. We fed him tiny doses of watered-down milk and he survived real good. We'd fetch him young fresh grass and those clover buds that grow into a tiny ball – they love that, rabbits. They eat them like anything. Those buds must taste sweet.

Sometimes we couldn't find our rabbit and we'd say to each other, 'Hope the dogs didn't get him.' Then we'd find him sleeping in the warmth of the dog's neck – the old dog was lying with him. Our dogs were fierce hunters but they treated that rabbit like a mate.

Visitors coming to the door would say, 'There's something here running round me very fast all the time. It's running all around me and I don't know what it is.'

'Oh,' we'd say, 'that's just our rabbit.'

He used to show off for visitors. He'd turn somersaults, jump in the air, jump on the table and spin around, then back to the floor. We'd laugh like anything. Oh, it was great to see him go through his antics.

When Ian was about four, he used to come with me when I went fishing. I used to take him to the place where we fished as kids. A lot of watercress grows there. A bit of water ripples through the pools, but even after floods some of the trout won't leave there because they're very territorial. Sometimes when we get the fish, we pick the watercress and put it on the eel or fish's neck and take him home looking very inviting to eat. Nice clean watercress on it.

This particular day Ian was very excited. We got to the river and all the fish took off and hid under stones. We had to watch them then. We could see a big trout under a rock with its tail sticking out. I said to Ian, 'You be my spotter.' Because when you're in the water, the reflections come, but if you're higher than the water, you can see where the fish are going. 'It went over there, Dad,' he said. 'Not that rock, Dad, this rock here. There he is, there's his tail!'

I watched the trout and he kept moving out. I thought, It would be a good shot for the little fellah. I'll let him have a go. I asked him, 'You want a go, Bud?'

'Yeah! Yeah!' Ian said, but he was nervous, though he'd seen me spearing.

'Here you are,' I said. 'Here's the spear.'

He took it and stood on the rock, looking at this big trout. 'Not yet, mate,' I said, 'not yet.' Ian was looking at me and he was starting to shake with excitement. I could see the spear quivering a bit. He was going to spear a big fish. I said, 'You'll be right, mate. Just when I tell you, you let the spear drop on him real fast.' And I went, 'Now! Now! Let him have it!'

He went *bang* with the spear, and the spear started bucking and he was hanging on and looking at me like this, with big eyes, as if to ask me, What am I going to do now? And the spear was jumping around in his hand. I said, 'You hang onto him, Bud, you hang on! Hang on! Don't let him get away!' He must have felt the vibration come through the spear. And he pushed the spear down and pinned the trout to the rocks at the bottom. I put my hand down and leant in the water and pulled the fish up on the spear.

'There you are, mate. Look at that!' Ian looked at the big trout with wide eyes. It was a great big trout too – I don't think I've seen one as big as that, before then or after. 'You're a big hunter now, mate. You won't starve when you know how to spear the fish, eh?'

'Yeah, yeah,' he said, as he was looking at this big fish. 'We'll go home now?'

'Okay,' I said, because I knew he wanted to go home to show his big fish.

I got a fern stalk with branches on it and put it through the fish's gills. He could carry it home then. He said, 'I'll take it! I'll take the fish!' and he took it up the big hill to his grandfather's house. When he was getting near the house, he walked faster and faster, and the fish was that big he was dragging it behind him. He walked in saying, 'Look, look, Gran! Look, Grandfather! *I* speared this fish! *I* speared it!'

'Aaah, did *you* spear it?' they said. They didn't really believe him. They thought I held the spear for him. But I convinced them, saying, 'Yeah, he done it. He done it all on his own.' And he was that happy! And we all had a good feed of fish that teatime. Enough fish for everyone.

That was the first spear he had, and ever since then he was always handling the spearing of fish and eels. And he used to show his skills to other people who wasn't used to it. He'd catch a fish anywhere that other people wouldn't, because he knew where to look. As the years went by, he'd say, 'Remember that fish I speared, Dad, when I was little?' And I'd answer, 'Ah, yeah, that was a beauty.'

I'll never forget that fish. It was the biggest brown trout – I couldn't put my two hands around it. That was Ian's initiation into hunting and he was that proud of it. Many other fish he speared after that, but he'd always remember that first big fish. I still think of that fish too. I can still see Ian standing on the rock telling me where the fish went. That's a special memory to me, because he's gone from us now.

CHAPTER 15

I could only work in the quarry off and on in them days because I used to get pneumonia every summertime from the quarry dust in my lungs. In the quarry you couldn't see your hand before your face for stone dust. Stone dust covered everything like salt, and you were breathing it in constantly. So to get work I had to go far away sometimes.

Our marriage started to break down a bit then, but I was still earning my children's keep and working hard. In addition, Audrey had to keep leaving me to go and look after her mother, who was getting sick, and everything just fell out of place very naturally.

In the end I was living on my own more often than not. Some of the kids lived with me – they'd go backwards and forwards between us. But I kept on working, hoping that everything would turn out all right. I was drinking heavily at weekends, when no one was with me, but I always went to work. Audrey and I had arguments, like any young couple reaching a crisis and not knowing what's going on. However, in the end I took it for granted that she'd left me, and I got on the grog more. But I always went on sending her money, and we ended up being friends.

I used to walk miles for a reviver after a Saturday night drinking. I'd walk past the house where Audrey was living with her mum and dad, and my little children used to stand watching.

One Sunday they came across to the road and asked me where I was going.

'Ah,' I told them, 'I'm crook today. I'm going to get a reviver in Panmure or somewhere.' I walked away sadly.

'We don't want you to go, Dad. We love you.'

'I know you love me,' I answered. 'But I've got to have that drink. I'm on my own and I want to do something – go for a walk. Go walkabout.'

I said goodbye to them at the gate and walked up the road about fifty yards. Then I looked back. My little children were still watching me. And I said to myself, What chance have them kids got, with a drunken father and their whole life breaking up?

I didn't even have a smoke. I sat down near a bush, with my children watching. And I thought, Look at me! Prepared to walk eight miles, get a bottle of wine and walk home again. I don't need it that much, do I? Then I thought, I've got to do something for my little kids. And I said to myself, Right-oh, Banjo. No more drink. From this moment on, you're putting your kids first. I looked in my pocket again and found some old cigarette butts. I tore a piece off an old newspaper what was hanging out of the bush and rolled myself a smoke. Then I turned around and walked back.

'Where are you going, Dad?'

'I'm going home now. I'm going to cook myself a feed and have a good rest, to be ready for work in the morning.'

'Aren't you going for your drink?'

'Not on your life. I'm going to look after you fellahs now.'

They ran home real happy, and met their mum at the door. 'Dad's not going away for a drink now! He's not going!' they told her.

And I saw Audrey shake her head as if to say, Yeah? And how long will that last?

I looked at her. But I didn't say anything, just kept on walking. I hadn't gone ten yards before a car pulled up beside me. Two of my white workmates yelled out, 'How are you going, Banjo?'

'I'm going all right.'

'Are you crook?'

'You can say that again!'

'We've got something here to fix you up.'

I looked in the car. On the back seat was a big box of beer. Two boxes, in fact. Just through habit, I was going to reach in and take a bottle. I looked back up the road. My children had seen the car pull up. They had left their mother and come back to watch. Still looking at them, I thought, What did you say not long ago, Banjo? You promised them something.

I said to the bloke, 'No, mate. I don't want a drink.'

'You *must* be crook!' they said.

'I'm crook all right.'

'Well, have a drink.'

'No, mate. Five minutes ago, I told my little kids up there that I wasn't going to drink today or tomorrow for a long, long time.'

'You must be *bloody* crook!'

'Look, mate. Start your car up and get going. I don't want any of your grog.'

They started the car and drove away with all the grog. I went straight home, cooked myself some nice soup, cut wood and went to bed.

I woke up fit the next morning and walked all the way to work at the quarry – five miles.

Next payday, I marched into the pub and ordered a lemon squash. Everybody laughed at me. But I went on drinking lemon squashes for about seventeen years. My kids grew up, went to school, got the best education they could get and good jobs afterwards. I took them and their white and Aboriginal friends to social clubs, gymnasiums and the YMCA. I taught them to box, and fitted right back into the community again.

I didn't really get back together again with Audrey, just off and on. But we remained the best of friends and would always help one another in times of trouble. My mother-in-law got sicker and she thought that was why Audrey stayed with her.

As our children were growing up, I taught them the basic things in our old language, but not really to speak it. Today they can say a lot of things without white acquaintances understanding, of course, if they need to. They can communicate with each other in a crowd.

Our traditional way of life concerning spirit things was also always part of our children's education when they was little too. At home they learnt that we always have something to cling to in times of trouble, something which guides us and never fails to warn us – just as the white man has Christianity.

We feel very close to people's spirits, and people from the spirit world let us know things. That's the Aboriginal tradition. Speak that way to any Aboriginal, and he'll understand exactly what you're talking about. I would tell my children that often the spirit of someone what has passed on will come to you in a dream, or you'll get a warning that a friend or relation is sick. Something strange happens, and you know it's a message from the spirit world. Aboriginals live alert to these things all their lives, but we don't tell people about them. We are afraid of being laughed at over things which are absolutely true. There's something *there*. I don't understand it myself, but we know it's there. We're not academics or scientists to work these things out, but the main thing is that we *believe* these things happen.

I have heard white people say who have spent time with Aboriginals, like here at the mission with us, that nothing happened to them in the white world the way things happen to them since they entered the Aboriginal world. They get feelings, as if someone's telling them an important message. And they might get signs from outside, like a dream or a bird. But if you heard Aboriginals talking about these things around a campfire, you would think we were talking a foreign language. I'll tell you about one of the things I'm speaking about.

One time when I was home alone – because my wife had gone to look after her mum – I was reading books by the light of an old candle burning beside my bed, because we never had electric lights then. It was about twelve midnight.

Somebody walked up the passage in my house and pushed my door open. I looked up into the doorway and saw a lady standing there. I thought it was Audrey, so I called out, 'What's wrong? Old Granny must be really sick for you to walk here at this hour of night.'

But the woman never answered me. She just stood outside the reach of the candlelight and kept looking at me, though I couldn't see her face much. She was standing in the shadow and I could only see the shape of her.

Then a funny cold feeling flowed all over me and the hair at the back of my neck started to stand up. I realised that this was a moorup [spirit]. I sat paralysed, staring at her.

After about fifteen seconds, I said, 'What do you want? Talk to me! Tell me what you want!'

The lady turned her back to me and stepped backwards into the candlelight. The candle lit up the whole of her head and I could see she had long black hair and was wearing a long, old-fashioned dress.

'Why are you doing this? What's wrong?' I sang out.

The lady walked out and up the passage, and I jumped out of bed and followed her, shouting, 'What's wrong? What's wrong?' I was scared.

The woman walked straight outside and disappeared.

This happened after I had given up drinking to give the kids a go, and I was stone cold sober. I'd had sober habits for years.

My wife came over a few days later to bring me some things. I told her, 'A moorup lady came here the other night and I thought it was you.'

She laughed at me but she started thinking about it. After a while, she remembered that before I got the house it used to be occupied by an old full-blood friend, Uncle Jack. And he would say to his nephew, Joe Alberts, 'Ah! I don't know why this woman comes in my room looking at me all the time. She don't belong here. And she won't speak.'

When Uncle Jack died, his nephew took over the house and his children used to sleep in that room. They complained that the woman was still coming in, standing looking at them. Joe then cut out two partitions so that he and the children could sleep in one big room. Nobody used the other bedroom again till now.

After that first night, that lady used to come at the same time for over five years, and I grew to look forward to seeing her. That old lady will be along soon, I'd say to myself, it's about her time. About two or three nights a month, she'd come. And I'd talk to her, saying, 'I'm all right, but thanks for coming to see me,' but still she wouldn't speak to me. She'd walk out through the door, same as always, and I'd follow her.

So I got to know her a bit, and that she didn't like drunks. She'd get real angry if drunks were in the house. She'd throw things at them, and someone even felt himself being choked by her once, and dragged around the floor.

One of my younger daughters was out picking mushrooms once when, from a distance, she saw the moorup woman standing at my door, and she thought it was her mother. She ran over proudly to show her mother all the nice mushrooms she'd picked. But when she reached the door no one was there, and the house was real cold. She ran over to her granny's and found her mother waiting.

The moorup woman appeared to a lot of people, but the funny thing was, my wife was still living. If Audrey had passed on before this lady came, I would have felt sure it was her spirit.

Maybe Audrey's spirit was coming to watch over us anyway, without her knowing it. Because I could have sworn it was her, though the woman wouldn't let me see her face.

CHAPTER 16

During the middle part of my life, I was sent to gaol a few times. Sometimes it was for standing up for my rights, and sometimes it was because I wouldn't tell on other people for something they'd done. For example, if someone had stolen a coat and the police said it was me, I'd just think, Oh good. Somebody's got a nice warm coat now that needed it, and be pleased for him. I wouldn't mind going to gaol about it. It was part of our way of life – we accepted it because we was Aboriginal. We accepted all sorts of bad things and went along with them. We couldn't fight against them things and be nasty. We just went along with them. We couldn't speak up for our rights – we had no lawyers. But it made big headlines when Aboriginals went to gaol, and full pages for little trifle things what Aboriginals done – it was their policy to demoralise us as much as they could. It was as if they *wanted* you to be bad.

One time I was in gaol, I was telling all the other prisoners stories that made them laugh. One of the warders, who everyone was scared of, noticed this and I could tell he didn't like me for it. You weren't allowed to be laughing and having a good time in gaol.

I'd found out we could ask to do our time working in the prison garden, so I lodged a request to see the governor about it. The warder who everyone was scared of bailed me up and started shouting at me.

'Want to see the governor, do you?' he snarled. 'What's the matter, sonny? Missing our grog, are we?'

'No,' I said, 'I'm not missing my grog.'

'Missing not having to work then, are we?'

'No,' I said. 'I don't mind working.'

And so he went on with a few more questions. 'Missing your women, are we?'

'No,' I said again.

'Missing your black mates, then?'

'No, sir,' I replied. 'All my mates are in here.'

Some of the prisoners around me started sniggering. The guard was furious now. Coming right up to my face, his eyes flashing and his face bright red, he yelled, 'Well what *do* you fucking miss then?'

'I miss the sound of little children's laughter,' I said.

The warder stopped dead, his mouth open. He didn't say another word, just sort of spluttered at me. After standing there for a minute, he turned tail and stormed off.

The other prisoners congratulated me on the cleanest fight and most resounding victory they'd ever seen – but I didn't mean it to be anything like that! I think the fellah must have lost a child or something like that. Maybe his wife had left him and taken the kids. Something horrible must have happened for him to always be so horrible to other people. I felt sorry for him.

He never came near me again after that, and if he ever saw me coming, he would *run* away. He wouldn't even look at me.

Another warder, who'd listened to all this, took me outside to the garden and gave me some work, saying, 'Any time you want something, come and see me.'

I met this young whitefellah in gaol in Melbourne once. It was the first time he'd been in trouble. The squatter what he used to work for owed him money, and he met some good people from another town what used to come to his church and they offered for him to spend a holiday with them. But they didn't know what he was going through at the squatter's place. He kept that to himself – how cruelly he was being treated. The squatter made him sleep out in the chookhouse if he didn't finish his chores. He thought about the people what befriended him at the church, and this young girl what he'd started to like too. She was the same age as him. He told me all this when he was in gaol. He wanted me to write them a letter, but I wasn't much of a letter-writer. I said, 'No, *you* write the letter, mate.'

He said, 'But I want you to do it because you might explain it better. I don't want them to know I'm in gaol.'

'But they'll see the letter came from gaol,' I told him. 'They might be sympathetic and come to see you, come to visit you. They don't expect you to be in gaol. I wouldn't expect a person like you to be in gaol either. If I met you outside of gaol, I'd say to myself that you'd never, ever go to gaol, mate, because you're too honest.'

But he had stolen this horse what was equivalent to the money the farmer owed him. And when they missed the lad and the horse, they sent out a warrant for his arrest. He was taken to court and sentenced for six months. First time in trouble in his life, and everyone in that small town was all against him. The fellah he stole the horse off had a lot of influence and money. He was a civic leader of his community, and the boy couldn't say nothing about him owing him money or the way he was treated. So he went to gaol and he was scared. And he got to working with me, and the warders left him with me because, being Aboriginal, I'd been in gaol a few times.

Anyhow, this young man was working with me, cleaning the warders' lookout towers. And one day he stood on a stool to look out over the prison yard, and he was singing out, he was real glad and excited. 'Come on, look, look, look! Look at this! Look at it! Look! Look!'

'What? Why?' I said.

'Come round, hurry up, look! Look!' he cried out at me.

I thought I was going to see a mass escape of prisoners or something. And I'm looking out the window, and looking all along the big brick walls, stone walls, and couldn't see anyone. I said, 'What are you looking at?'

'Look! Can't you see it?'

'Tell me what it is, mate. What is it? What are you looking at?'

'The green grass! Look at the beautiful green grass!' he shouted.

And I looked at him. What's this bloke talking about? I came from the Western District, where there's always been green grass. I said, 'Yes, it's green grass. So what? Didn't you ever see green grass like that before, mate?'

'No,' he said, 'that's the first time in my life.'

Turned out he came from a really dry area up in the Mallee somewhere. See? He was that excited about all the green grass. And then I realised, Oh, the poor lad. He must have been suffering a long time, this lad.

He told me he'd never, ever go back to gaol. I never wrote the letter for him, but he said he might go and see the good people. He wanted me to stay in gaol with him till his time finished and go with him to explain why he was in gaol. I said, 'They won't allow me. But you do that, and they will still love you. They'll be wondering where you are, and how you dropped out of the picture. They don't know *where* you are. You're not going to your church, and no one seems to know where you are. And the local people probably won't tell them where you are.'

So I had to leave gaol before he did. Years after, when I went back to gaol, there were all these young fellahs in the remand yard. One of them came up to me and said, 'Do you know me?'

I looked at him hard and said, 'You resemble somebody I met a long time ago, but he was in gaol too. And this young fellah said he would never, ever come back to gaol again.'

And he said, 'Well, I'm that man.'

'What happened, mate?' I said.

'I never went home when I was released from gaol,' he told me. 'I never went to see them good people what befriended me, I never even went to see my mum. I went straight through to South Australia and I've been living with Aboriginals along the riverbanks. I was in and out of gaol ever since.'

I said to him, 'When I first met you, I would have bet on it that you wouldn't go back to gaol.'

Fact is, if they would have treated him properly, he would have never, ever been *in* gaol. But he lost faith in everybody. Even himself.

Because he befriended me in gaol and I was the Aboriginal what looked after him, he looked for other Aboriginals to look after him when he was released from gaol. Eh? And living in an Aboriginal camp in them days meant drinking and fighting and thieving. Living on the fringes of white men's towns, and that's how this young white-fellah was. And he told me, 'Although I was in and out of gaol all this time, I'll never, ever forget how you looked after me.' He took off a new jumper he had on – it was wintertime – and he gave it to me. And he only had a shirt on underneath.

I said to him, 'What about you, mate? It's cold in here.'

He said, 'No, you take this, take it for looking after me.' And I've never, ever seen him from that day to this, and that was years ago. I never even heard of him again. Any news of people in trouble – murders or accidents – I always looked for his name, but I never seen it. I wonder what happened to him.

Chapter 17

The time came in the 1960s when my dad came to base himself on the mission once more, after thirty years of living in Melbourne. But he still made trips back to where Mum was working in the city. And my mother would come home from time to time too. But she always liked to be near work, and there was much more work for her in Melbourne, in cafes and people's houses. She also used to visit her own homeland, Cummeragunja Mission.

My youngest brother Bert stayed with Dad. Poor fellah – he worked hard all his life but he was an alcoholic. The drink more or less killed him. We used to call him Gunboat, after an African-American fighter, Gunboat Jack. My brother became well known everywhere as Gunboat because he had the same mannerisms.

Gunboat got fed up with going to and from hospital when he was dying, so in the end they kept him in. We all went to visit him. He must have thought I looked sick and in need of a drink, because he told me to ask the sister for money. 'I've got plenty of money what I never spent because I was in hospital,' he said to me. 'Take it all, I don't need it now.' He knew he was dying.

'I don't want it,' I said. 'That's yours. You never know what you might need.'

But he insisted. 'You get the nurse now. I'll call her.'

'No, mate, don't do that. That money's in your possession. You keep it here. I don't want anything.'

I took nothing, and I never have taken anything from a sick person.

I don't know what happened to that money after he passed on. I never inquired who got it. Money doesn't mean a thing to true Aboriginal people. If somebody else got it, they must have needed it. That's okay – no arguments about it.

One time, while I was working at the quarry, the message came that my dad did not expect to live through the day and he wanted to see me. He'd been in hospital for a couple of weeks.

I went in to where he was lying on his sickbed. We had a yarn about everyday things, then he burst out urgently, 'You're not going to leave our tribal land, are you, son?'

'No, Dad.'

'Don't you ever do that. It's our spirit-land. It was good enough for your ancestors and mine. It was good enough for me to rear a family on, that spirit place. It's the only place we have to cling to, to feel one with our ancestors. You have to promise me that you'll stay on there.'

I said, 'I'll go away and come back, but I'll always call it my spiritual home.'

'That's what I mean,' he said.

My dad had heard long ago about an old law that if one Aboriginal person was still living on former mission land, it could not be taken over for non-Aboriginal purposes. It could never be declared vacant while one occupant was left.

He said he was going to have a rest now. 'I'll see you later,' he told me.

'All right then, Dad,' I said.

I still stayed near his bedside, walking up and down, watching him sleep. As I watched him, I knew he would not be with us much longer. I saw him take his last deep breath and I realised that he had gone to the lands of his tribal ancestors.

The nurse who had kept walking past, glancing at him, came up to me and said, 'Your dad looks as if he's sound asleep.'

'Yes, he *is* sound asleep,' I said.

Next time she came past, she went over to feel his pulse. Then she panicked and yelled, 'Look! You get away from here!' very angrily.

But my dad had called me specially to come and hear the things he'd said about his spirit-land, and it was right for me to be there. I didn't leave, anyway. The nurse saw the doctor, and the doctor came and told me, 'We did all we could.'

'I know you did,' I said. 'My dad was happy with the care you gave him here. I saw him take his last breath, and the nurse didn't realise that I knew he'd passed away.'

I was glad that, when my dad was on his last, his only wish was to find out how his son would cope with the land and his belief. He wanted to be sure of the spiritual side to my Aboriginal life. And I promised my old dad on his deathbed that I'd never leave here. That's why I'm here today, through all the terrible things what happened.

Because of what my dad told me, I've been confident that our land would always be regarded as Aboriginal country. Despite all the hardships, the trouble about government and ownership and land rights, this land was always occupied by Aboriginal people. We never forsook it or left it vacant. Somebody always remained here like a guardian of the spiritual sites where our ancestors roamed. That's what our bush means to us – a spiritual place where we can come and go. It's not just a tree or a river, it's something sacred what money can't buy from you. It's something there forever.

The young nurse didn't understand that Aboriginals are used to death. We know when our friends pass away. From childhood, we have looked after dying relations. We hear their last wishes. Aboriginal people are used to such things. From birth, we live with death. We all know what to expect when our time comes. That's the Aboriginal way of life – we share the hardship as well as the happiness. It wasn't the nurse's fault that she didn't understand that.

My old mum lived on for years. She was near a hundred when she passed away in 1985. She kept a real nice garden outside her home at Framlingham, and had a fire going every day.

'I always have a fire going, even on a real hot day,' she'd say. 'I need it to look into the Dreaming.'

She had always been in the battle for fair treatment for everyone. She held out a helping hand to everybody, no matter what race or religion they belonged to. That was part of her life, to help everybody. She was a great fighter for Aboriginal rights in particular. She fought for equal conditions in the Aboriginal community around this area, around her homeland Cummeragunja, and other parts of Australia where Aboriginals were ill-treated. She used to tell us stories of Cummeragunja Mission, about how all her playmates were dragged away there. She was never taken to the orphanages – I think she must have had strong parents what fought for their kids. If the parents protected their children and hid them away, they sometimes survived. When there was no one around to do that, the little ones were easy to grab.

My brother Frank, who went to North Queensland as a fighter, fought in the Sydney stadium and then married an Aboriginal girl in Queensland. He had a family up there and lived there all his life. He even boxed during World War II. He's passed on now, and I'm the only brother left. Another link with the bark-hut days has been broken.

One night in 1973 I had a terrible dream. In Aboriginal tradition, dreaming about dirty water means death.

I dreamt an old buggy was floating down the river with my wife and our youngest daughter Fiona on it. And the water was all dirty. I struggled out through the water to get my wife and child. But I lost Audrey, she went right under the water. I grabbed little Fiona and swam to the bank. And when I looked back, I couldn't see my wife anywhere.

Soon after I had this dream, our eldest daughter Pat drove her old grandfather's car past me when I was walking along the road. 'Hurry up!' she said, 'Something's happened! Mum's lying on the floor. She's collapsed.'

I ran back to the house and picked her up off the floor – me and her old dad. We laid her across the bed. She was dying.

She reached out to me and grabbed my hand and pulled me down. And she kissed me. Then she put my little girl Fiona's tablets in her hand – Fiona used to have epilepsy – and said, 'You'll have to look after yourself now.'

My little girl was only nine and she cried out, 'Don't let Mummy die! Don't let Mummy die!' Fiona ran and found a spoon and put it in Audrey's mouth to stop her from biting her tongue, because she thought her mum was having an epileptic attack, as Fiona often did. Then she kept running outside and turning on the tap and putting cold wet rags on her mum's forehead.

Meanwhile Pat drove to Purnim to ring up the ambulance because we didn't have a phone. Then she came back and said, 'What'll I do? What'll I do? They refuse to come!'

I told her, 'Go back and tell them they've *got* to come. It's a real emergency.'

Twice more Pat drove to ring up the ambulance. But they said, 'We don't go to the Aboriginal settlement unless the police have notified us first.' They were no doubt thinking, It'll only turn out to be a drunken fight or somebody hit with a bottle. They didn't look on

Aboriginal business as urgent. It had nothing to do with them as far as they were concerned.

In the end they said they'd come, but they took the longest time. All the while, my poor wife was dying and Fiona kept crying, 'Don't let Mummy die! Don't let her die!'

'She's not going to die, my girl,' I said, 'she's not going to die.'

Fiona was sitting at the head of the bed sobbing, holding the cold rag on her mum's forehead. Just before the ambulance man came in, I knew my wife had taken her last deep breath and passed away. I didn't tell my little girl that her mum had already gone.

'Don't let Mum die, Dad,' she kept saying. 'Don't let Mummy die.'

The ambulance man walked in and said in a rough voice, 'Where's this person who's supposed to be sick?'

I just stood there saying nothing, holding Audrey's upper body in my arms where she lay across the bed. Little Fiona watched us, sobbing. She was expecting some great miracle.

The ambulance man felt Audrey's pulse and said in the roughest voice, as if the whole situation was just a nuisance, 'We've wasted our time coming here. The woman's already dead.'

My little girl screamed and ran away. And that's how she found out that her mother was dead.

The police came out afterwards and had a look around, looked for tablets. We had no tablets. A routine check-up, I suppose. My wife died of a heart attack.

The moment Fiona screamed has been with me ever since, and all her reactions since then seem to me to come from that scream. Whenever a person close to us dies, Fiona relives what happened to her mother, and the man's horrible tone of voice saying, 'This woman's dead.' It's there all the time; that goes for me too. For every Aboriginal I have met, the raw agony of the way our loved ones died is with us always; we feel how they felt in their last moments on earth, and we feel our own grief from when that was happening. Then when another person close to us dies, we relive every detail of all the deaths we have watched before. Some white people say, 'It's all in the past now; put it behind you and get on with your life.' But that's not the Aboriginal way – there is no past. Everything is still happening; the spirit of how the person felt then is still in that place, and still in our heart. We have to take the bad with the good, because knowing that we are connected to the spiritual world makes us Aboriginal.

Part Three
1975–2000

CHAPTER 18

It meant so much to me that Audrey had kissed me while she was dying. Even though we were no longer together, we had become the best of friends and a great support to each other. I still loved her very much, and wished all the time that we could be more than friends.

After Audrey's death, I had nightmares about my wife every night for the next three years, and started drinking again. It was terrible. The nightmares only finally stopped after Dr O'Callaghan in town gave me some pills to help me sleep.

I would often walk up to the cemetery and sit by her grave and talk to her. Many times my spirit felt like throwing itself onto the grave and begging her forgiveness for everything.

Audrey's and my children all took courses after they finished school. As I said, once I gave up grog for them when they were little, I encouraged them in every way. They had to cope with an undercurrent of prejudice, but a lot of their white mates stood by them. Most of our children married, and they have brought me more grandchildren and great-grandchildren.

My son Lenny worked as a public servant for years in the Commonwealth Employment Service, and in the police force as the chief commissioner's advisor on Aboriginal matters. He was also an administrator at the Gunditjmara Co-operative.

In the late 1970s and 1980s Patricia also worked at the Commonwealth Employment Service, then at the Ministry of Conservation. Later she enrolled in the teacher training course at Deakin University in Geelong and graduated with a Bachelor of Arts in Education. After teaching around the Warrnambool and district primary schools, she returned to Deakin as a lecturer in education. While working there she studied part-time and then graduated with another degree, the Graduate Certificate of Natural and Cultural Heritage Interpretation. These days she also writes and performs her own songs, and many of them have some of our traditional language in them.

Bernice worked for more than twenty years as Aboriginal liaison officer to hospitals. Her job meant travelling all over south-western Victoria to liaise with Aboriginal clients, medical people and welfare workers. When she first started at the job in 1976, she covered the north-west and central parts of Victoria – towns including Horsham, Dimboola, Rupanyup, Ballarat and Warracknabeal. There were no local co-operatives for Aboriginal people back then, so her job was real important. Ian worked for Social Security in Mildura and was the Aboriginal cultural officer for our district. Elizabeth is researching a history of our family, and Fiona, who paints and works with textiles, has sent her designs to an exhibition in Sweden. Helen worked as a kindergarten assistant for a while and then became an Aboriginal liaison officer at Bairnsdale Hospital. Another daughter, Lee-Anne, was a secretary for the Gunditjmara Co-operative and for a lawyer's company. She also earned her qualifications to enter the hospitality industry.

I'm proud of them all.

Life is never easy for Aboriginals fighting for their survival and their integrity. But then we met the Baha'i people what respected us for trying. The second time they came, we had a bit of a gathering and a sing-song at the old mission church. They told us about their principles and how they had learnt to understand the Baha'i Faith, what they called their religion. It struck me as something different – more sincere about respecting all religions and different cultures.

These people seemed to understand Aboriginal principles, but they didn't know what I realised – that their principles was the same as Aboriginal ones! They were as close as they could be. And my half-sister Dolly, what gave them a lot of hospitality over the years and later became a Baha'i also, used to mention how we'd all been reared up from babyhood that we'd just have to keep on forgiving white people. Because they'd never ever understand our rules of politeness.

And now at last a big change had come. These people had got close to our hearts straight away and given us hope. And we saw that it could be the beginning of all sorts of better things. The Baha'i Faith says the world is one family, the world is one earth, and all of humankind are the citizens what live on this one earth. We're all different cultures, but we can still get together as one family and laugh and talk and be friends with one another; we can break down the barriers of racism, prejudice, and everybody can be brothers and sisters. It would make everybody happy.

I was very interested in it all. I thought, I'll go along to meetings with these Baha'is and see what it's all about. So I went to a great many conferences and met different nationalities from all over the world. It wasn't how I'd understood religion to be.

Everybody was glad to see you because you was Aboriginal, you was their brother. They'd come up and put their arms around you and invite you to their homes. White South Africans, black South Africans all mixed together in one happy family. At last I thought, If it's good enough for them, it's good enough for me. So I joined up in August 1975, and I'm still with them.

Soon after, Camilla came with her daughter to see me in hospital when I had pneumonia. Her little girl Ruth sang a song for me and she brought me some of her birthday cake. She told me the cake would make me well. I told her that if she went on singing to me the way she was doing, and being good to me, it would make me better quicker than the doctor's medicine. And I was right – I got better real quickly because I felt so happy when this little girl sang for me.

Later, Camilla told me that when she and Ruth came to the hospital she was scared stiff because Ruth sang to me in French. She was afraid I would think they was snobs! But in meeting us Aboriginals this Baha'i mother met people who could see into her heart. She said it was a wonderful relief when she realised this. We found Camilla very easy to understand. We knew that her daughter's friendship and her song were gifts to us from the heart.

A lot more Aboriginals joined the faith like me, and I've never looked back since. Joining the faith has strengthened me and helped me face the struggles of modern life which Aboriginals find themselves in. And I'm still going all right. I go in the pubs and have a drink of lemon squash with my mates. They respect me for it. White mates, black mates, any mates at all – a lot of people there in their forties and fifties I knew since they was little kids. They're still my mates. I get on well with them all because I'm an ordinary person with understanding for everyone else. The more you speak with people, the more you understand them. You know their problems, their happiness and their sadness, and you're there with them all the time.

In 1975 my son Lenny went to work for the Department of Labour and Immigration in their office in Bairnsdale. I'd been thinking that was where my first child, Helen, my long-lost daughter, might be living, though she'd be all grown up now. The only clue I had was that her mother, Agnes, was from there.

'If you go up there,' I told Lenny, 'you might see my long-lost daughter. She's been searching for me for years and we still haven't found one another.'

Lenny left for Bairnsdale, in Gippsland. While he was there, on one overcast day an Aboriginal man, Keith Morgan, knocked on the door of his house as Lenny was leaving for work and said, 'My wife would like to see you.'

'All right,' said Lenny, 'I'll call in later. Do I know her?'

'No, but she's your sister,' Keith said.

Lenny then went to Helen's house and knocked on her door. Helen said that when she opened the door she saw her son Adrian's likeness in Lenny's face. The long-lost brother and sister embraced on her doorstep, laughing and crying. They was glad to see one another. That's the Aboriginal way of life, to accept all members of your family.

Helen's foster-sister Marion was there, and said, 'Supposing *I* had opened the door? Did you both just *know* who each other was, or would Lenny have hugged the wrong woman?'

Helen had heard a Clarke from Warrnambool was coming down that way and thought he might be family, but didn't know for sure.

That very day, Lenny sent me a telegram saying I was to go to the Tattersalls Hotel and wait by the phone. I didn't have a phone at my place. He wrote he would be ringing me up about something important.

I didn't know what was going on but I had great hopes, deep down. I went to the bar of the hotel with an old boxing mate of mine, Nulla Austin. And then the phone rang. Someone called out, 'Is Banjo Clarke here?'

'Yes!' I said.

It was Lenny on the line, like he said he would be.

'How are you going?' I asked him.

'All right,' he said. 'How are you fellahs down there?'

'All right. Did you ever find my long-lost daughter?' I quickly asked.

'She's right here in my office,' he said.

My mate Nulla, who knew nothing about the situation, had followed me down to the phone and burst out laughing when he heard my words.

'Listen, Nulla,' I said, 'shut up, eh? I'm about to talk to a daughter I never saw before in my life. We've been searching for each other for thirty years. I don't know what she looks like, I never even spoke to her before. This is serious.'

Nulla got all quiet then. 'Yeah? It *is* serious then,' he said. I think he was nervous too.

Lenny explained to me how he had found his sister. Then I talked to Helen. It was the strangest conversation I ever had in my life.

'Hello?' I said.

'Hello,' she said.

'How've you been going, my girl?' I asked.

'All right, Dad. How've you been going?'

'All right.'

Long silence.

'Where've you been all the time?' I asked.

'Everywhere,' she said. 'All through the camps with these people who were like Mum and Dad to me. I was waiting for someone to point you out, but they never did.'

'Never mind, my girl, I'll catch up with you now.'

That was all the conversation for a long time. I didn't know what to say. I tried to keep on talking but there was no answer. Then my son got back on the phone.

'Where's my daughter gone?' I said.

'She's still here, Dad. But she just can't talk any more – she's crying too much.'

And that was it that day in the Tattersalls Hotel. When I was young, every Wednesday that hotel was like a country fair, with farmers in big hats and rubber boots boasting of what money they'd got for their cows or bulls. Aboriginals used to camp in the now-demolished saleyards opposite, sheltered by high walls and welcomed by gates that were always unlocked. Because of that, I always felt surrounded by the spirits of dead friends and family in that place. And now Tattersalls Hotel had become like a sacred site for me, because it was where I first found my long-lost daughter.

Later, Helen wrote me the most beautiful letter that ever I got. She told me she was so happy to find me, and that she had six children. So I had six grandchildren I didn't even know about, all these little mates up there in Gippsland. Six of them!

I said to everyone, 'I've got a big tribe now! A big tribe!'

In the letter she said, 'I won't cry and search any more, because I've found my dad. I've found my dad at last.'

So this big family came to me from out of the blue. All beautiful little kids, and one lad of hers grew up to be a good footballer. And now I've got about thirty grandchildren and sixty-seven great-grandchildren in all.

Helen and I soon found we had a lot in common. The biggest thing was our love of sharing with others. Like me, Helen has always had an open house for children in need, as well as her own. She told me she'd often not know how she was going to pay the next electricity bill or something, but she'd never turn anyone away. Helen still goes to the local park on scorching hot days, and on Christmas Day, to find travellers of all nationalities hanging out there. She invites them home for a shower, a cool drink and a bite to eat. I'm real proud that she practises those Aboriginal principles like me.

Helen and her husband sometimes come to visit me and we always keep in touch. I see my grandchildren too. And one day, when we all get together, we're going to take a big photo. It'll be the biggest tribe that ever you've seen.

And I'm the creator of all them young people, eh? By accident.

CHAPTER 19

Once my little mate David, Camilla's second child, went to Melbourne to stay with his dad's doctor friend. He watched these people cutting their hedge. David had spent a lot of time with me in the bush and he'd seen me make things from nature. So when he saw a twisted limb in the rubbish what they had cast aside there, he took it out and said, 'I'm going to take this home to my best friend Banjo. He'll make a snake out of it.'

He hung onto it and hung onto it, and finally brought it home to me, a real twisty little snake. I had it for a long time. I worried about the fact that the snake had two tails. I thought, There's not many snakes around with two tails.

One day my mood felt right to cut one tail off. Then I rubbed the rest of the stick down with stone and sandpaper, gave it scales, and put bright beads into its bulgy head for eyes. I also gave it a forked leather tongue.

The snake gives you a scare at first, because you don't know whether it's alive or a stuffed one, or what. And a bigger one what I worked on gives you an even bigger scare. It rears up at you. I took it from the pine tree in David's paddock. His family says that it contains the feel of all snakes.

I know that David will keep both sculptures forever. He's over six foot now, and graduated from Melbourne University as an engineer. He always comes to see me when he returns to the Western District. We'll be friends for life, his sister Ruth and him and me. I used to look after them a lot when they was little. They never, ever forget. It's one of them special friendships what lasts forever, what cuts across any differences in age or colour or religion.

From time to time I borrow back the snakes, and a basket I made for Ruth, and take them with other artifacts around the local schools. I talk to the little children, giving them more understanding about Aboriginal culture. My son Lenny has come to speak with me there sometimes too. The schoolkids' parents wouldn't have had much chance to understand us – all they learnt was demoralising stories about Aboriginals. White children used to be taught to look on Aboriginals as nothing. That Aboriginals were lazy, shiftless thieves. All the worst things you could say about a person was planted in white people's minds about us.

These things started in the early days, when they took the Aboriginals' land – all the grassland and bushland for their sheep and cattle. They said that Aboriginals were lazy because they never had farms. But Aboriginals had other things. We knew how to catch our food in fish traps, and how to govern the land without destroying it. Everything was sacred to us. We looked on the land as a mother who knew how to care for us, and we knew how to care for her. We never did much damage because we knew that if we hurt the land it would get sick and die, like a mother. She would no longer provide food for the people.

We had to look on things that way because we were directly dependent on nature. No big commercial factories like today, with money everywhere. No people fighting over money and dying for it. Aboriginals never had them things. We lived in harmony. Oh, we had tribal wars all right, but they were over in no time. Wars today seem to last forever.

I tell sad things like this to the children in the schools. I warn them before I start that some things are going to be sad. 'But,' I say, 'if I don't tell you the sad part you won't know the real history. This is real history that I'm speaking about, history that was hidden from the public all these years.

'We're not angry about it,' I say. 'We're just sad. I don't blame white men for their barbaric ways towards us. White men came to this country in chains and were treated like animals themselves – how could we expect them not to act like animals? White men came here from cramped ways of living and saw all this space, and all this land. It drove them insane!' [To Banjo and many of his people, greed was always regarded as a form of insanity.]

How can you bear grudges, how can you be angry, when it happened to indigenous people all over the world? Of course it shouldn't have, but lots of people in authority say that it never happened. But it did. Our Elders were very particular about telling us the things what happened from the very first days that the white men got here: our people was put on missions and not allowed to leave, and handed out so little tucker that they was starving and dying by the hundreds of ordinary flu and measles, and things like that. Others were put on small islands away from their homelands, and died of broken hearts looking over the water at their own spiritual place. Especially around Tasmania – on Bruny Island and such, where Granny Truganini was born. 'Put them away on an island – let them die out,' they'd say. 'When all Aboriginals die out, there'll be no more Aboriginal problem. We'll save thousands of pounds' worth of government handouts.'

When I talk to the school children about all this stuff, they become very sad but they say to me, 'It won't happen any more, Banjo, because we know something about your culture and the spiritual way you feel, and the spiritual way you think of your Old People.' That makes me real glad to hear them say such things.

I tell them about my country and the spirit world and the people before us. They say they've never heard that way of speaking. I tell them that all different-coloured people are beautiful, like the flowers in a garden. I tell them our stories from the heart, the way we feel, and what things mean to us. I tell the kids all the positive things that are happening today. How Aboriginals are coming up stronger now. How a lot of us are educated now, and going the right way. Even Aboriginal culture and languages are coming back again.

The Olympic gold-medallist runner Cathy Freeman is an Aboriginal Baha'i young lady who's going very well despite the opposition. But once you're a sportswoman, you're accepted today, whatever your colour.

Even that used to be sad. In the early days, when Aboriginals became good at sport, they often had to pretend they came from another race – not Aboriginal. They had to register under a different nationality. Why was that attitude created?

When I was young, a lot of the good teenaged athletes went away from the mission to Melbourne to try to further their careers. The police told them to go, but they were just trying to push them aside. The young fellahs would turn up in the ghettos in the big cities and start drinking grog in parks and empty houses. A lot of them went to gaol, and quite a few died there – of stress and heart troubles and things, and from disillusion with life because they left their homeland.

But when they did join in sports, they beat everything in front of them. Only little children they was, but they was great athletes. We've got one young fellah today, he could be a champion runner, and we hope he is, because a lot of good athletes came from here. His name is Geoffrey Ugle, who we all call Possum. Lionel Rose's father came from here too, and he was a good old fighter like his son.

He never took it up serious, but Lionel did and he won the bantamweight championship of the world.

The only hope Aboriginals had in them days was to meet good white people what gave them the heart to carry on and to be sane about it. But a lot of Aboriginals lashed out through frustration. The only legal way to express it was in the boxing ring. They wouldn't get into trouble then, or be locked up for nothing. That's why so many Aboriginals was good boxers. A lot of them had never seen a glove until they got in the ring. And they'd be fighting good white athletes what trained with gloves every night in proper gymnasiums. [Despite Aboriginal people only constituting 1 per cent of the total Australian population, 15 per cent of Australia's boxing champions have been Aboriginal.]

But we never had a gymnasium. We just worked in the bush with an axe or something, cutting wood or labouring somewhere, and we'd wait all day without a bite to eat to get a fight that night. And when we did fight, we would fight barefoot sometimes or borrow someone else's shoes. When in the ring, you'd hear people call out racist insults at you too, a lot. That's the sort of thing what happened here, and not only in the one place, but everywhere.

I believe the solutions for all the different races of the world is to just *understand* one another and each other's cultures. Go up and speak to people! If you can't speak their lingo, don't turn away saying, 'Ah, I don't understand him.' Go up and shake their hand and say, 'I am your friend. Speak to me about your culture; I'll speak to you about my culture and we'll be friends.' Don't fight or be angry. You get nowhere with anger. Same with violence. It only reduces us to the level of those who act violently towards us, and if we get into that cycle, there's no end to it. So just be happy! That's the best way.

CHAPTER 20

Mission kids of my son Ian's generation often resented being looked upon as different and called names when they went to school in town. But when we, their parents, were young, we had to put up with all them things. That was just part of our life. If we were insulted we had a good old knuckle-up sometimes, but after the fight we'd forget what it was all about. Ian, more than any of them, was deeply troubled. And his troubles brought him down. But he had white friends too. White girls and boys who were friends with Ian still come to see me. They stuck by him all those years. Ian never forgot his desire to do good for his people. And he never hesitated to help anyone, no matter what. That fact got him into trouble later.

One night Ian was lying down at home on the mission, in real agony from a back injury he'd got when he was woodcutting for a farmer that day. Then one of his cousins rang up from a hotel in Warrnambool, asking Ian to come and pick him up. Ian was rung up for them things all the time by his mates. He'd never say no to anyone asking him to give them a lift. That sort of sharing is an ancient tribal custom to us fellahs. If an Aboriginal on the mission buys a car, it is his duty to drive everyone else around in it. And often the driver will never end up where *he* wants to go.

So that's what Ian did that night – he got up from his bed, even though he was in real pain, and drove into town to pick up his cousin. His brother Lenny had told him several times, though, 'Keep away from pubs. These days the crowds there live on a cocktail of drugs and alcohol. Anything could happen.'

Ian arrived at the pub and found everyone watching TV. There was some show to do with blackfellahs on and some racist remarks were said by a few white people there. One man turned to Ian and said, 'Of course, none of this applies to you. You have European features.' There were great roars of laughter from some of the other people in the pub because Ian with his dark skin was clearly an Aboriginal man. And he was real proud of his heritage too.

'Listen, mate,' Ian said, 'I don't hold that comment against you, because you don't know. But if white men hadn't raped my ancestors, I'd have no white blood today.'

Some more racist remarks were uttered, and two of the man's relatives who were with him said they'd had enough. 'Come on, we're going now,' they said, and one added, 'If it weren't for you I wouldn't be in the pub tonight anyway. I didn't want to go. No way.'

The man they were talking to took a few steps after them, then turned and walked back to the bar. There were words spoken between him and Ian's mate, who he'd come to pick up. Ian's mate, who often got into fights, suddenly swung his fist at the man. An all-in fight began. Chairs were thrown. Ian didn't want to be in it. No way – he didn't want to have anything to do with the fight. The bartender ordered the white man out. He knew that fellah had started it.

Later, when Ian left the pub and went outside, the white man suddenly appeared again, running straight at Ian, his right fist back and moving. Ian's instinct was to defend himself. He moved awkwardly because of his sore back, and raised his arm. But somehow in the struggle the man's relative, the one who hadn't wanted to be in the pub that night, got between them. Ian hit the man once.

The poor fellah fell and hit his head on the concrete kerb. I suppose he'd been trying to stop his relative. He didn't move and Ian was
real concerned for him. A crowd began to gather. 'Look after this fellah,' Ian said to the white people around, 'and get him to the hospital
straight away. He's hurt.' Then he went to his car and drove home.
He came in real quietly and sat by the fire. No matter what I said to
him, he wouldn't answer me.

Finally I said, 'Come to bed, son. What are you doing sitting
here?'

'Waiting for the police,' he answered.

'Then I'll wait with you,' I said, and asked no questions.

We sat in silence for hours. Finally Ian spoke again. 'I think I've
killed a man,' he said.

The whitefellah died in hospital and Ian was sad ever since. He kept
saying, 'What about his little children? There shouldn't have been a
fight. Other people started that fight and I wasn't even in it. All I was
doing was trying to stop them. Then I had to hit hard to defend
myself and that's what happened.'

He was distraught about the children losing their dad. Not only
that, but Ian was arrested and charged with the man's murder. Lots
of Ian's friends and youngsters came to see him off and lend him
support when the police put him in the van to take him to
Melbourne. But they didn't bother to lock the van door. 'You won't
run away,' the police told him.

He was taken to Pentridge Prison but was later let out on bail.
That was unusual, because people who were charged with murder
aren't normally let out on bail. He came home to live with us, and for
the months leading up to the trial he couldn't sleep at night, and

would pace the floor for hours. But he showed enormous strength. 'I have to be strong,' he said, 'or my family will go to pieces.' He had to report to the police station every day, but otherwise wasn't allowed to leave the mission.

Terrible racism arose in Warrnambool against all us Aboriginals because of it. Little innocent black children on their way to school had rubbish tipped on them and things thrown at them. We had to keep them at home because it wasn't safe for them to be out in public. We also had to set up trip-wires around our place on the mission because we were frightened out there. Several carloads of whitefellahs had driven out from Warrnambool to our place yelling, 'Let's kill the blacks!'

When the preliminary hearing came up at the local courthouse, everyone was expecting the charge to be reduced to manslaughter, but the local magistrate kept it at murder. Months later, when the trial opened in the Supreme Court in Melbourne, the judge there reduced the charge to manslaughter. Ian pleaded not guilty. It was a relief when he was acquitted. The presiding judge said, 'I am very impressed with this young man. I believe in him.'

Ian came home a free man but he was never quite the same.

Two or more years after all this happened, in the early 1980s, Lenny and I were in a hotel. Lenny said hello to some young people and they said hello back. He asked how their mother and family was going. I realised that they were two of the children that had lost their dad. Lenny explained to them that Ian had never got over what he'd done.

After some more conversation and me buying drinks, the children sent a message to Ian through Lenny that they forgave him. They added, 'A lot of white people were going to do this and do that to you, we heard, but we had nothing to do with them.'

Ian didn't know what to say when he got the message – it changed his life. He realised more fully than ever before that not every white person was bad. It gave him hope. He saw at last that anything could happen when unhappy people didn't understand. His outlook on people had been changed altogether.

One time I was sitting in the bush with my children and their young mates, and we were yarning about various things. It was then that it struck me that the land still belonged to us because it had never been taken from us – when I was a boy we still lived there in bark huts, in the traditional way. We loved the land because it was our spiritual home and we wanted to hang onto the land. I told the young people that the bushland still belonged to us, not only because of our feelings for it, but also on white men's documents.

They asked, 'How's that?'

'Because it's never been officially taken away,' I told them. 'When Aboriginals were gathered together here in the early days, the bush was defined by law as our recreation and hunting ground for as long as we would live around these parts. I remember my dad saying one time in the bush – I was only a little fellah, about four or five, and I was sitting on a heap of wood – "You know, this land will never be taken away from us. This is our tribal land, but if we leave here, it will be officially vacant and anybody can take it. I heard it from a big government man, many years ago. He said, If you're gonna stay on that land, stay on it, because if everybody leaves, it can be sold or leased to the white man – but as long as one Aboriginal is left living there, they can't do nothing."

'Years later, all this land rights thing has come along and I'm thinking, *That's* what old Dad was telling us years ago! It came in handy because I happened to be there as a kid when Dad was in the humour to tell me these words.

'Anyway, the government tried to build an agricultural college here in 1890, but they found they couldn't because we were still here. The forestry commission took over then, and controlled all the wood going out of the bush. Aboriginals got jobs off the farmers because woodcutting was more or less the only work around. The farmers paid royalties to the forestry commission and we cut as much wood for them as they wanted. We refused to pay royalties ourselves because it was *our* bush. We said, "People should be paying royalties to us."

'We always cut the wood with respect. We didn't cut a bit out of a tree and leave the rest to rot on the ground. You don't do them things. Trees are important for oxygen and fresh air and rain. They attract rain, and keep the soil together with their roots.'

Ian and the other young people started discussing how trail-bike riders were churning up the ground in the forest, making huge gutters for the water and soil to run down in winter and scaring the animals so that you didn't see them much any more. It was then he decided to put a blockade up and fight to get the bush back properly, and that's what we did. We blocked off the road into the forest and put up a sign saying 'ROAD CLOSED UNTIL TRIBAL LAND RIGHTS GRANTED'. It was like old times – Aboriginals had something to do! We didn't have to sit in stuffy houses staring at four walls. We slept under the stars again and had a big fire to cook the food that we gathered for everyone.

White people in town seemed to think that all bush was national park, that the beautiful things were not there before their forebears discovered them. But we *lived* for thousands of years with the waterfalls, the trees and rocks before they came, and we knew that everything had a reason for being there. When the barricade went up, at first a lot of people thought we were mad, but then they started to say, 'It *must* be their bush.'

We got in all the newspapers, big and small, and on national television as well. Then finally, in May 1987, with the help of several good whitefellahs, including Malcolm Fraser, Jim Kennan and Clyde Holding, the federal government made the Elders of my family the official forest caretakers. We travelled to Melbourne to be given an official copy of the framed document stating we had inalienable title to 1089 hectares of bushland.

Ian got on the front cover of the Warrnambool *Standard* newspaper that day [29 May]. The headline read 'This Land is Ours'. He took the journalists into the forest and they wrote that he told them 'the title to the land will help restore the identity of the local Aborigines . . . This move now acknowledges our historic right to the land.'

My son Lenny worked hard to get the bush back as well – he worked at it for a good sixteen years. He travelled to Melbourne and all over with us, meeting with politicians and such. He said, according to the newspaper, 'Aboriginal people have been receiving false promises for the past 200 years. This title is very symbolic. Changes such as this will aid our people and their spirit.'

We owe a lot to the university and school students of the 1960s for their help in the years before the blockade. Rotary, Apex and the people of Wangoom helped too. Students came here in their dozens, and camped with us. They are successful doctors and lawyers and such now, but it would be good to see them again. They put fences around our open paddocks and built two dairies. And they found helpful government documents in various archives and gave us copies. We knew a lot already about the bush being ours, but it was nice to have written proof. I don't think the government liked what the students were doing to help, because it was trying to get us to leave the land.

Not long after we put up the blockade and closed the bush to trail-bike riders, the animals started to come back and breed. Them little poteroo fellahs – me and Ian saw different coloured ones after a while, some grey, some black, so there must be plenty in there, way up at the top end where hardly anyone goes.

When I was young, we learnt all the animal habits, all their individual characteristics. I still enjoy sneaking up on the wallabies on my way home from a day in the bush. The wallaby creeps up to the old bush track where all the green grass is, and bends over eating the nice green grass. You spot him, so you stand still. He'll stand up and look around, but you stand still and he'll put his head down again. You get closer and stand still again. He'll look around. He seems to feel that something's there, although he never seen you move. He probably thought you were another stump, standing up in the middle of the road. He's thinking, It's a bit funny. That stump been way up there before, it's a bit closer – how come that? He goes more often, looks around real quick again, he don't eat for as long as when he thought he was on his own. He gets a bit panicky – he knows you're there but he can't see you. And when he starts to eat again, you sneak up a bit closer, and he'll sit up there and he'll listen and he looks around, and he looks towards you and he looks real hard. You've really confused him. You stand real still and he might think, Aah! That's nothing, and he goes to eat again. Then all of a sudden he thinks, It *must* be something! And he'll take off into the scrub. They panic. They take off. You can hear sticks breaking and all, they go that fast! You never yelled at them or nothing, they just realised that somebody was there all the time watching them.

One farmer says the kangaroos are getting a bit too many. He wants us to put a kangaroo-proof fence up at the edge of his paddock. We'll have to work that out because we don't want to disrupt the farmer. We have to work in with him and make him happy too.

We've seen too many bushlands being destroyed. We didn't want that to happen here, no matter who is the owner. You've got to have animals. That's part of nature, part of Australia – part of every country. Native animals are entitled to live here, same as anyone else. We've got to share our hospitality with the animals, and be their friend.

The old mopoke, he's a traditional message-bird to us fellahs. If anybody is sick or has passed away suddenly, three or four hundred or even a thousand miles from here, a mopoke will start calling in a strange way close to us, changing his voice and sounding excited. Even if he sings out nice and quietly, there could still be somebody a bit ill somewhere.

Then we'll tell each other, 'Something's wrong. Maybe somebody close to us has died a long way from here.' We'll wait to hear word that somebody what belongs to our tribe is very sick, and not expected to live.

Things like that have been handed down to us, probably for thousands of years. And we've still got that way of living. Aboriginals didn't have phones in the early days, or write letters. So God must have worked things out so we'd find out news through other means. People living with nature have to know when the weather's going to change. We know when a storm's coming up, or when there's going to be a long dry or a wet season. You live with all them things. And we notice things about animals too.

So when the mopoke sings out in the gully or close by in the bush and he starts to change his voice, we say, 'Hey, look out, mate! That old mopoke's giving us a message.' My son Ian, who was a great believer in those things, would exclaim, 'Come on, we don't want to hear no more. Let's get inside. He's got a bad message for us, that fellah.'

And sure enough, that night or next morning, we'd get word that somebody met with a terrible accident. Nine times out of ten, that has happened.

The curlew is a frightening bird too. There's always been something happening when he screams. He doesn't come as often as the mopoke, but he's a bird to take seriously too. You think a woman's getting killed or screaming for help when you hear his cry in the middle of the night. People what haven't heard him before get the biggest fright of their life. A chill goes down their back and they never, never, want to hear that bird again.

It was in 1989 when my granddaughter Nancy – Pat's daughter – was going with this young white man. She wasn't going with him long. They lived in a house together. He wasn't racist, but one day he took a bird home to show her. And when my granddaughter saw what sort of bird it was, she grabbed a stick and belted him across the arms. She yelled at him to take it out and let it go.

I didn't know anything about the incident until he tried to tell me a week later. He said, 'You Aboriginals have certainly got some strange ways. When Nancy saw the bird I brought in, she belted me across the arms. She shouted at me to take it out, and I did, because she frightened me. She wasn't like herself at all. She said, "We don't do things with that bird. We keep our distance from him." She did tell me its name, but I've forgotten.'

I asked, 'What sort of bird was it?'

'Oh,' he said, 'a kind of owl.'

'Was it a mopoke?' I said.

'Yes, yes. That's what she called it. I threw it away. It all seemed silly to me. What does that bird mean to you people?'

'That bird means death,' I told him.

'Oh,' he said. 'I've got a lot to learn yet. Anyway, I threw it away.'

Nearly a week later, Ian was outside. It was getting dark and we heard a mopoke down in the gully, yelling, screaming, calling and changing his voice. And Ian sang out, 'Quick, Dad! Come here quick! That mopoke down in the gully, listen to him. I've never heard him panic like that before.'

I listened and I said, 'Ah, whatever it is, something terrible's going to happen tonight, mate. I've never heard him call so mad in all my life – he's hysterical.'

Ian whispered, 'Come on, Dad, get inside. Get inside, don't listen to him any more.'

We went in and stayed up waiting for the news we knew was coming. It got later and later, and in the end I went to bed.

At 5.30 a.m. my son came into my room. He cried, 'Dad! Dad! Wake up! Nancy's dead! Nancy's dead!'

I couldn't believe what I was hearing. We'd seen her a couple of days before, looking healthy and fit. 'What happened?' I asked.

'Car smash,' Ian said.

Later, we found out she had great internal injuries. And she was sitting there for hours before anyone found her. A horrible death.

It always seems to be a bird what brings messages. That's Aboriginal life – everything has a spiritual meaning.

Nineteen eighty-nine was a very bad year for us. In addition to losing Nancy, there were other great losses as well. In May of that year me, my mate Lenny Lovett and others went to the World Indigenous People's Conference in Darwin. Lenny Lovett and I met indigenous people from most parts of the world – South America,

North America, Brazil, Canada, the Philippines, Hawaii and even Japan. The destruction of land for money seems to be having the same effect on indigenous families everywhere.

Aboriginals arrived in Darwin from all parts of Australia to attend the conference, and it was good because it gave the opportunity for real people to confide the truth. I met a young Aboriginal girl there, and the fear in her eyes and her expressions was striking when she told us stories about the 'little people' back home. She was reliving things what happened. 'If you go over my way, Uncle Banjo,' she added to me, 'you have to take two or three people with you. Don't you go on your own, because the gooligahs [little people or fairies, similar to nett-netts] don't let you come back.'

Then she asked me, 'Could I call you Pop? You put me in mind of my own grandfather, but he's dead now.' And she went with me everywhere during the two or three weeks of the conference.

I encouraged Lenny Lovett to absorb the sacred paintings of Kakadu, and feel how much the Aboriginals there respect them. Our own sacred paintings in the Grampians, what Lenny had the job of looking after, are just as holy.

'Well, it's like you said, Uncle,' Lenny told me in Darwin, 'this has been a big thing for me. From now on I won't listen to people who want to manipulate me and tell me what to do with our sacred places. I'm going to guard them and respect them. I have realised that being Aboriginal is important. I'm going to learn all the history that I lost contact with.'

Lenny Lovett went to the casino that night, but he felt sick and rang a taxi to take him back to the hotel. Before the taxi arrived at his hotel with him, he had gone to his Dreamtime.

When everyone at the conference heard the news, they dedicated the meeting to Lenny, and they explained at a memorial service for him how much being there had meant to him. Then they took up a collection for his wife and little children. His body was brought back here and buried in the tribal country where he was born.

CHAPTER 21

After the court case and all that business, Ian tried to avoid all the situations that could bring him down again. He got a job as cultural officer and then director of the Gunditjmara Aboriginal Co-operative and traced our Aboriginal history some more. His previous job had been to go all over western Victoria with the Aboriginal Archaeological Survey team, fencing off sacred sites. He organised cultural talks in schools between Elders and the children, and taught them things. They all loved him. He always found something worthwhile for youngsters to do who had been on the wrong side of the law. Then, after a while, I got these feelings I tend to get when something bad is going to happen. I rang up my son Lenny in Melbourne.

He asked me, 'How are you going with Ian?'

'Ah,' I said, 'couldn't be better. We're the best of mates. I've never seen him like it before – he's doing everything right. But I'm worried about him.'

'Why?' Lenny asked.

'I've just got a feeling that something's going to happen. That he's going to be taken from us.'

'Well, you want to watch him then.'

I just couldn't shake these worried feelings. I even rang up my Baha'i friends and told them that something was wrong, that I was worried about Ian.

We had a gathering at the Aboriginal Co-operative that day and everything went well, even though there was often a lot of in-fighting and bad feeling between some of our tribe's clans. But this day Ian tried to shake hands with a man he'd had words with a couple of weeks before. The man refused and Ian took it really hard. I wondered why it bothered him so much. He had been used to knock-backs all his life, but I think he knew he was going to his Dreaming. And he wanted to go free, with no enemies left behind him.

Soon after, he brought my youngest daughter Lee-Anne home to see us. We hadn't seen her for ages. And Ian's girlfriend Ange was with us that night too.

'This is going to be a special night,' he said. 'I'm going to cook all the food. But first I'll chop a load of wood for you.'

It was a cold June winter's evening. It got dark quickly, so I went out to cut a log for the open fire. I was cutting away when Ian came over and said, 'What are you doing there, Dad? I told you, this is going to be a special night. I want to do all the work. I've got my sister out here and I'm going to cook tea.'

This fellah's sick all right, I thought.

He began to whistle and sing while he worked at cutting the wood. He never used his chainsaw, he was using my axe. He was cutting at a great rate and wheeling it to the wall. Back and forth, tipping lots of wood out from the barrow and going back for more.

Soon I had a big fire going. All the meat was there, ready for him to cut up, because he had insisted that he would do it. His girlfriend Ange went out later on to see him and found him stretched out beside the barrow.

'Pop! Pop!' she screamed.

'What's wrong?'

'Ian! Ian! He's lying by the barrow!'

I ran out. The barrow was skew-whiff and the wood had fallen out and he was lying beside it.

'Are you all right, Bud?'

He didn't move, he just went on lying there, so I said, 'Come on, let's pick him up.' So we lifted him up and carried him inside and laid him on the floor. 'Come on, Bud! Wake up, wake up, what's wrong, what's wrong, what happened?'

He just lay there with no go in him. I told Ange, 'Do that mouth-to-mouth resuscitation!'

She did it, but then she said, 'I don't know how!'

Everyone was panicking. Poor Lee-Anne had never seen anything like it.

'Ring the ambulance!' someone shouted. 'Ring Lenny!'

I knew Ian was going and I started wailing and singing out. 'Come on, Bud! Here's your father!' I touched him on the shoulder. 'Come on, Bud!' He reached out with a feeble hand and grabbed mine, and pulled it towards him and looked up into my face. He smiled at me.

Then he just faded away, as if he went to sleep. I was still calling his name and going out and looking up in the sky and calling his name. All these years, when Ian was home, on different summer evenings when the moonlight came out over the bush, he'd say to me, 'Come and look! Come and look at the moon. Isn't it beautiful? Look at all the trees lighting up.' And he'd go on, 'What makes it more beautiful is that it's coming up over our own spirit-land. The burial ground and everywhere is lighting up.' He used to take special notice of the moon. He loved rainbows too, and would make us all come outside to look when he saw one.

Ian was still lying on the floor when the ambulance men came and put the machine on him, but it was too late. And I was walking behind him when they took him out on the stretcher. I was still calling out, 'Come on, Bud! Don't lose, mate! Come on, my boy!'

They were wheeling him out to the ambulance, and the police

were there too. Then something happened. That big moon that Ian always watched with such love rose up over the hill. As it did, it shone right on him and his whole face lit up.

I ran towards the ambulance. I grabbed Ian – I'm sure he was still awake – and I showed him the moon. He felt cold, but I'm sure I saw his face smile again when that moon shone on him.

The night Ian died was a special night, with the big moon in the sky like that shining on him. I've never seen anyone pass away so peacefully as my son.

My feelings that we were going to lose him proved right. Ian had died of a heart attack like his mother had done also. He left six children behind. He was only thirty-nine. I know he's still supporting us in a spiritual way. His spirit is still with us today. He was a real fighter for this land.

CHAPTER 22

After Ian died, I bought a horse and wagon that I promised him I would. I paid for it using some compensation money I received from working in the quarry. After years of suffering with pneumonia from all the stone dust that had accumulated in my lungs from my time working there, they had granted me some monetary compensation.

The money didn't last long because of our sharing nature. None of it was spent stupidly, though. It cleared up some of my family members' debts, and bought them the things they needed. And I paid cash for a few old things I really wanted myself.*

The horse and wagon had been Ian's and my idea together. Ian had wanted to buy a big Clydesdale horse and wagon so he could take children in the bush. He wanted to teach them about Aboriginal ways of life and beliefs. He was going to show them how to make things out of what was growing in the bush, and help them absorb the atmosphere of living and working in the bush. He said they'd make spears and boomerangs, and learn how to survive in the bush.

'We'd better go and get the horse, Dad,' Ian said.

---

*Banjo always saw himself as an ambassador for all Aboriginal people. At the menswear store in Warrnambool that cashed his cheques he would normally give money in credit, waiting for when he decided to buy the next thing. He would never be in debt, but he seldom came out even either – he liked to be in front. And if he heard of an Aboriginal who did not intend to pay their debt, he would normally pay it for them.

'Ah, leave it for another week,' I said. 'We'll go and get him soon. No worries.'

But it was in that same week that Ian died unexpectedly. He never had the pleasure of driving the horse we'd both saved up to buy. Yes, he'd put money towards that too. And he died just before all the things he'd dreamed about started to happen.

That was a sad time when he passed away and I was left with the horse and cart. And I began to do the things that he'd wanted to do. I drove to the shops in the cart pulled by the big young Clydesdale horse. I took little children and schoolchildren and adults for barbecues in the bush. Driving up the old bush tracks, I showed them where the Old People camped and explained how the happy laughter of children would ring throughout the bush. I got them used to the bushlands.

Once I had a group of sixteen Aboriginal kids from the Gulf of Carpentaria come to visit. Where they come from there was no horses, so having a ride on the wagon was a new experience. We'd come back from the bush with children clinging onto the cart laughing, me holding the reins, and my great strong horse Prince going flat out down the road. Everybody loved to see us, and the children loved it too.

I tell all the people that visit about the things what used to happen in the Aboriginal community, and where the children played. I tell the children about the little nett-netts that looked after us kids when we were little. Nett-netts are like little fairies or elves. They are only a couple of feet high and look like a two- or three-year-old child. They are the shadows of children's spirits that became separated from them when the children waiting to be born left the Dreamtime to be born into the real world. So the nett-netts made their way into the real world too, to find the child they belonged to so they could protect them.

When I was a little fellah, the nett-netts liked to live in the rocks along the river and in the scrub. And when we used to go along the river spearing fish and hunting, we'd always look out for them. We never saw them but we knew they was there. They'd always keep tabs on us, and kept us being good little kids. Them nett-nett fellahs were really good people to us little fellahs, and we'd hunt really well to try to please the little people. We'd be happy kids hunting and playing by the river, and our laughter would ring through the hills and the valleys because we knew the little nett-netts was there to guard us from trouble and look after us. We didn't want to bother them because we knew they were there to guide us. And that helped keep us out of trouble, so that was a good sort of a thing! We thought, We won't get into trouble because them poor little nett-netts will worry about us and put themselves in danger trying to save us from the river and everything. So we'll be good and do everything right because they are following us around everywhere, behind that big rock, and behind that tree.

And that's why I want to tell all the little children today about things like that, about the Aboriginal lifestyle and the way we feel, about the Aboriginal Dreamtime world, about all the beautiful things that happened and the beautiful bushland. Because all the bush is being cut down now, and the rivers are being polluted. Everything is going wrong because people don't love nature. She can't provide for her children now. She's trying to fight back but everyone's too greedy.

The federal government has given a company permission to build a uranium mine at Jabiluka in the Kakadu National Park in the Northern Territory, a classified World Heritage Area. But don't they know that all the leakage, the radioactive waste comes into the waterholes and the rivers and destroys all the fish, and the trees die and people get sick? That's something the tribal Elders in the far north of Australia have been talking about for thousands of years – what they've called 'the monster in the ground'. From generation to generation, the Aboriginal people up north have warned their children about that monster. But the modern-day man and the scientist say, 'Ah, that's not a monster! That's something of great value to the people.' But it's that monster what makes the uranium and the atom bomb which has the power to kill everybody, like the poor Japanese when the Americans dropped the bomb there and finished the war. That was the big monster that done that, the monster what the Aboriginals spoke of for thousands of years. They said this monster was going to destroy everybody and burn the place and set the world on fire. And that was shown when the atom bomb was dropped. Aboriginals have always said, 'Don't you touch that monster. It will destroy everybody.' And that story was told for thousands of years, from generation to generation. The Aboriginal people knew all about the good things and the bad things in the earth. They weren't scientists, they just loved and respected the land where they lived.

As well as speaking to children in schools and taking them into the bush to teach them about the old ways, I've done a bit of acting on television. I was on *The Flying Doctors* once, and *Rush*. But I wouldn't call myself a professional. Whatever I do, I like my work to be artistic, not just labouring.

Sometimes I hear that friends of friends overseas want something made that is genuinely Australian, such as a boomerang or a basket, and I'll make it for them, from the bush. But I don't do it commercially. It's the same with most of my family. We don't believe in capitalising on what we can make. Or in doing anything just for the sake of money.

CHAPTER 23

As soon as the white man put his foot on Aboriginal land, Aboriginals was denied life from the word go. White people came to Australia in large numbers and looked at the vast land and saw all the riches they could make: they saw future mansions, beef cattle and sheep grazing. They didn't look at how beautiful nature was, or what it provided for the people already. The white man tried to make us all think rich – to see the land with the fences they was used to and think of the money that could be made. But Aboriginals didn't have big farms or money, because they didn't need them. The land provided everything for them, and she looked after them.

I don't know if it was guilt about what they'd started, or homesickness or what, but they tried to destroy everything native to Australia, and all the things Aboriginals believed in. They destroyed the human beings too. The native animals were massacred – they were different from what white men were used to and they didn't get used to them, much the same as they didn't get used to Aboriginal people.

But we Aboriginals thought in a different way – we got feelings for the bush, and feelings for people. Aboriginals just lived for day to day. We lost a lot of our culture when the white man came. Our Old People wasn't allowed near our children, and our children were taken away and put in dormitories to learn how to be servants for the white man. Our Old People wasn't allowed to talk in the old language to them. Everything native to Australia was a nuisance, or punished for being there. My Elders said, 'If the white man doesn't want to be friends, that's okay – so long as we're left in peace. We can see the white man destroying himself, so there's no need for *us* to take revenge. They've done so much damage to Aboriginals and to the country – leave them to it, because they'll destroy themselves in the end. We're all right, we'll get a feed, we'll get tucker somewhere.'

White people say, 'We're all the same now – live in the same country, eat the same food . . .' But when it comes to principles, there's a great big gap. That's because white men didn't understand the real way Aboriginals think and interpret things. And that's where the big breakdown comes. 'Oh, we live together. We could do the same work . . .' But when it comes to talking about things, Aboriginals talk different. We might have lost a lot of our language and everything, but we've still got Aboriginal principles.

I don't want to be turned into a white gentleman. I don't want to hear people say, 'Forget your colour, forget your tribal ancestors.' We can't do that. Many migrants arrived in Australia over the years, and they don't forget their ancestors. The Irish go back and see their people too – so do the Scots, the Italians. They pay homage to their homeland. Just like we do in Australia – we pay homage all the time to our tribal land here.

I am still Aboriginal and always will be, that's the main thing I always try to put across. I still have my Aboriginal identity. But bad things happened to us here. Our race died out in different areas. Young white people came into our society, and the Aboriginal colours faded away. We used to be only black, but now you see all different colours. But we love them little children too. They belong to us, they live like us and they understand Aboriginal ways.

I'm glad I've lived this long to tell my children and my people all about the old Aboriginal people I grew up with and all the kindness they had, and all the hardships they went through – shifted from one mission to another like cattle getting drafted here and there. And all they wanted to do was come back home to their land where they was born, but some were taken to foster homes, orphanages or other missions where they didn't belong. Some of them came back later on in years and found that their people had passed on. They hadn't had the privilege to have lived with them and understand what went on in the early days, like I did.

And you know, all those obstacles we had in front of us everywhere, most Aboriginals never took offence at it. They just got used to it and they carried on, doing their own thing and hoping that one day things would change, and things would be better, and they never held any grudges. The Old People survived by looking at nature and saw its beauty, instead of looking at their own hardships. All the bad things that happened to them, or they saw happen, or looked bad for them, they'd make a joke about it, or would sing a song about it, and they'd start laughing then and they'd see the funny side of life, and have a good old laughter with everyone. And I think that's the gift they had to keep them going on.

But most of my old friends have died now. Many died of sadness. I try not to get angry because we have to try to teach the children not to be angry at the way we have been treated. Anger gets you nowhere. You've got to have patience instead, and think of the good memories.

Yes, all them things happened, but I'm still here today and I do the best I can without any vengeance, or any grudges or anything. I just want to tell people what happened so they can live with it and understand it and make it better for the Aboriginal people in the future – for them to get on in life without prejudice and racism and everything else. They was pushed long enough back into the background, and now they're getting a bit educated. But I hope they still stick with their Aboriginal identity too.

Years of being a Baha'i has helped me a lot. When I joined the Baha'is in 1975, I asked Camilla to help me not drink, and I've been aware of the prayers of the Baha'is for me over the years. This awareness made me extra strong in 1988, when white people were celebrating two hundred years of European rule here in Australia. I was listening to it on the radio and I had a whole lot of grog near my bed. I decided to give it up again out of respect for my ancestors, who didn't know what grog was before white people came. I went out and all my Aboriginal mates were saying, 'Don't celebrate in '88, Unc.' I said, 'I'm not. Here's my grog.' They drank it, and I never. I liked my beer and going in the pubs. But giving it up was the easiest thing in the world. I haven't touched it since. It's just a question of your beliefs, and the respect you've got for your Elders. The way they was treated and how they suffered and died in the gutters and gaols and parks as alcoholics, through white man's corruption. Them Old People must be watching me, I think, and I was glad to give up grog for them.

I think that if Aboriginals studied the Baha'i Faith they'd come back to their real selves again, because the Baha'i Faith is so like the Aboriginal way of life. The Baha'i writings say that in the future humankind will be so sensitive that no one anywhere in the world will be able to sit down to a meal if they know that somewhere in the world a person is starving. Aboriginal feelings are like those writings. We feel united with everyone. Sometimes we get terrible feelings because we know something terribly bad is happening. And we start to cry as if somebody was telling us – but nobody is telling us. We can feel it. Aboriginals can't explain them things, and it's frightening too. You don't know if it's going to be yourself or somebody close to you, so you wait patiently for the message. The warning makes you able to bear it.

It's still like that. White people have got these things, but a lot of them don't care for these things any more. But these feelings inside of them will govern them in the future. Like in the Baha'i writings.

One night my cousin John Austin died trying to save a mate from a fire. He went to visit his sister and found her house on fire and everyone still asleep inside. He ran in and woke everyone and got them out. Once they were all out on the street, they remembered that a friend had been sleeping on the couch inside and was still in there. John ran back in to try to save him. While he was looking near the couch for the man, a burning beam fell on him and pinned him down, and he died there. The man he was trying to save escaped but later died from his burns.

That same night I felt all these terrible things. I felt real hot but it was a cold night. I was sweating all over, my chest and everything. I was that scared I started to cry, and I thought, Either I'm going to die or somebody close to me is dying. And this was happening to young John at that very moment. See, going through that fire! That's what I was feeling. White people get intuitive feelings like that too, but it don't mean a thing to them if they don't listen to it. They say, 'I had this funny feeling,' but they shut it off.

The next morning, after I'd barely slept all night, I tried to find out who had been burnt. I was still feeling hot all over. I didn't have a phone, so I couldn't call anyone to ask what happened. I was just about to start walking the twelve miles into town to find out the news when my daughter arrived. She kept asking me if I was all right, because I looked that terrible. Then she told me my cousin John had died in a house fire the night before.

Everybody is united and the same, I think. But Aboriginals have that real strong spiritual gift about them, because in the world they lived in – nature – that sort of spiritual thing governed their everyday lives. And so we still have it today.

Everything in life has got to be in pairs of opposites that unite and make a whole, like religion and science. Nothing is really separate. Everything has to take into account everything else. Aboriginals believe mostly in what they can see and feel and hear, things like that. Everything spiritual has its physical part, and everything physical has its spiritual part. For example, once my aunt was looking after her six-year-old son. She was worried because he was crying in the back room as he was hungry, and there was no food in the house. She suddenly heard him stop crying and she thought, Poor little fellah, he must have fallen asleep. Then she went and looked in the room at him, and saw him sitting on the bed eating a big piece of bread and jam. Yet there had been no food in the house. She asked him, 'Where did you get that food?' And he answered, 'My brother gave it to me.' But his brother had died the year before.

Things like that happen to us all the time.

I can see it would save the world if people got back to Aboriginal principles. It will never rectify anything unless we do, one way or another. Aboriginal culture has so many positive gifts to bring to the world. People say, 'Oh, those ways don't exist any more.' But that's *why* there's big trouble today, because they are no longer practised everywhere. And they could easily be. My people have just got to look at themselves and say, 'I'm Aboriginal, I shouldn't be like this. I should be thinking the traditional way, with Aboriginal thoughts.' Behaving that way kept the peace for sixty or seventy thousand years. If that's finished, the world will finish. All trouble starts when people say, 'That's finished.' You are not Aboriginal any more when you say that.

Love – great love – is Aboriginals' strength. Aboriginals have respect for all people, no matter where they come from or how poor or how bad they are. You've got to give everyone a chance. We treated other people the way we wanted to be treated. We had wars to uphold our laws, our spiritual principles, but we still respected the human being – all human beings.

To go to the funeral of someone you know is very important in the Aboriginal community. It's real important even for children to go. Because every Aboriginal what passes away is leaving less and less behind in Aboriginal culture. Aboriginals would go to every other Aboriginal's funeral if they could, whether they knew him or not. They'll look upon him or her as a friend what went through suffering and racism like the rest of us. That's why we always pay respects even at a stranger's funeral. You do your best to go to it and say farewell to your brother or your sister. That's part of Aboriginal life. Even if you never heard of him before. You hear, 'Oh, a poor Aboriginal got killed, or passed away, the other day.' 'Oh yeah, when's her funeral?' they'll ask. And you'll go. It's a natural thing. They don't say, 'Oh, I've never met her before.' Or, 'I don't know him.' They go, mate! Because he is one of us. That's how it is. That's the sort of feeling Aboriginals get when they hear of an Aboriginal dying or being killed somewhere. You feel grief for him. It's just one big family that's suffering all the time through the white man's occupation and racism. That's the deep sense of unity we all have for each other. No matter where you are, it's still that same thing. I would go to every human being's funeral in the world if I could, to show my respect for him or her for being a human being.

In 1993 we organised a big Songlines concert at the Warrnambool football oval. We called it the Peek Whurrong Coming Home

Concert. Richard Frankland, a Gunditjmara man, was the main Aboriginal behind it. People of all races were supposed to forget their prejudices for one day and join one another in song. A lot of stars performed, like Shane Howard, Neil Murray and my nephew Archie Roach, and a lot of young girls and boys showed off their talent. My granddaughter Jemmes – Ian's daughter – came to take part as well, with her Native Cultural Group of dancers from Mildura. In my day there were no Aboriginal bands, but an Aboriginal can get on the stage and sing and play anywhere now. My grandson Lee Morgan is doing well that way. He lives in Melbourne now and is a professional musician, but he always comes back for special events like this.

There'd been trouble in our area just beforehand – young people on drugs not knowing what they were doing – and racism had reared its ugly head again. So when I was asked to open the concert, I ended my speech with the words, 'Let us destroy the drink and drugs that are destroying our young people.'

It went on late into the night. We watched the gates strictly, and no alcohol was allowed in. A huge crowd of Aboriginals, Maoris and white people – all nationalities – was there, all enjoying themselves. Towards the end, a big fog rolled in over the football ground. It felt real mysterious, with lights shining through and music in the background.

My children here in Warrnambool have all helped put a concert on like that since 1996, one that celebrates Aboriginal culture and reconciliation. They've had wonderful musicians like Archie Roach, Shane Howard, Neil Murray and Judith Durham come play at it, every year. They call it Tarerer. That's an Aboriginal word for how all the coastal Gunditjmara clans used to gather together in this area once a year. It was a great time for celebration – there'd be dancing, singing, storytelling and laughing. The missionaries put a stop to all that, though.

I've opened the Tarerer concert a few times now, and in 1999 the Mayor of Warrnambool presented me, as Elder of our clan, with a Sorry book, signed by hundreds of people from the town saying sorry for the bad things what happened to us. That was a real special night.

I've been asked to open the Port Fairy Folk Festival too, every year since 1995. [Banjo's son Lenny has now been asked to carry on the tradition.] I always say something like, 'Let us all be united and enjoy ourselves, like one big happy family.' I spoke at Deakin University once too, at an unveiling of *Tuuram Cairn*, a permanent sculpture by Chris Booth and the students 'to encourage remembrance of the recent suffering of this land and its Indigenous peoples'. [Banjo's daughter Fiona has since collaborated with Chris Booth on a sculpture in central Melbourne.] There I said, 'My people used to camp and roam all through this area. Thank you for remembering them.'

All these things have shown me how much white people are changing for the better. It's given me hope that all the different races will one day stop fighting and be friends.

Chapter 24

My grandkids went for a walk today and found some of the old places. I was glad. There's a dam near the old mission that always has some water in the bottom. They musta found that. They arrived home looking like a lot of little tadpoles. Mud everywhere, and on their faces. Looked as if they'd been rolling in it.

One of them, Caleb, had got his boot stuck in it and they all helped him get it out. Then they all got into it. They musta thought they were bunyips, playing in the mud hole. They musta had great fun. I didn't tell them off. 'That's all right,' I said to them. 'I did the same thing when I was a kid.'

I washed all their clothes four times over, and split a few logs because there was no fire to dry them. All the kids are clean now, but my grandson Kirrae is wearing somebody's big jumper and baggy shorts. He had a shower and sung out for a towel, and I went in and brought it to him and his face was still black. I said, 'You've forgotten to wash your face, mate.' I did that for him. Talk about mud! They had mud all over, their clothes too.

I've shown Kirrae where things happened in the bush, and he knows it like the back of his hand.

I remember a few years ago, the kids had found an old water tank in the dam. It must have blown there in the last storm, and they got the idea to roll it out. They got inside and were laughing and running around inside it – gee, it looked powerful! You couldn't see them most of the time, just their monster tank rolling over the paddocks everywhere, over and over, like a big drum making thunder. It was open on one side like a loudspeaker. The cows and the horses came up and circled it while it was stationary, and you could hear the kids laughing away. Then they tumbled it over again all of a sudden, and gave the animals a huge fright. It was fun watching them.

For a long time, it seemed to us that white adults thought the way to make children grow up was by squashing their feelings. But to us, a lot of white adults were not really adults at all. You are not truly grown up until you experience *feelings* – the right feelings – with the whole of yourself. Aboriginals want to treat children as children, and not force them to be adults. It's better for them to be children as long as they could, and come out of that gradually.

When I was growing up, when little children overheard adults talking about a problem, they wouldn't know what the problem was but they knew it was a problem. They'd say nothing, because they've got to work this out in their head and listen to the Old People. That way they'll get strong. As they grow up, they get used to these things gradually – it's not pushed on them straight away in my community. You've got to teach them gently about the harsh things and the troubles. Teach them softly – no sudden shocks about something hard, about the terrible things that happened. Don't frighten them. Little children grow up that way – they'll think about it, and get to feeling.

When something bad happens, they'll feel emotional about it. That's why, when a parent or an uncle dies, young children put their arms around one another and cry like anything and not even be ashamed of it, because they are regenerating a good emotional thing in their heart around one another. That's their feelings. They learn to cope with their troubles and all the things that happen while they're growing up. They're not cut off, and not plunged into it. If they meet the harsh thing straight away, without it being explained to them gently, I think that affects little children's minds. No, tell it to them in a real kind way, and they will understand better, grasp it better when they're not forced into understanding. That's the way I see Aboriginal people doing things – gentle things.

When I was a little fellah, kids used to be hunted away if the grown-ups had any argument. Children were not allowed to see or hear anything. That way we wouldn't know if it came to a case for tribal punishment. Any disagreement, children were not allowed to be there. It would upset little children to see grown people having a fight. That was all through my childhood days, you know, until I was a young man. Children wasn't allowed to listen to arguments. I think that was a good thing too, because young kids these days, when they get into arguments, they get more aggressive than kids did when we was kids, because they've seen other big arguments. It's like they was trained to do it because they're there when there's real big arguments, like between husband and wife – kids have been drawn into it through their parents. That's why a lot of cruel things happen today with children. You see all these things happening – aggression becomes part of them, part of growing up. I don't think it's very nice. So even today I try to stop people from arguing in front of children.

That's why children in our community wasn't allowed around when grown-ups were having a fight, and weren't allowed back until everything was quiet. The children still have respect for what's happening, but they're not involved in it themselves, though still understanding that it's happening. Children couldn't solve any arguments or problems anyway – it was left to the community. But if there was a split-up or separation between their parents, the children would play a great part in that, like fetching both parents together again so that they wouldn't split up. It would mostly be the children doing that.

And the Old People wouldn't listen to gossip from the husband if he took the children from the wife; they would not allow that man to condemn the wife in front of the children. They would not do that. The children would know there was a mistake made somewhere, but the Old People would speak of the mother who'd made the mistake with love too, and not condemn either one of the parents in front of the children. The way they used to do it was, 'Let the children love both parents. And as they grow older, if they're not back together again, the children will realise that they parted somewhere along the line, and the children will love both their parents, instead of saying, "Oh, don't go with your father, kid – he's no good, he left you," or, "That woman left me with all you kids." Little children will grow up and they'll learn themselves what happened, and they won't make one be apart from another. They'll love everyone.'

That's how the families stay together. They've got love around for everybody. A lot of things like that happened in Aboriginal culture and a lot of it still happens today among Aboriginals with principles. I don't think it's fair at all to turn children away from one parent to the other. The Aboriginal people didn't think that was fair. That's your blood – that's your father, or that's your mother, or that's your brother.

There was nothing to be said about anyone unless they was there to protect themselves or defend themselves against accusations. You can't talk against anyone if they wasn't there. That's different today too; people like to hear gossip, or create gossip. If Aboriginals had their way, they'd be punished real severe for creating gossip and for creating troubles. That's against their parents' law.

Aboriginal religion is lived every minute of every day. It's a basic feeling towards people. If you feel you can trust somebody, he's your friend and you are his friend. All these things are drifting away in our society and they've got to be grabbed and brought back. Everywhere in the world, children are doing their own thing and getting into strife. That's why the world is falling to pieces – children are not guided any more.

When I was young, your tribal father or mother needed not be your real mother or father. Your other adult relatives were your guardians too. And if you did wrong, they were the ones who'd punish you, like a mother or father. That went on till I was in my thirties. That way, people in their thirties still had respect for their aunties and uncles.

Aboriginal children are never lost if they have that extended family. When Aboriginals talk about being brought up in orphanages, they often say, 'I had an older brother or sister who looked after me.' Older children often protected younger children in the institutions where they were taken after being stolen. But some poor kids who were alone simply died. When children were together, though, they looked after each other. You would never see an older Aboriginal child tormenting a younger one. Little white kids – a lot of them are lost because they've got no extended family to care for them when they go astray.

That's what held Aboriginals together, respect for the Elders and the community. Them things are not regarded as sacred any more – listening to Old People. There's something *real* wrong when Aboriginal children don't listen to Elders.

I'm specially careful about rearing up my grandson Kirrae. People tell me that sometimes he seems like an old man.

My own Old People learnt me how to be a trusted member of the Aboriginal community. You had to be a special person before they'd tell you things. They could foresee a day when Aboriginal values would be forgotten and they wanted to prevent that happening. But as I grew up, they gradually got more silent and never spoke out around the campfires like they used to when I was small. And many who knew the old language stopped speaking it too, because the church people who would come out and visit the mission wouldn't let them. A lot of that language has been lost now.

CHAPTER 25

One day, after shopping in Warrnambool, I called in at our local store on the way home. The phone rang while I was there.

The storekeeper looked at me. 'It's your house!' he said.

'What about my house?'

'It's on fire!'

My daughter was with me and we raced home. Coming over the hill two miles away, I could see my old house going up in smoke.

The firemen were already there when we arrived. The men jumped in through the window and grabbed a few boomerangs that my son Ian had made. Nothing else got saved. I just stood in the rain and ashes and looked.

A strange thing happened later that evening too. Another fire started at my home and it finished off the back part of the house that was still standing and a caravan. The firefighters said it couldn't have been from the original fire – they'd completely put it out. It was like someone was trying to get me off my land.

Some firemen invited me to stay with them until a new house could be organised. They were white people and you could see they had no prejudice. Things were changing, I could see. Being turned away from pubs, being served last in shops, people saying nasty things to you – these things used to happen so many times we never took much notice. Not until we sat down and talked. 'Remember that bloke? He said this, he said that.' Then we'd have a good laugh. We had to accept that them things happen. It was a life of struggle.

When it became publicly known that my house was burnt, people what knew me or had heard of me arrived from all over the place to offer to help. That really touched me. But the people who came round to show me their support were mostly white – that amazed me. Not many Aboriginals came – that saddened me. Some Aboriginal organisations in Melbourne did lend a hand, though. You always help other human beings in times of trouble, *always*. That's an Aboriginal principle. Even if they're your worst enemy – all that should be forgotten in times of trouble. The Old People taught me that from when I was a little fellah. But that principle isn't always practised in the black community any more.

White people came with blankets, food, and offerings of help. A man drove in and left a caravan behind. He said, 'There you are, mate. Live in that.' And he drove away before I could even thank him. I lived in that caravan for two freezing winters, almost knee-deep in mud outside. As soon as white people knew I was in need, they behaved towards me the way Aboriginals used to towards each other. It showed me how much things are changing – white people for the better, but some black people for the worse.

There was difficulty in getting a new house built, though, and the white folk said, 'We'll get you one. We'll lobby the government.' Farmers too offered to help, although they were worried and confused about land rights. Troublemakers had been saying, 'The blacks are going to take your farm and your land,' and yet, when it looked like I might be pushed off *my* land, it was white farmers and other members of the white community what came to help me.

In the days following the fire, when it came down to fundamentals, I got a clear perspective on the real relations between white people and Aboriginals. Nobody said, 'Oh well, we'll leave him there. He's just another old blackfellah. He'll build a bark hut somewhere.'

I would have done that, no worries – even if I died of pneumonia. There was no way I was going to leave my tribal land. The more hardships I had, the more determined I would be to stay there. You don't leave your spirit-land in times of trouble. That's what my old dad always taught me, and made me promise him.

But no, the white people wanted me to have a house. And that gave me reason to live, so I could tell the story of what other people did for me. Because one day my descendants or someone else might be in difficulty. Then they'll remember the story of when Banjo's house burnt down and white people came from far and wide to help him. And that will give them hope. It's a better story than saying, 'The white people came and condemned him.' It tells the truth.

It was hard for me to accept help like that because I'd never, ever done it before. I'd worked since I was a little fellah to support myself and my family. But people told me they wanted to do back to me what I'd done for them. The government gave me money after lots of hassles, but they didn't want me to build my house where I wanted, overlooking the big gully where I used to roam when I was a little kid, hunting and spearing fish and eels. Most of my little black mates from them days have gone to the Dreamtime land of their tribal ancestors. There are only two or three of us left out of the mob of children what used to hunt along that river.

You'd hear our laughter echoing around the cliffs and waterways, and cries of, 'I speared a big fish here!' and, 'Come up this end, I've got another one here!' You'd hear us calling each other all along the river. Little barefoot kids we were, running over the big rocks like mountain goats. Nobody slipped and fell or hurt himself. The rocky river was like a smooth highway to us.

To have my house built overlooking this beautiful bend in the river, I had to have a private road made. This was going to be expensive.

Funds were raised for me all over the place. A white girl and my old Aboriginal mates from Melbourne helped organise a benefit concert, though most of them were battlers themselves – sleeping in parks, being kicked from pillar to post. That lot proved to me that some Aboriginals still have Aboriginal principles. They collected over three thousand dollars for me at the concert. My grandson Lee and his friends went out busking in the street. He collected five or six hundred dollars, and it all went towards building my house.

An architect came up from Melbourne. I'd never met him in my life, but he had heard about my troubles. He asked me what sort of house I wanted. I said, 'Only a small one.' He had a look down the cliff and went for a walk on his own by the river. He climbed back up and said, 'I've got it now. I'll build a model and send it to you.'

He designed me a beautiful little house. Carpenters were notified and they came and built it. It was hard for them because they'd never done one like it. The walls are curved the way the river bends around, so my house contains the atmosphere of its environment. Now I'm going to grow trees against the walls, to make it a real part of the bush.

So I'm pretty lucky. And it's true – no matter what situation you're in, or how bad people say you are, there's always someone who'll give you a go, someone who'll hold out a hand to you and treat you as a human being. I reckon I'm probably the first Aboriginal in Australia to have the kind of house he wanted, built where he wanted it, with some government financial help.

Once my new house was built, I had a nice warm bed and a roof over my head and all my troubles were just about disappearing. But every day trouble comes up – it's part of life. You've just got to learn to live with it and tolerate other people.

When I was a little boy on the mission, we lived together in peace and harmony. Everybody got along, shared with one another, and respected each other. But over the years, all these changes came. Governments stepped in, wanting to make amends for all the terrible things that happened to us in the past. They wanted to make things right, a bit easier and better for Aboriginals for all the wrong what was done to them. (The good white people think that way now about the past, and are often more honest today than ever before.) So they started giving houses and land for Aboriginals and set them up with money, to try to give us chances. They decided that all people with Aboriginal blood can be classified as Aboriginals if they want, and apply for the benefits of that.

Then all of a sudden politicians came – Aboriginal politicians – seeking power and money. A lot of them had left our community when they were young and lived in white society and done the same things as whites, had a white-man education and even identified as white. But they suddenly came back 'to look after my people'. And they've got proper jobs now, administrative, and powerful, and as 'leaders of the Aboriginal community'. They are the biggest authorities on Aboriginal problems, and yet they've never lived with the problems! They never identified themselves with us: 'Yes, I'm Aboriginal. I fight for my people's rights.' If there was ever some trouble on the missions – somebody stole a sheep, or been sent to gaol – some of these Aboriginals who had left would say, 'Oh see, those Aboriginals out there on the missions are still the same. Got nothing to do with me, I don't live out there.' You know, they'd cast themselves off from their Aboriginal community when it suited them. They didn't want it to be known that they belonged to Aboriginals. Some of them never came back to visit, or only came at funeral times.

But many who have returned now are looking for handouts and they've already got thousands – they've got homes, they've got land, they've got beef cattle, and still they're crying out for more. And the real people what was bred and born and lived here, they're still struggling. Those that worked hard all their life and are getting a pension now and things like that, and our grandchildren, are living in poverty and we can't help them because we've got nothing. When I was young, the traditional way was to share half of everything with others. Now money and greed is the goal of many younger Aboriginals today. It's unbelievable how greed and power can destroy people.

It's different values now, money and greed not only destroying the people what's greedy but destroying the other black people what's got nothing. Their own people are doing it to them. Intimidating and threatening them, causing disunity and power struggles. That's where Aboriginal principles are being destroyed. But they can't see it. They never had that power before in their lives. Because a lot of things happened what the white people done to them, they're taking it out on their own people. That's the worst part of it. And they're using the good white people up and trying to make them feel guilty for what happened in the past.

So much has gone wrong in Aboriginal society, and it is many of these black leaders what are hurting Aboriginal culture. We've got few real honest leaders left. And those that are honest can't push their power and do their work without somebody else trying to overthrow them. I might come across as resentful about all this, which I am in a way, but it just shows me the way Aboriginal people are changing. But I would rather die than compromise my beliefs and principles.

What I'm saying is, to be Aboriginal, you've got to have Aboriginal principles. Then you're Aboriginal, no matter how fair your skin might be. You must look at Aboriginal problems through the black man's eyes and have respect for the black man, and not put anyone down. If all Aboriginal people pulled together with one voice, we'd have a powerful argument. With no one fighting one another.

Our young Aboriginal people have a lot of opportunities today, more than ever before, but if you forget your past, your Aboriginality, you're not a real person any more. It's good when our people are educated at university or whatever, because right education is what's going to help all the races understand one another. But our educated generations must also go on identifying as Aboriginal and living by Aboriginal principles.

Right now, there's so much fighting going on among us and it must end. Friends are turning into enemies, and everyone is suspicious of each other. The other members of our clan are trying to take our bush off us. Yes, our sacred bush, which transforms us for the better when we go into it! Where we feel the spirits of the good Old People healing us! Where the bush animals are happy and free! What will happen to them if it's not looked after? There will be no more animals for the children to see. They will only be in picture books.

There's sadness in the bush now. Many trees are dead and the koalas killed them.* The old bush is crying out and yet people are fighting over it and destroying it. We have to leave it as it is and let it grow back wild again, like mother nature wants it to. We've got to protect the land where we were born. That is why we fought to get it back from the government in the first place. The land is like a mother to us. She can't provide for us if we allow her to be destroyed.

---

*The koalas, which were introduced into the area, were free of chlamydia, a disease that prevents population explosions. They overpopulated, and also marched on the surrounding farms.

It's like those places overseas where a conquering country wants the oil or gold or copper and kills the forest people to get it. Where it pollutes the rivers and lays the country to waste. Where soldiers chase journalists yelling, 'Kill, kill!' when they try to report the truth. Where foreigners leave, followed by hundreds of refugees. Then the conquering army goes away and leaves the inhabitants with nothing, without a country. I don't like to think about it. We're suffering in this spot exactly like those countries overseas fighting for their independence. The bully countries come in, put soldiers with guns in the streets, shooting innocent, unarmed people who want their independence. Shooting them even when they hide in the churches – there's nowhere sacred to hide. And yet there's so much beauty in those places too. It seems like they are blind to it all.

All my family has here is the bush now, and that's all we want. It's our spirit-land. And yet the other members of the clan are trying to take it away from us. If it goes, we're gone too. Our children will be like wandering spirits without a homeland. What will happen to them? They will have nowhere to call a spiritual home. I don't want my grandchildren ending up in the cities, in trouble, on drugs, in gaol. They will lose their identity and won't know where they come from, and neither will their children's children. We know where we come from and where we belong. That's the Aboriginal way of life. That's part of your living, to know where you're from. That's why a lot of these people today are lost and lashing out at everyone, because they've lost their identity.

It's something for people what's doing us wrong to look at *themselves*, what they're doing. If they can look at themselves and say, 'We're doing wrong to them people up there [Banjo's end of the mission]. They've got nothing, we've got everything – there must be something wrong with that. Why've we got all this and they got nothing?

235

Is it our fault? Are we not doing things the right way?' Them themselves have got to look at it.

People ring me up from everywhere, white and black – they're concerned too. They don't like what's going on. They can see it all. They never met these other people [other members of Banjo's community], but they can see there's something *wrong* somewhere. Every day we wake up knowing that there will be niggly, trifling things to wear us down, like our water turned off constantly [after Banjo's death, the water was turned off for an entire year], or our gate will have been opened and our horses driven onto the road and the pound rung up about it. I've coped with a lot of big things during my life – my wife dying through injustice, other members of my family dying through injustice – but trifling things wear you down even more somehow.

It's a new century now, and are we going to put up with all this *again*? After all we went through? It's a terrible thing, putting up with that all the time. They're trying to wear you out, and they *never* – so far. But little things, like water dripping on a stone – it wears the stone out in the end, eh? See? That's how they're trying to get to us.

When I was in Melbourne during the Depression, the buildings blocked my view of my Dreamtime tribal home. I came back to our land to get married and raise my children, and thought things had got better when we got the land back from the government. Now my own people are trying to take it away from me again. They should stop the politics and violence and sit down with the old tribal members to see what they want to do. When Aboriginals are given land, it should be shared and not just grabbed by a selected group.

Getting a committee together to manage the bush, with both sides represented on it, as I have done recently, has been my big move towards reconciliation with my own people. But not long ago, the committee members from the other side decided to meet while my descendants were away attending a funeral. I was too sick to go to the funeral, but a kind lady offered to take me to the meeting and I didn't want to upset her. Once I was there, without my glasses of course, because I had to hurry, the people made a big fuss of me and they got me to sign a paper – as a matter of course, they said. I'm a pretty innocent sort of a bloke, and because I'm Aboriginal it's not natural to me to take much account of the written word. I trust word of mouth, where usually I can trust seeing people's expressions and feeling their feelings.

My son Lenny came into my bedroom later that night and asked, 'So you went to the meeting. How did it go?'

I was lying down and I answered wearily, 'There's a paper on the table out there. It should tell you something. They're all with us now.'

Lenny went out and came back with the paper. 'Do you know what this really says?' he asked. 'Do you know what you've signed?'

'Just that I attended the meeting,' I answered, even more wearily. 'There were other names listed there.' I was still lying down.

My son stood in the doorway and talked to me gently, obviously afraid of alarming me. He said with great sorrow that he understood I didn't take no notice of such things, but it was a time when my signature had been important.

In the deep silence which followed, I slowly realised that my son's quietness could only mean that I must have signed the members of my family off the committee managing the bush. I had signed my own people away.

I hadn't been told that was what that paper meant. How does anyone recover from such a thing?

Soon afterwards, the following notice appeared in our newspaper [the *Standard*]. It was signed by the chairperson of the committee managing the bush:

FRAMLINGHAM FOREST

Please be advised that as of today any authority issued on behalf of Kirrae Whurrong Aboriginal Corporation for the cutting and/or removal of firewood and/or off-road vehicle use in the Framlingham Forest is hereby revoked.

And, until the completion of a forest management plan:
- *Any person found cutting or removing firewood from the Framlingham Forest will be charged with trespassing.*
- *The use of trail bikes and 4WD vehicles within the forest area is prohibited.*

My mate David Fligelman has a four-wheel drive, and he always takes me around the bush in it when he comes to see me. And I like to gather firewood from there *every day* so that I can survive in the cold, and sit by the Old People's graves in the bush and talk to them. And this notice told me I couldn't do that any more. But they're not going to keep me out of the bush. Never, never. We've been getting wood there ever since I was born and we've *never* destroyed the bush. We *clean up* where we cut wood and you only see a stump left. And then the grass grows and the bush animals come and eat it, and then all the little trees grow up in there, from the seeds where we burnt the branches we didn't want. We've been conservationists all the time. Before white people ever *thought* about it.

But now you go into the bush and you see trees lying everywhere in the ferns, and you can't walk through the bush for logs lying around what they cut down and walked away from. They're left there to rot away. That's desecrating the bush. Yet they think nothing of it.

But it's a spiritual place to us. It's like white people's church is to them. You wouldn't go into the white man's church and smash it up. They'd soon put a stop to that. Seeing the bush getting cut down is like having bits of myself being cut away.

The bush should be left as it is, without people being bosses over it. We can look after the bush as *one people*, not one group intimidating another and saying they are bosses of the bush. That don't go along with me. We all belong here. Why should they penalise *me* for going into that bush? That's my homeland. That's my spiritual home. My old dad cut wood in there when I was a little kid. That bush belongs to us, belongs to everybody.

Yesterday it was the middle of the afternoon and I was going for a walk. I'd just stopped to have a sleep in the old caravan there for a while. There was a north-east wind blowing. I sat down in the drain near the pines and I seen this thing come towards me out of the pines, like smoke. I thought I'd dropped a cigarette butt or something in the caravan. I looked across and nothing was there, but it was coming out of halfway up the pines. I looked and looked. I couldn't believe it. It was like a big mist, and when I looked at it harder it was sort of silvery and soft, and it blew real slowly away from the pines. It definitely came out of the pines. And I don't know what it was. When I had a good look, it wasn't smoke – it was silvery. And it had sort of real silver spots in it. Like tinsel things, something like that. The last bit finished and it all went to the east away across the paddocks. Up that way, across the road, past me. I was watching and it went away over in the paddock and just disappeared into nothing.

I don't know what it was, but it filled me with the sense that something good is going to happen here. All these bad things I've been talking about happen, but a lot of good things are going to come out of it. It will make the people enjoy themselves, without none of these politics or anything. I've seen a strong promise for the future. I would like to see a building erected there, on just that spot, where all nationalities and all ages and all walks of life could get together and learn about true Aboriginal principles and how to use them out in the big world, and in their own lives. Where children could come from everywhere, and people with a spiritual hunger – down-and-outs and even rich people. All to learn about the bush, bush law and bush craft. About how to use the land properly. Especially to tell the little children. It would be like the bush school I grew up in, where I learnt all that I know today.

World peace is inevitable. The world has gone from tribes to city-states to nations, and international unity is obviously the next step. But the world can have peace either the easy way or the hard way – everyone can either become more positive *now*, or allow their greed and corruption to cause a disaster. A disaster so terrible that people will want to turn their backs on their previous negative ways and create a society based on different priorities, something closer to Aboriginal traditions.

In the same way, unity among *my* people is inevitable. There must be an end to cruelty, and unity between the rival groups at the mission must occur. But we too can have it the easy way or the hard way. Either we can come to our senses and start working towards it today, or something will happen that is so terrible that both our sides will not be able to bear any more pain and we'll have to start working together and co-operating.

I want us to cross a bridge to which we will never return.

The Framlingham Forest is the most important asset of our people. It is more important than financial assets or commercial enterprises. The forest belongs to nature and you have to be kind to her. You need to look after mother nature as you look after your old mum. Everywhere you walk in that forest, there are story places. They give us feelings and they give us dreams. It is our church, our spiritual place. It's my homeland. It's the homeland of my ancestors and my people. It's the spirit of my people. It's where they lived, where they roamed, where they sang and told stories. Without the forest, there'd be nothing for me in life. If the bush was destroyed, I would just die with it.

I would like to live quietly in peace in the forest, without being a radical or a politician. All my children and grandchildren feel the same way about the forest. My son Lenny says the forest is for all Australians to enjoy, and that we have to instil into the younger ones what the forest means so they will look after it. When he was going to the technical school in Warrnambool years ago, he used to see the tall pine from the forest's cemetery on the horizon and it would always make him long to return home. Lenny's son Kirrae loves the forest too. He spends most of his time in there, learning about it. He's even taught his dad a thing or two. And one day he'll teach his children.

A lot of great songs have come from this forest. A lot of song-writers, black and white, have come here and been inspired by it. Archie Roach's song 'Weeping In The Forest', is one of them. [See page 265.]

I am not a politician, just a man of nature. White children come to the bush and I tell them stories about the bush. I tell them about the spirits of the forest that are still there and about the Dreamtime land.

It's the Aboriginal way to have feelings for your area, for any part of the land. If you didn't have feelings for that part of the land, you wouldn't have feelings for anything anywhere. No matter where Aboriginals roamed and lived and camped, it was all spiritual to them, you know, a sacred thing. Them spiritual feelings for the land mean everything to us Aboriginal people – that's our life. It's part of our soul, and we're part of its soul. You can have Aboriginals what don't live on the land, what are living in the city, and they're lost souls. They've got nothing there to cling to: they know what they want but they haven't got it. That part of spiritual feeling is not with them in the big cities.

I know this forest like the back of my hand. It's part of my life to live with scrub and trees – it's my home. A lot of people say, 'That's just another tree,' or 'That's just another gully,' but all them things are spiritual things to us. The bushland was always very important to us – it was work, it was shelter in the winter, there was plenty of wood for our fires. It was all-important to have bushland near. It was very important.

Any excuse at all, I like to get into the bush. I love that old bush. And once I do go into the bush, it's hard for me to go back home again and get into the house. Looking at walls all day makes me crazy! I always go into the bush in the evening. I go in there for hours and hours and sit down, and come home when it's all dark.

I like to look into the distance and into the Dreamtime land, and see all the tribal people. And I often think how beautiful it must have been, with all the little huts here and there and all the children's laughter in the bush. These days you don't hear any laughter in the bush.

Whenever I've been away in the city or had hard times, I couldn't get back to my homeland in the bush quick enough. All I've wanted to do is head deep in, to where some old camp used to be, sit down there and feel the peacefulness. That's where I like to go in difficult times – if I'm depressed, have been in town too much where I don't fit in, or I've heard too much hustle and bustle about politics or land rights. I never mind about the hardships, the racism and the big debates of the world when I'm in the forest. That's why I'm still in one piece. I go into the spirit-land to see my friends and my Old People. Then I'm able to face the big world once more. I come out of that forest real strong again. I'll face up to anything again and not weaken.

We once had an old camp deep in that bush. I like sitting there because you feel the old Aboriginal spirits watching you, standing somewhere behind the trees, in the shadow of the gums. I see with my mind's eye all the Old People living around that area, and hear the little barefoot children. The leaves will rustle with laughter and everything will have a happy atmosphere.

I feel happy having my own people watching me, and it makes them happy to see me because they know I'll never forget them. That makes the spirit-world happy, you know, that we don't forget them. That's the sort of thing I believe in. The people are there in spirit. Little children are whispering and laughing all around. You know that they have come from your heart. They might be passed on to that land beyond, but their spirits are still here. And that's what makes things strong for you, you know. For once you've got your land where your ancestors roamed, it's a very strong feeling, and without this, if someone came and cut all these trees down for farmland, we'd be lost people with nothing to cling to, no spiritual side to our life. Our connection with the forest links both our past and our future.

I look forward to my death. I know I'll be in the best grave there is. The young fellahs always take special care. They get down and dig and sweat, with all their thoughts going towards you like a gift. The old fellahs like me tell the young ones what to do. They take special pride in it because they're doing something for your last resting place. It's got to be perfect, not just a hole in the ground. One day someone came along with a machine to dig a grave in our cemetery. 'Don't do that,' we said, 'you're disturbing the Old People.' The way we do it is hard, but it's the way it should be. We do it with our hands, and even on the hottest or the coldest day out. We're all friends, digging together. That grave has to be perfect. It's a very beautiful, peaceful place. A lot of my friends and family are here.

I'll never leave here. My heart and spirit will never leave the bush. I do not understand the notion of 'title' and 'ownership'. Who can own the forest but God? It is a cathedral to me, a special place where I can feel my ancestors' presence. It's my homeland, the spirit of my people, where they roamed, sang and told stories. Whether you are black or white, you need to love, respect and be kind to this cathedral, and never, *never* undermine it.

When I used to travel all around as a young man looking for work, I tended to move in a circle because my forest homeland was calling and pulling me back so hard.

You always come back to your homeland. You always come back.

AFTERWORD
(by Banjo's children)

Our father passed away unexpectedly in the Warrnambool and District Base Hospital on the morning of 14 March 2000 after a short illness. Shane Howard played the didgeridoo as more than thirty loved ones crammed into the tiny room and waited.

A few days later, we took Dad back to his home at Framlingham, where we had kept a sacred fire burning. In accordance with Aboriginal tradition, all Dad's male relatives, including his many grandsons, dug his grave over several days. His Baha'i friends rubbed his body with rosewater. He looked like a king in his coffin, his hands clasping his favourite nulla-nulla, a large boomerang by his left side, and he wore a headband of black, yellow and red, the Aboriginal colours. His bearded face looked magnificent and noble.

In the days following his passing, obituaries for Dad appeared in the *Age*, the *Australian*, and as far away as the London *Times*. His funeral was conducted in his 'cathedral', where the forest gives way to the field, just metres from his chosen gravesite. A marquee was erected for the service, but the unanticipated crowd spilled out into the field and all around, numbering into the thousands. The mission road endured a gridlock of traffic akin to a city street in peak hour. It was the largest gathering of mourners the town of Warrnambool had ever seen. One of the many speakers at the funeral service quoted a proverb: 'It is appointed unto man once to die, and after that the judgement.' He stretched out his arms as if to encircle the crowd and said, 'Well, this is the judgement.'

Towards the end of his life, Dad was greatly troubled by the disunity among his own people on the Framlingham Mission; by the fighting over the control and distribution of government funds, and the ownership of the surrounding forest. 'The bush should be left as it is, without people being bosses over it,' he always said. 'We all belong here. That bush belongs to everybody, not just one group.' However, just months before his death, he found himself in the Federal Court in a wrangle with his own people, only to lose any legal rights he once had to the forest. It caused him immeasurable pain, which he expressed to Camilla in one of their last interviews.

Dad is buried on his tribal land, at a point we all called 'the pretty place', on the brow of a hill overlooking the Hopkins River. Lenny found him there one day, just weeks before he died, sitting alone by a small fire. Dad told him that he wanted to be buried there when he had gone, and not in the mission cemetery where all his family lie. This surprised us at first, as he took care to visit the cemetery almost daily, tending the graves of Old People, little children, and all his mates and ancestors aged between. On reflection, we believe his wish to be buried on his land was to ensure that we, his children, would never leave it, and to fulfil his promise to his own father, made almost forty years earlier, that he would never leave it either.

Two months before Dad's death, Bernice and her daughter Karana spent two weeks at his home caring for him while he was unwell. To Bernice this was the most cherished and instructive two weeks of her life. They sat up together night after night while Dad told her many stories about his childhood and the history of our people. He had much to say, more so than at any other time of his life. As was his way, some things were lessons but many were directions. We now realise that Dad had a strong sense he was being called to his Dreaming. Some evenings he and Bernice would take the kitchen chairs outside and watch the sun set over the forest, while Dad talked about how it once thrived when he was a boy, before being diminished by logging and damaged by an overpopulation of koalas. On these nights the forest would come alive with the reds and golds of the sunset, as if to illustrate Dad's tales of how it once flourished with life and health.

At other times during Bernice's stay, she would hear Dad whistling and singing a particular tune to himself while making a cup of tea, tapping the teaspoon in time to his song. She didn't take much notice of the lyrics, but after his death she recognised them when Radio National replayed an old interview with Dad in which he sang the same words:

> I remember my childhood when Daddy was strong
> He toiled and he laboured the busy day long
> He tried to be honest and neighbourly fair
> Now he waits for the Master to call him up there
>
> He's my old crippled Daddy
> I love him so dear
> But I wandered away from his side
> I'll go back home today and I'm going to stay
> Before the Great Master calls him away.

Bernice then realised the message, and Dad's wish that he wanted her to fulfil. She and her family immediately left their house in Warrnambool and moved into Dad's small but much-loved home on the mission, overlooking the river where he played as a child. We were certain that he was at peace, knowing she was there.

After many months, Lenny and his son Kirrae offered to look

after Dad's house so that Bernice could return to her own in Warrnambool. Kirrae is very happy to be living in his grandfather's home, surrounded by his memory. We are sure Dad is also happy that Kirrae is there, overlooking the same river and forest where he hunted and played as a child.

Now, as Dad's descendants, it is our turn to fulfil the same promise that he made to his father – that we will never leave our tribal land, and that we will never forget the Old People who have gone before us.

Helen, Patricia, Leonard, Elizabeth, Bernice and Fiona Clarke

General Policing Department
Warrnambool Division

214 Koroit Street,
Warrnambool 3280
Victoria, Australia
DX   219606
Telephone   03 5560 1198
Facsimile   03 5560 1115

5 June, 2000

Libby CLARKE

Reference   Banjo CLARKE

Dear Libby

I understand that there is some confusion about whether Police attended your father Banjo's funeral and in what capacity they attended.

Your father was a great man who was respected and revered by all who had the good fortune to meet him. His influence went beyond his physical presence to the four corners of the Earth and this is evidenced by the tributes that flowed from overseas at his funeral.

Members under my command expressed their desire to attend Banjo's funeral as a mark of respect. It was felt that we could assist in a meaningful way by escorting his body to his final resting place. We were also aware that this would be the biggest funeral Warrnambool has ever seen, which in itself would create traffic problems on Banjo's final journey to his beloved forest.

As the Officer in Charge of the Warrnambool Police District, with my senior management team, I saluted your father's body as it passed from the service to his final resting place. Again, this was as a mark of respect in the same way that I would salute a fallen comrade.

Libby, I hope by this letter you see that your father was respected by all and was and is someone we can all still look to for guidance long after he returned to his forest.

John ROBINSON BM
Chief Inspector

WRITING BANJO'S LIFE
(by Camilla Chance)

In July 1975, on a fine midwinter's morning in Warrnambool, a beautiful place on Australia's south-eastern coast, a group of friends belonging to the Baha'i Faith and I set off from my house. Barwoo, a sixteen-year-old Aboriginal from Mornington Island, in Australia's far north, is among our number. He has been staying with my family and wants to meet local Aboriginals. I have not yet met any Aboriginal people in Warrnambool in the three years I have lived there, though I knew a few city Aboriginals and was struck by their poise and strength. They still believed in the fundamentals of their ravaged culture, and obeyed its laws. I know the Framlingham Aboriginal Settlement is nearby. Maybe we could drive out there, I tell Barwoo, and see if we are invited in?

We travel by main roads. Everything along the way has a powerful intensity. I see hills and green trees as if I've never looked before. Great expanses of sunshine move toward us, then shade. A rainbow arches across the road.

A few minutes later, our group of many different nationalities is sitting among pink lilies and yellow-white jonquils outside the mission boundary. We do not want to be disrespectful and enter uninvited, so we wait to be asked in, as is the traditional Aboriginal way. Laughing a lot, Barwoo strums his guitar and sings for us. My four-year-old daughter Ruth joins in. The rest of us hum softly.

The next thing we know, a woman is standing beside us. 'I'm Molly,' she says. 'Come with me and I'll introduce you to the people in some houses.'

Suddenly I understand that whatever happens today will have depth and significance for all of my life. We follow Molly to the nearest weatherboard dwelling, the home of Auntie Mary Clarke. Government-built and below the standards required for housing white people, the thin-walled house nevertheless exudes hospitality, light and happiness. Many people are inside. We are surrounded by faces with more strength and gentleness than I've ever seen in my life. I sense broad feelings of love and attraction from all of them. The strongest feelings come from a man with the kindest and gentlest face of all, whom I'm told is Auntie Mary's son. His name is Banjo.

My daughter Ruth runs towards him with open arms. He bends, picks her up, holds her against his chest and exclaims, 'Eeeeee!' as if he is squeezing her as tightly as he can.

Banjo later said of our first meeting, 'We were drawn to one another.' From the moment he had seen our happy group of many nationalities sitting on the grass, he wanted to be part of it. He told me that as soon as we met, he knew that things were going to change for the better for us all.

A few months after our first meeting, Banjo had a stay in hospital during a bout of pneumonia. I visited him there often. He was very interested in learning more about the Baha'i Faith, which I had discovered at the age of twenty-two. It instantly appealed to him as he recognised its teachings as a true extension of the Aboriginal principles he had grown up with – love, unity, forgiveness, equality and sharing. They were the same principles that I had responded to when I first encountered Baha'i people. I went to one of their meetings in Switzerland and was amazed and overjoyed to discover so many different races and social classes sitting together in perfect harmony, happiness and love.

I grew up in a wealthy, semi-aristocratic family with servants and all the luxuries, but was dismayed that we had so much when others had so little. I also hated being treated as somehow higher and better than other people. I was once horrified to have porters and others grovel before my baroness grandmother and me when we alighted from a train at a station. I longed to find a community in which everyone was equal and had love for each other. That community I found in the Baha'i Faith, and I discovered it again when I met the Aboriginal people at Framlingham that day in 1975. Instantly we all knew that deep down we were the same, despite our different social and racial backgrounds. We could see into each other's hearts. There have been plenty of bad times in my life, but meeting the Baha'i people and then the Framlingham Aboriginals were both highs.

Banjo and many other Indigenous people bonded with me because my own experience had prepared me to believe their stories. My parents had been angered and horrified by the fact that, as a child, I had a keen sense of justice, compassion and love for people outside our social class. In response, they did their utmost to crush my mind, my heart and my soul. On a daily basis I was told I shouldn't love; I shouldn't share; that being soft-hearted was a terrible fault. They tried to destroy me emotionally and spiritually for my beliefs. This was a similar experience to that of so many Aboriginal people I met later in life. My parents had the same uncaring attitudes as the white people about whom I heard terrible stories from my Aboriginal friends. These friends had suffered at their hands, whether on missions, as stolen children in orphanages, or just in daily life.

When Banjo was discharged from hospital, I invited him to my home so that he could continue his recuperation, and he stayed with my family for three or four months. It was a very special time for all of us, particularly for my young children Ruth and David.

Towards the end of his stay, I remember Banjo telling me about a troubling dream he had had about David, and explaining why he had wanted to build a fence along the cliff behind our house, below which the Hopkins River runs.

'I started worrying that your little fellah might fall way down into the river,' he said. 'I had a terrible dream about him – he was in a car or a little home, floating along the river with lots of bits of wood around him. So I built a fence right along the cliff. It is like a strong arm protecting David.'

We did not know it at the time, but Banjo had had a premonition, more than twenty years in advance, of David's near-drowning in 1998, when the van he and his girlfriend Eliza were sleeping in was washed into the ocean during a flash flood in Mexico. Before David had left on his trip, he made a special journey home to Warrnambool and spent time cutting wood in the bush with Banjo. In among their usual quiet conversation, Banjo told David that if he ever needed him on his long travels, he should just close his eyes and Banjo would be there for him.

In the first few weeks of 1998, while David was away, Banjo again started having dreams he could not explain. He would see water rushing in through the windows and doors of his house, and could do nothing to hold it back. Every night the dream would return. It frightened him because, to Aboriginal people, dreaming about water means death.

During February, David and Eliza were travelling along the west coast of Mexico on the last leg of their journey. They camped overnight in a small caravan park on the coast. It was the middle of winter and the weather was unsettled, so they were the only campers there.

That night, Banjo and his grandson Kirrae were watching television at Banjo's house when a documentary about floods and natural disasters came on. The program completely unsettled Banjo. He realised that it was David who had been in danger in his nightmares. He said to Kirrae, 'David had better come home this minute,' then immediately telephoned me to tell me the same thing. What we didn't know was that as we spoke, an El Niño-generated storm was sweeping over California and northern Mexico. At 4 a.m. the retaining wall behind David and Eliza's van collapsed, sending a flash flood through the caravan park. The water swept the van over a cliff and into the sea. They managed to scramble out of the van and jump into the ocean. Once in the water, they were swept further from shore in the huge surf. The sea was full of debris – mud, logs and sticks – and the night was completely dark except for two distant streetlights. Each time a wave rolled over, they had to force their way through the mat of debris to reach the surface and struggle for breath. After about twenty minutes, they lost hold of each other.

The waves were relentless. David couldn't see Eliza and was reaching complete exhaustion. He began to feel his arms and legs go numb from the effort and the cold. He knew that he would not be able to struggle much longer, and for the most part, he says, he can't remember caring. It was then that he closed his eyes and heard and felt Banjo there with him, reaching out with his 'strong arm' in the dark, urging him to make one more effort to swim ashore. It was enough to help David back to dry land, but Eliza was lost.

We are certain that Banjo Clarke saved my son's life.

Despite the deep love and spirituality that I sense in Eliza's family, I cannot begin to imagine their terrible suffering at losing this young woman, whom I'd looked forward to being my daughter-in-law. Despite our faith, my son's grief is boundless and my own is great. I am no stranger to grief, tempered by gratitude for having known such magnificent souls. My friend Rodney Wicks has written:

Such was the nature and depth of the relationship between Banjo Clarke and Camilla Chance that the puerile-minded could not comprehend the 'spiritual bond' between an 'uneducated' elderly Aboriginal man and an Italian finishing-school product, a surgeon's wife. They were interdependent soul mates, crossing a host of cultural and class barriers, the most wonderful and admirable examples of Baha'i unity and friendship.

Banjo gave validity to my own natural reactions to things, and gave me the strength to express them. Aboriginal culture has so many gifts for the world, and through all the cruel and sad times Banjo was always patient, not losing hope that one day the world would graciously accept his people and their wisdom. That is why he asked me to help him write this book, and it was an honour to work on it with him.

Recollections
of Banjo Clarke

The Power of One Good Man
Martin Flanagan

Last Tuesday week, I met Rajmohan Gandhi, grandson of
Mahatma Gandhi, and asked him if the secret of his grandfather's
power had been his belief that there is an innate goodness in
human nature. 'I believe it was,' he replied. He said that at an
early point in Gandhi's life he studied history and concluded that,
despite the misery and mayhem of the world, human goodness
was a historically verifiable fact. Rajmohan gave me a copy of *The
Good Boatman*, his biography of his grandfather, which is
dedicated 'to all who prize freedom without hate'. In return, I told
him about Banjo Clarke, who had died that morning in
Warrnambool Hospital, having lived that principle as well as
anyone I had seen. (In this, and certain other respects, I place
him alongside an Australian from a very different background, Sir
Edward 'Weary' Dunlop.) In this culture, it is customary to
describe such individuals as true Christians, but in Banjo's case
that would be a serious error. An Elder of the Kirrae Whurrong
people, he gave his religion as Baha'i.

Banjo Clarke lived and died on his people's traditional lands –
the Framlingham forest, east of Warrnambool. Born in 1922, his
schooling lasted a total of two days. After seeing a teacher strike a
student, he returned to the forest, sat with the Old People and
learnt from them. In those days, the character of Aboriginal life
on the Framlingham mission was still strongly traditional. Banjo
could recall the presence of the invisible lawman, the kadaicha

man, who visited after a member of the community took a wife against the skin laws of a tribe in another state.

Last December, I wrote an article on Banjo for the *Age* [21 December 1999]. It was a difficult time for him; a dispute over control of the Framlingham forest was causing him acute distress. After the story appeared, however, he told me he was walking down the street in Warrnambool when a whitefellah said to him: 'We shoulda been talking to you blokes years ago.'

David Fligelman, the son of a local doctor, has known Banjo all his life and would probably count himself as one of his children. His mother, Camilla, introduced Banjo to the Baha'i faith, which, according to Lenny Clarke, appealed to the old man because of its compassion for all living things.

On Monday, Fligelman delivered Banjo's eulogy to a crowd of about two thousand people at Framlingham. Afterwards, a local said that what I had to understand was the range of people from the white community who were present – police, bikies, church groups, unionists, farmers. One of the speakers was the Mayor of Warrnambool, David Atkinson, while a message of condolence and respect was received from former Prime Minister Malcolm Fraser.

Arriving at Monday's service, I was met by a man in his fifties who had grown up on a neighbouring farm and played with Banjo's kids. He'd come from Melbourne to attend. Afterwards, he said to me in a slightly puzzled way: 'This is unusual. I know most of these people. This has been like a concert.'

A contemporary corroboree was how it was later described to me. At some point in the event, which lasted half the night, all the people who needed to be heard were listened to, all the songs that needed singing were sung. Those who performed during the more formal part of the proceedings were Andy Alberts, Shane Howard, Alan Harris, Lee Morgan (Banjo's grandson), Paul Kelly, Rebecca Martin, Neil Murray, the Kuyang Yandaa Dance Group and Archie Roach.

Archie was Banjo's nephew. Stolen from his family as a child while living at Framlingham, he returned as an eighteen-year-old, felt nothing, got drunk and went back to Melbourne. He returned ten years later with his wife and two sons and in response to his questions, he was told he should go and see Uncle Banjo. Archie's first sight of him was an old man running towards him with tears streaming down his face. Later, Banjo took Archie around, showed him where his family's shack had been, where he had played, the tree underneath which his mother was born, the part of the forest he played in as a child. In Archie's words, 'That old man put me back in the story. Nobody else could have done that for me but that old fellah.' He wrote a song about the experience called 'Weeping in the Forest'.

Archie sang this song at the graveside. It was to have been broadcast but the radio microphone didn't work. David Arden, a deeply quiet man who sometimes performs with Archie, shrugged his shoulders and said, 'Did it the old way.' A voice in the wind.

The grave is not in the forest, nor does Banjo lie with 'the old people' in the Framlingham cemetery, but he is on Kirrae Whurrong land on a bluff above the Hopkins River. I do not pretend to know the exact reason for this, but I suspect it has to do with the dispute over the forest and ensuring his people never leave the place.

Over the years, as Banjo's reputation grew, many travellers arrived at his door. No one was turned away. Nor are they turned away from Lenny's place, an old farmhouse down the road. If Banjo was a knight, Lenny was his valet or squire at arms. When we went back to Lenny's place on Monday night, a white kid beset with problems was sitting slumped behind the wheel of a car in his front yard. The kid lives with Lenny but used to visit Banjo each morning. 'Basically,' says singer Shane Howard, 'Banjo saved lives. He made order from the chaos.' Howard says Banjo Clarke's Dreaming is for all Australians, black and white. The song he wrote with him, 'The River Knows (Kuuyang)', is from *Clan*, the album he made after returning to the Warrnambool area and rediscovering this amazing old man living in a forest with too many dead trees and a river that has fewer and fewer eels. The song begins: 'Who's gonna save this country now? Who'll protect its sacred power?'

It wasn't only people from Australia who came to meet him. Last year a Kosovar musician arrived with a Dutch cellist and together they filled the forest and its valley with their music. Then there was the El Salvadorean peace activist who had survived a murderous civil war and spoke no English. She felt Banjo understood her.

The visitors' book he was given a couple of years ago even contains the signatures of two One Nation party activists. 'We talk with the devil if he stop and have a yarn,' said Banjo, and laughed, a soft gleeful chuckle that seemed to have a life of its own. Thought is now being given to making his simple home into a keeping place.

I think of Banjo Clarke first as a man, one whose early consciousness was impressed by the discipline that accompanies traditional Aboriginal life. As a child, he saw others his age die through lack of medical care. As a young man, he knew hunger and imprisonment. During the years of assimilation, he saw members of his family abducted by the authorities.

He was a member of a proud fighting people whose number includes Lionel Rose, a world champion when those words meant something, and Reg Saunders, whose life is the great Australian war movie waiting to be made. Banjo had been a tent fighter in his youth. It wasn't that he didn't have anger; it was that he identified anger as a destructive force and kept it in check. As I told Rajmohan Gandhi, it was as if Banjo Clarke decided the way to defeat the enemy was through moral example.

Mahatma Gandhi said of politics that unless it works in the village, it doesn't work. Banjo worked in the village. The Warrnambool *Standard* gave two-thirds of its front page to the news of Banjo's death and more than that to its account of the memorial service. In a stable culture, what happens in one village spreads to the next, but in our technologically isolated and increasingly frantic age we care less and less about our neighbour. Banjo Clarke never thought of his as being anything but himself. As a youth humping his billy, he sustained himself by thinking there had to be a good person around the next bend.

In the course of the service, I asked Ken Saunders, a Gunditjmara man now living in Melbourne, if he thought there could ever be another like him. He slowly shook his head and said he doubted it. Later, after seeing the white boy lost in grief over Banjo's death, I asked the same question of Lenny Clarke, upon whom a heavy weight of responsibility has now fallen. The thought brought a sweat to his upper lip. 'We can do it,' he said, smacking his fist. He said we, not I.

In Banjo's final years, when Lenny feared the old man was getting lonely, he sent his youngest child, a boy called Kirrae, to live with his grandfather. Banjo invested in him knowledge about the spirit-land and its creatures.

Kirrae Clarke's mother has red hair and freckles. Now aged nine, the boy has thick lips, snowy white hair and stands as straight as a spear. Banjo Clarke was the opposite of whatever it means to be a racist.

A decent young man from Warrnambool named Gerard Finnigan travelled with his mother to Monday's service to pay his respects. He said Banjo had always represented to him 'a way of blacks and whites relating that wasn't political'. That matters, because so much of politics – and race politics is potentially its most dangerous form – is about appearance, and Banjo Clarke went several dimensions beyond that.

In the end, the issue left by his life is simple enough. Do we want peace in and with this land? Are there enough of us who have what it takes?

This piece is a revised version of an article that appeared in the Age *in March 2000.*

Weeping in the Forest
Archie Roach

Uncle Banjo told me
Before the children went away
Life was good and life was free
Not like it is today

Children running everywhere
And the trees were looking after
Little spirits, dancing there
Among the sweet, sweet laughter

Oh but there's weeping in the forest
Now that the children have gone
And the trees at night get no rest
But they were there when the children were born

Uncle let me fly away with you
And let me see the things you see
When children laughed as children do
As they played among the trees

Oh but there's weeping in the forest
Now that the children have gone
And the trees at night get no rest
For they were there when the children were born.

Banjo and Mandela
Tanya Waterson

South-west Victorian Aboriginal Elder Banjo Clarke was the 'same quality of person' as world-renowned South African leader Nelson Mandela, State Aboriginal Affairs Minister Keith Hamilton has said.

Speaking in Warrnambool on Wednesday, Mr Hamilton said the late Mr Clarke was one of the most amazing men he had met.

'I've met Nelson Mandela, and Banjo was the same quality of person,' Mr Hamilton said. 'He was just one of the most remarkable men I've ever met in my whole life.

'He was one of the people you could just sort of listen to and he made lots of progress about building a better understanding.'

Mr Clarke had tremendous respect from Aboriginal and non-Aboriginal people, he said.

'He provided a strength which was almost an inner strength which radiated out. He claimed – and I believe – that he got his strength from the Framlingham Forest.

'He built lots of bridges in a community that has historically had a lot of tensions between Aboriginal and non-Aboriginal people and I gather that was because of the respect that was given to him.

'He was recognised across all of Victoria as a great source of knowledge and a great source of wisdom.'

Mr Hamilton said the government had had discussions with the Warrnambool City Council and member for Warrnambool John Vogels about establishing a public memorial to Mr Clarke.

The popular Aboriginal Elder died in March 2000, aged seventy-seven, after a short illness.

He was born Henry James Clarke in a bark hut in Framlingham Forest and is remembered for his compassionate nature and his love of the forest where he was born.

This piece was originally published in the Warrnambool Standard *on 2 August 2002.*

Walk on, Uncle Banjo
Judith Durham

I somehow feel that I was already being impelled to focus on the content of this piece for Banjo, because the request to write it reached me when I had been concentrating strongly and vividly on the lyrics of a song called 'Walk On'. You'll realise the significance of this when I tell you that the song's message is to commemorate and celebrate the great souls that every so often come to this world and show us the way, bringing us hope and creating harmony and inspiring peace among us.

Uncle Banjo is one of these souls. He is a great man still, a true humanitarian who will always be an icon in the community, an example to the Australian nation and the world. What he achieved through his warmth and humour, his generosity and humility, is known far and wide – but as often happens with rare souls of his ilk, it is through death that his true level of attainment as a human being can be valued and demonstrated.

The connection between myself and Banjo becomes more and more significant. How I wonder where it all really began in a spiritual sense, but our first meeting was as we sat, literally side by side, in the audience of Gary Foley's wonderful week-long seminar, Understanding Black Australia, at Melbourne University around 1991. I was impressed by the great respect and love bestowed upon Banjo by those close to him, and for the first time in my life I understood the value of an Elder to a community, and how our white community often misses out on this opportunity to revere someone older and wiser, and to learn enduring values.

Much later, as one of the many delightful surprises ensuing from the 25-year reunion of The Seekers, I discovered that my fellow Seeker Athol Guy had close connections himself with Banjo. In memories dear to his heart of when he was brought up on a farm in Warrnambool, Athol told us how his uncle had been best mates with Banjo all those years ago. So special.

From such humble beginnings, Banjo's light permeated the hearts of all around him in ever widening circles – ever brighter – irrespective of colour or creed, and the world became a better place.

Banjo's book can lift our spirits still, to heights of love and harmony. His telling of his story is an instrument of the greater universal consciousness, and he has transcended the bondage of the ordinary by showing us that, if we are open and childlike, loving and grateful for all that sustains the world, happiness and contentment truly come, from somewhere beyond our comprehension.

Thank you, Uncle Banjo, for what you gave us all in life. Thank you for the gift of your book to inspire us and remind us to be caring and useful human beings while we spend our days on this physical plane.

Smoke Under the Bridge
Paul Kelly

All day long I've been walking
And mostly to myself I've been talking
The lonesome night is too quickly falling
In this unfriendly town
It's cold when the sun goes down
So I'll head for the river and look for smoke under the bridge

Once I had a place I could call my own
Now wherever I lay my head is home
Ran into some trouble back on down the road
They didn't like the look of me
Someone took a hook at me
I'll keep my eyes open for smoke under the bridge
Keep on hoping for smoke under the bridge

I'll keep on looking for smoke under the bridge
Keep on walking to smoke under the bridge
A little shelter, a friendly fire, some company under the bridge
I'll keep on walking
I gotta keep walking
Gotta keep walking

Uncle Banjo Clarke
Shane Howard

On the day of the funeral of Clare, the mother of my four eldest
children, a number of images were etched indelibly on my mind.
The image of Uncle Banjo Clarke, standing outside the church
with his family beside him, is one of those. I didn't know him or
his family very well at the time. They would not have been
missed, but still they bothered to be there for me and my family.

I became a frequent visitor to Framlingham in those days. My
father says that 'the attentive ear is the sage's dream', and I
enjoyed listening to Uncle Banjo fill in the details of the history of
the Warrnambool area from an Aboriginal point of view. He told
me about his people, about the Old People and the old days. He
taught me about the migration of the eels and how best to spear
or net them.

He was a great storyteller. He told stories that would make you
burst out laughing. Stories of mystery and intrigue. Stories of
history, of life on the mission in the old days. Stories of the Old
People. Stories of little triumphs along the way. He had hundreds,
possibly thousands of stories of immense hardship, racism, sorrow
and inhumanity. But despite all the odds, Banjo didn't become a
bitter man. He reinforced the importance of honourable
behaviour.

I know when I talked with him of hardships I was having in
my own life he wouldn't comment on them directly. Instead he
would sit listening at his table or by his fireside and then

discreetly tell me a story of someone he knew who had suffered greater loss. Everything is relative, and I always came away from Uncle Banjo's place with a sense of acceptance and humility. Sure, things could be better, but they could just as easily be worse. Count your blessings and be grateful for small mercies.

It is not an exaggeration to say that the Uncle Banjo I knew, in his later years, was about the business of saving lives on a daily basis. He was a source of wisdom and calm in a chaotic world; the centre of a turning wheel. He reconnected many members of the community that were part of the stolen generation.

At the heart of his world was the belief that it is the simple things in this life that matter most. Family, community, tolerance and compassion. Uncle Banjo would often say to people, 'Just be happy,' and as simplistic as that first sounded to me, I soon came to realise that being happy is a choice we make. Every day.

Unmarked Graves
Neil Murray

What happened to the Aboriginal tribes of western Victoria? Where is the clan I should have been born into? Where are their sacred sites and dreaming lines and what are their songs and dances? What is their language and what is their law? What is my skin name and what would my totem be? I'd carried these questions for half a lifetime. There was no one to ask. All shot, poisoned, diseased and removed long before my time.

'Uncle Banjo,' I'd hear over the years, whenever eyes got misty over too many beers or the loss came near at creekbed flagon parties or I happened to stumble into someone who seemed to know where I came from and what it was I was after.

'Go see Uncle Banjo,' I'd been told.

At Framlingham, finally, I found him, a spry old man with a twinkle in his eye, joking and laughing in front of a small two-roomed cottage on a ridge above a river that trickled through the stone of ancient fish traps.

'G'day, mate,' he said waving me inside, 'have a cuppa tea, feed there too.'

I sat down in his spartan kitchen and held onto my questions. There was a boomerang over the fireplace.

'You know I've been away a long time,' I ventured, 'I went away to the Northern Territory and lived with the blackfellahs.'

'Yeah,' he said, casually cutting me off, 'that's what usually happens.'

Uncle Banjo told yarns. He told life stories. He told histories. I just listened. None of it seemed to be what I wanted to know. But I couldn't speak. I couldn't think. I was confused. The weight of my questions had made me weak. Finally he said, 'My grandfather helped round 'em up, brought 'em here.'

I lifted my gaze. He was pointing over and beyond the gully to an old pine tree leering above the tree line.

'See that pine tree, that's the old mission cemetery. You wanna see 'em?'

Through the scrub down the end of a track, Uncle Banjo opened a rusty old gate and we stepped into a solemn clearing beside the gnarled and leaning pine. His hand swept slowly through the still bushland air indicating the gentle dip and hollow of the ground we walked on.

'All the tribal people are buried here,' he said softly.

Oh sweet Jesus the bones beneath my feet. I stepped lightly, painfully, and stuck close to him.

'Did you see them?' I asked, my voice a whisper. He shook his head. We walked to more graves along the fence.

'. . . and here . . . my daughter, son, brother, father, mother, grandfather and grandmother.'

We walked around, he pointed out his relatives and ancestors. Then he stopped.

'We'll all go back . . . to that spirit world from where we came.'

Then he didn't speak for a while. We just stood there. He stared at the ground. I heard the cough of a koala. A roo paused from grazing to look at us while the grief washed over me. And out of me my questions, gone.

'See, we don't like to make it flash with headstones or anything, just leave a stick or something and I remember,' he said cheerfully, putting the chain on the rusty gate as we left.

'I remember every name.'

This piece was originally published in Neil Murray's One Man Tribe *(Northern Territory University Press, 1999).*

The Storyteller
Susan Pickles

In 1990 I was working at a school in Melbourne, teaching physical education and geography. I was also the Year 8 co-ordinator, and as such was involved in the school camping program. This was primarily recreation-based, but I decided to include some historical, cultural, environmental and industrial elements in order to enrich the experience for the students. I chose Warrnambool as the destination because I knew it well, it has a rich history, and I wanted the students to be able to go surfing.

Noticing the Aboriginal flag painted on the roof of the Gunditjmara Co-op in Warrnambool, I approached the centre and met Len Clarke, who was then in charge, and proudly nursing his newly born baby boy Kirrae.

I asked him if it would be worth bringing a big group of city-based teenagers to the co-op to listen to some Koorie history from his people.

Len replied, 'Better still, take them out into the forest and let the old man tell 'em a few stories.'

'All right,' I agreed, thinking that if the 'old man' didn't relate well to thirteen-year-olds, we could try something different next year.

Once the students and I were in Warrnambool, I followed the map Len had given me and found his father, Banjo Clarke, waiting under the big gum tree on the corner of his property, just as planned. Banjo waved to us and climbed on board our bus. He directed us to the picnic ground of the forest, where he began to tell the students about his life growing up in the bush on Framlingham Mission.

Banjo's ability to tell a story stirred our imaginations. Standing there amongst the trees and grass, we could easily imagine the little huts scattered through the bush and the kindness of the old people, who, despite being forced to live there, still hung onto their Aboriginal traditions in order to make life on the mission a happy place. We could almost hear the laughter and chatter of the little children hiding and running through the bush, playing with one another, as Banjo described what once was.

Banjo explained how things had gone wrong for many families living there. People became lost in the huge gap that existed between Aboriginal and European culture. Children were forcibly removed from mothers, fathers, sisters and brothers, never to be seen again, or, in some cases, returning much later in life to try to find what had been taken from them.

Many times, after hearing these stories, students would say to me, 'But how could people let this happen? Did it really happen? Why didn't policemen try and stop it? Someone needs to write down the things that Banjo is talking about so that everyone can find out what terrible things were done to these people.'

Banjo's words, his delivery of history, and most of all, he himself, impacted greatly on every group of students we brought to him in his forest home – sometimes fifty teenagers, sometimes as many as seventy in a group.

When we left Banjo that first day, he raised both his hands above his head and said, 'You are all welcome to come back and visit me any time – my door is always open.'

Having travelled to the Northern Territory and northern

Queensland a few times to areas where I hoped to meet
Aboriginal people and learn something of their culture, I could
not refuse Banjo's offer. Next time I was in Warrnambool, I
decided to call on him, but I felt nervous – would he remember
me? Would we have anything to talk about?

I didn't need to worry. Banjo did remember me, and welcomed
me into his home like a long-lost family member. We talked about
how much the kids enjoyed meeting him and what a valuable
opportunity it was for him to pass on history first-hand to young
and interested minds.

Banjo began ringing me from this time on and we never spoke
for less than an hour. He always liked to finish on a humourous
note. Laughing loudly, he would say, 'Okay Bud, better go now.
I love you, see ya.' He was such a faithful and constant person in
my life. I often wondered why someone as ordinary as myself
could be treated as so special by a person as highly respected as
Banjo was. But it was ordinary people and the lost souls of the
world that Uncle Banjo had a special place for, and I know so
many others came and went through that open door at Banjo's
house as I did. It was incredible just how many times, when life
had got on top of me, Banjo would ring that same day because, he
said, I had been on his mind. 'You need to go out into the bush,
mate. Clear your head, slow down a bit,' he would say.

With that encouragement, every school holiday I would do just
that. Banjo would stoke an especially big fire and make a bed for
me on the floor. I would cook dinner for us both and then he
would tell me story after story until I couldn't keep my eyes open
any more. I saw that there was a common theme in all his stories:
that compassion and acts of kindness were powerful tools that
could disempower hate and prejudice. 'People often behave in the

same way as they have been treated,' he would say, and, 'the spirit world and the natural world work together.'

The more Banjo taught me, the more I was able to prepare my students for their meetings with him. For seven years I took groups of teenagers to see him, and he warmly and enthusiastically received every one of them. They were always such positive encounters, and Banjo did a lot of one-on-one chatting with the kids as well. He made them all feel at ease, even special. He was like a grandfather figure to them – maybe that's why many people refer to him as 'Poppyman'. I know that just meeting and talking to Banjo would have helped the students offset any racism and stereotyping they might encounter further into their adult lives.

No one left Framlingham unaffected by their time there, least of all myself. During these years I had become engaged to a young man whom I desperately wanted my family and friends to approve of, but that approval was not forthcoming. Knowing how unconditionally Banjo accepted all people, I headed for Framlingham with my fiancé. Of course he received my partner warmly, as he did everyone, but he was uncomfortable about me marrying him. The engagement later broke off, and I did not know how to withstand the great disappointment and despair I was feeling. A wedding date had already been set and I couldn't bear the thought of being alone in Melbourne on the day I had hoped to be married. The only place I felt I could emotionally survive was Banjo's home. He had always treated me as if I were his own daughter.

We did a lot of crying and laughing that weekend. I remember he told everyone who came to his house during those two days that I had been 'just about to walk down the aisle, but decided it would be nicer to spend the weekend with Uncle Banjo. Bet they're all wondering where she's gone!' Then we'd laugh and laugh.

I survived that time of my life and other difficult times with Banjo's support. I have since met and married a wonderful man whom Banjo was especially fond of, and he did us the honour of attending our wedding. The night I went into labour with our first daughter, there was a message on our answering machine from Banjo saying, 'Hey, what's going on up there? Just wondering if everything's okay.' Before we had a chance to call him, he had rung the hospital and tracked me down, just hours after giving birth, to see how I was, and to hear the baby's healthy cry over the phone.

Banjo died a few months after our second daughter was born. I miss him more than I can express. But I have many, many wonderful memories of him, and think always how fortunate I was to have had him in my life for ten years.

Your Paradise
Trisha Smith

The bush
It was your Paradise
Your chosen
Natural home.

Amongst the
Gnarled and twisted trunks
And ghost-like
Stretching branches,
You nestled with
Your feathered friends
And furry, forest folk.

You knew each
Rustle, chirp and sound
In such an intimate manner.
You touched the bark,
You breathed the breeze,
You cherished
Each new sapling.

You found your solace
In the bush,
It provided simple answers.

A canopy of wisdom,
Against a troubled world.

The twigs,
They were your quills.
The dew,
Your fluid ink.
Your pages were the spreading leaves,
All bound
With silken gossamer.

You shared your
Wise ways
And your home,
With such a generous heart.
You walked the tracks
Of peace and love
With rhythm,
Never tiring.

The natural choir
Of the bush bursts into a
Farewell symphony,
To gently guide
Your precious spirit
On its final journey.

The orchestra,
Magnificent,
Beyond all human ears.

Performs with such perfection,
To welcome
Your special soul.

Transformed
Into the very sap
Of every limb and leaf,
The gentle foliage
Embraces you –
Eternally protected.

Wisdom Man
Andy Alberts

Let me tell you all a story about a wise old man
His name is Uncle Banjo, always doing the best he can
Now you may see him walking through the streets of your town
He's a man that's always smiling, he never wears a frown

At night time we'd go walking through the forest on our land
You'd laugh and tell me stories about our tribal clan
Our midnight firing embers show your smiling eyes
The next thing you know the night is gone and the dawning breaks
the skies

Oh stand up words of Wisdom Man
Don't let them push you round
You know they think they can
Please be strong old Wisdom Man

I've seen him in the papers talking of his land
They write his story, take his picture, but they don't
understand
All the hurt, pain and anger that he feels inside
'Cause the raping of his mother earth his pride has been denied

Oh stand up words of Wisdom Man
Don't let them push you round

You know they think they can
Please be strong old Wisdom Man

You see all troubles and hard times in this world today
That's why he teaches us young fellows that we may know his ways
Like the old fellows before us, said Uncle, they all come and gone
They all made that sweet, sweet journey to the Dreamtime and
beyond

So you see all you young Koories
When living through your lives
Remember Uncle Banjo told us
Always to be wise.

SOURCES

TEXT

The lyrics to 'The River Knows' (writers Shane Howard, Neil Murray and
Banjo Clarke) on pages vi and vii appear by kind permission of Jointed
Venture/Mushroom Music/Rondor Music/The Clarke Family; the footnote
on page 39 is from the Warrnambool *Standard*, 6 May 1916; the obituary
on pages 67–8 is from the *Standard*, 29 September 1925; the article on
pages 70–1 comes from a private collection and its original publishing
details are uncertain; the letters by and about Louisa Briggs on pages 72–6
are from the National Archives of Australia; the article on page 103 is from
the Adelaide *News*, 6 December 1947; the article on pages 259–64 is from
the *Age*, 24 March 2000; the lyrics to 'Weeping In The Forest' (writer Archie
Roach) on page 265 appear by kind permission of Mushroom Music; the
article on pages 266–7 is from the *Standard*, 2 August 2002; the lyrics to
'Smoke Under The Bridge' (writer Paul Kelly) on page 270 appear by kind
permission of Mushroom Music; the extract on pages 273–5 is reproduced
with the permission of the Northern Territory University Press; the lyrics to
the song 'Wisdom Man' (writer Andy Alberts, from his album *Gunditjmara
Land*) on pages 280–1 appear by kind permission of the writer.

PHOTOGRAPHS

Page 1 (top left) portrait held in the Tasmanian Museum and Art Gallery;
page 5 (bottom) the *Standard*; page 6 (top) the *Standard*, (bottom) courtesy of the *Age*; page 7 (bottom) the *Standard*; page 8 (top) courtesy of the
Victoria Police, (bottom) the *Standard*; page 9 (top left) the *Standard*,
(bottom right) David Owen; page 10 (top and bottom) the *Standard*; page
11 (top) John Collyer, (bottom) the *Standard*; page 12 (top and bottom)
the *Standard*; page 14 (top) the *Standard*; page 15 (top) Karana Morgan;
page 16 (top) Karana Morgan, (bottom) the *Standard*.

Why Weren't We Told?

HENRY REYNOLDS

Why were we never told? Why didn't we know?

Historian Henry Reynolds has found himself being asked these questions by many people, over many years, in all parts of Australia. The acclaimed *Why Weren't We Told?* is a frank account of his personal journey towards the realisation that he, like generations of Australians, grew up with a distorted and idealised version of the past. From the author's unforgettable encounter in a North Queensland jail with injustice towards Aboriginal children, to his friendship with Eddie Mabo, to his shattering of the myths about our 'peaceful' history, this bestselling book will shock, move and intrigue. *Why Weren't We Told?* is crucial reading on the most important debate in Australia as we enter the twenty-first century. Winner of the 1999 Australian Human Rights Award for the Arts.

'This is a fine and engaging memoir. It is also a fascinating book about the writing of history, by one of its master practitioners in this country.' – Michael Duffy, *The Australian*

'*Why Weren't We Told?* urges us to continue to search for the truth about our past in order to prepare for and safeguard our future.' – Andrea Durbach, *The Bulletin*

'A must-read . . . I found the story of Reynolds' intellectual and spiritual journey moving and thought-provoking.'
– Noel Pearson, *The Age*

Black Pioneers

HENRY REYNOLDS

Black Pioneers is an important new edition of *With the White People*, Henry Reynolds' challenging account of the role of Aboriginal and Islander people in the exploration and development of colonial Australia.

In this book, Henry Reynolds debunks the notion that indigenous peoples have contributed nothing towards the creation of a prosperous modern society, that modern Australia rests on the sturdy foundations put down in the nineteenth century by the European pioneers.

Black Pioneers pays tribute to the labour and skill of the thousands of black men, women and children who worked for the Europeans in a wide range of occupations: as interpreters, concubines, trackers, troopers, servants, nursemaids, labourers, stockworkers and pearl-divers. Some of their intriguing stories are here revealed.

Featuring a timely new introductory essay, *Black Pioneers* is an essential contribution to Australian history at a time when examining our shared past has never been more critical.

Jackson's Track

DARYL TONKIN & CAROLYN LANDON

In 1936, Daryl Tonkin and his brother, Harry, leave home in search of adventure. They find themselves in West Gippsland, Victoria, and set up a timber mill at Jackson's Track – a dreamtime place, a place that was paradise.

A bushman dedicated to his work, Daryl discovers happiness there – and unexpectedly falls in love. But Daryl is white and Euphie is black, and neither of them is prepared for the conflict their forbidden love ignites.

Set in the heart of the Australian bush, this spellbinding memoir recaptures a community and a way of life now vanished from sight. It tells of one man's courage and determination to pursue what he knows is right.

An unforgettable true story of joy, of tragedy, and of hope, which has won the hearts of Australians.

'Thought-provoking and timely, this book is a must for anyone hoping to understand Australia's past'
– *Herald Sun*

'A classic of its genre' – *Sydney Morning Herald*

'Don't miss it for quids' – *The Australian*

Butterfly Song

TERRI JANKE

They say if you live on an island for too long, you merge with it. Your bones become the sands, your blood the ocean. You and those who follow you will always be a part of it.

Tarena Shaw has just finished her law degree but isn't sure she wants to be a lawyer after all. What place does a black lawyer have in a white legal system? Does everyone in Sydney feel like a turtle without a shell?

Drawn to Thursday Island, the home of her grand-parents, Tarena is persuaded by her family to take on her first case. Part of the evidence is a man with a guitar and a very special song . . .

Butterfly Song moves from the pearling days of the Torres Strait to the ebb and flow of big-city life, with a warm and funny modern heroine whose story reaches across cultures.